PUBLICATIONS OF THE TEXAS FOLKLORE SOCIETY

MODY C. BOATRIGHT, Editor
WILSON M. HUDSON, Associate Editor
ALLEN MAXWELL, Associate Editor

NUMBER XXVI

Texas Folk and Folklore

XXVI

PUBLISHED BY

SOUTHERN METHODIST UNIVERSITY PRESS

DALLAS

Texas

Folk and Folklore

Edited by

MODY C. BOATRIGHT

WILSON M. HUDSON

ALLEN MAXWELL

Drawings by
JOSÉ CISNEROS

SOUTHERN METHODIST UNIVERSITY PRESS: DALLAS

1954

PRINTED IN THE UNITED STATES OF AMERICA
BY WILKINSON PRINTING COMPANY: DALLAS, TEXAS

Dedicated to

J. Frank Dobie

Editor for the Texas Folklore Society

For twenty years

From 1923 to 1943

Preface

The state of Texas is fortunate in possessing a rich and varied folklore. When white settlers from the Old South came in bringing their slaves, they found the Mexicans in possession, and before them there were the Indians. These four racial groups maintained their several identities, and, except for the white plantation owner and his hands, they also had different languages, religions, and cultures. Hence their folkways and folklore were distinct and characteristic. However remotely, Spanish, English, African, and native American influences were at work, modified by and adapted to conditions of life in Texas.

Another basic cause making for variety in Texas lore and customs is the variety of Texas geography and natural resources. East Texas with its pine trees and rivers constitutes a totally different sort of country from West Texas with its sparse vegetation and dry, eroded mountains. The Great Plains, formerly the pasture of the buffalo, sweep southward between the two and link Texas with an environment extending from Canada to the Gulf of Mexico. The low coastal plain lies in a great arc from the Sabine to the Rio Grande, flanked by long sandy islands and shallow lagoons. This is the destination of the ducks and geese that fly down with the first northers. There was, and is, a great variety of fauna and flora in the state, each form adapted to its locality. From east to west the annual rainfall declines steadily, so that alligators, water moccasins, and squirrels are exentually replaced by horned toads, rattlesnakes, and prairie dogs. The settler in East Texas lived in a log cabin and the settler in West Texas in a sod dugout or an adobe hut. When oaks that are huge on the coast try to follow a stream backward to the west, they grow smaller and smaller until they become dwarf species beyond the headwaters.

Variety in geography led to variety in occupation and hence to variety in the folklore arising from the way a people make a living. The eastern third of Texas is farming country and the rest is naturally suited to ranching. Oil and gas are found in almost every part of the state. Farming and ranching have pro-

duced their lore and customs in Texas, and so has the oil industry. In some irrigated areas of West Texas, farming, ranching,
and oil work are carried on side by side. Since World War II a
great new petrochemical industry has developed along the
Gulf Coast between Port Arthur and Corpus Christi; no doubt
this development will make a contribution to folklore also.

Seeing the opportunities for the collection of folklore in
Texas, John A. Lomax and L. W. Payne, Jr. organized the
Texas Folklore Society in 1909. Members of the Society have
been active in every field of folklore from that time down to the
present day. The first volume of the Society's Publications was
edited in 1916 by Stith Thompson, who later became one of
America's leading folklore scholars. Mr. Thompson was succeeded by J. Frank Dobie, who continued to act as editor for
the Society for twenty years. Mr. Dobie exercised a determining
influence on the work of the Society. He himself was very active
in collecting, and he encouraged others to be active likewise.
He planned and edited volume after volume. The storehouse
of Texas folklore upon which we can now draw would not have
been filled without his efforts.

Texas Folk and Folklore is composed of materials published
originally in the first twenty-five volumes of the Texas Folklore
Society. The number of the volume in which each article or
item first appeared is shown in the Appendix, which also lists
the titles and years of publication of the individual volumes.

We believe that this book ought to be as much fun as an old-
time cowboy dance. Like the cowboy who rode about carrying
the news of the dance, we say to you, "Everybody invited and
nobody slighted!"

MODY C. BOATRIGHT
WILSON M. HUDSON
ALLEN MAXWELL

Austin and Dallas
October 30, 1954

Contents

NEGRO TALES AND JOKES

STORIES AND SONGS FOR CHILDREN

LEGENDS

Illustrations

INDIAN TALES

Kiowa-Apache Tales

J. GILBERT McALLISTER

HOW COYOTE GOT FIRE FOR THE PEOPLE AND MADE THE SUN

A long time ago all was darkness.

Coyote arranged a meeting with some animals. The ones that met were Black-Hawk, Jackrabbit, Prairie Chicken, and Turtle. Coyote said to these animals, "I'm looking for you, I have heard about you. Let's see if we can make daylight. Maybe we can find fire for the people. Somewhere I saw fire."

In a high bank Coyote had found a cave, and in it some people had day and fire. These were the only people that had fire and daylight. They kept these things for themselves.

Coyote said, "Let us study how we are going to get these things."

The birds said, "You are the one who knows something."

Coyote said, "Someday I am going to go down there and look around. I want to see who watches the doors. You fellows wait until I come back."

Coyote went down there. Pretty soon he saw one of the little bugs. It was Dragonfly, who could look just one way, which was straight ahead. Coyote reached out and caught Dragonfly. He said, "What are you doing here?"

The Kiowa-Apaches are a branch of the Apaches who became associated with the Kiowas as a tribe but retained their own Athabascan tongue. They have a tradition that they joined with the Kiowas because they were too few to hold their own against the other Plains Indians. The Kiowa-Apaches now live near Apache in western Oklahoma. They used to hunt buffalo between the Canadian and Red rivers in western Oklahoma and the Texas Panhandle.

1

Dragonfly said, "These people want me to watch the door. My eyes look straight ahead. If I say, 'Open the door,' they let me in."

Coyote said, "Well, little bug, I've got you now. Tell the people to open the door and I'll let you go. If you don't do this, I will kill you. If I let you go, you can fly away and they can't see you in the dark."

Dragonfly called for the door to be opened and Coyote let him go.

The door opened and Coyote saw the room and fire and some animals dancing. They were having a big time. They were just like chiefs who keep things for themselves. Coyote went in. They saw him and said, "How did you come in? Who told you to come in?"

Coyote said, "I just came in by myself."

They said, "You're crazy. You go back."

Coyote said, "I want to join in. I'll carry the food for your fire. I want to join in your dance."

So they let him dance. Everybody was having a good time. Coyote kept getting closer to the fire. "Look out, your tail might burn," they called to him. He said, "I don't care, I'm having a good time." He wanted to get lots of coals. He meant to pass them on to the animals who were going to carry them to Turtle.

Coyote danced and danced. Then he put his tail in the fire. He got lots of coals on his tail and then ran out. They saw him and chased him. When Coyote got tired he called to the birds. Black-Hawk got the fire and Coyote went into his hole. Black-Hawk took the fire to Jackrabbit. The people chased him, but when he was tired he passed the fire on to Prairie Chicken. Then Black-Hawk hid. Prairie Chicken flew with the fire to Turtle. The people who were chasing the animals had just about caught up. Turtle took the coals, put them down his neck, shut himself up in his shell, and lay down. The people tried to make him open up, but they couldn't. Then they threw him in the water. Pretty soon they all gave up.

Coyote was watching and he saw the fellows go back. Coyote got Black-Hawk, Jackrabbit, and Prairie Chicken together. They took the coals out of Turtle, put some wood together, and made a big fire. Coyote said, "Now what are we going to do with this so that all the people can use it? Let's make the sun out of it so it will be daylight."

The animals said, "Well, you know how to do it, you make it."

So Coyote made the sun. "Now where are we going to put it?"

The birds flew up to the highest mountain, but Coyote said that everybody couldn't see it from there. So he talked to the sun and said, "I'm going to throw you right up into the sky. You stay in the sky. You go all around and come back, so that all the people everywhere will have daylight to see by."

Then Coyote said, "Now what are we going to do with fire? Let's put fire into the rocks." So he put fire in rocks and ever since that time rocks hold the fire. People can strike a spark from these rocks and with wood make a fire to cook their food. Then Coyote took the rocks around and gave them to everybody.

That is how Coyote made the sun and gave people fire-rocks.

HOW THE APACHES GOT HORSES

A long time ago the Apaches had no horses, only dogs. Then one time some horses came to a pond of water to drink. The Apaches saw them and asked Mole to go over and get them. Mole went under the water across the lake. He saw that an old mare was the leader of the horses, and went after this mare. When she stooped down to drink, Mole made ripples, and these ripples became a rope and got around the mare's neck. Mole had a hold of the other end of the rope and led the mare to a tipi in the village. The other horses followed. That is how the Apaches got horses. They were the first to get them. They didn't abuse them. It was forbidden to hit a horse on the face or with a bridle or with a saddle blanket. A long time ago when they gave horses away, they cut off the forelock and pieces of warts from the horses' legs. They rubbed these together and then over themselves. It was good to do that.

HOW COYOTE GOT THE BUFFALO FOR THE INDIANS

One time the Indians had a big dance. When the dance started, everybody was there but Crow. Later when he came into the tipi somebody smelled fat on him. They asked him what he had eaten, but he told them nothing. They arranged to watch him when he went back home. When everything was over Crow crawled out and flew straight up. Everybody watched, but he flew so high that nobody could see him but Dragonfly, who doesn't blink his eyes. Dragonfly watched until he could see where Crow was going down.

Next morning the Indians went there, and found Crow in his tipi. His wife was with him and they had a little girl walking around. Crow was by a big flat rock which lay over the fireplace and covered a hole. There were buffalo in this hole, but the Indians did not know this.

Coyote had a scheme to find out what Crow was eating. The chief called all the people to a meeting. Coyote said, "You all move away in the morning. I'm going to turn into a little puppy." They all moved in the morning and left Coyote there. He changed himself into a little yipping puppy, but he forgot to do something about his moustache and his eyes, and they looked too wise.

Crow's little daughter was looking around. She heard the puppy yipping and soon found him. She took the puppy and ran up to the hill where Crow and his wife lived. They told her to throw the animal away. "That is not a dog," they cried, "look at his eyes. They are too wise for a little puppy." But the little girl wouldn't give up the pup, just as you can't make a child give up her pet today.

When Crow started to get the meat they covered up the pup's eyes, but there was a little opening and he could see what was going on. So when Crow went into the hole and brought up some meat, Coyote knew just where to go.

After a while Crow and his wife left. Coyote got away from the little girl and ran into the hole. He opened the hole and scared the buffalo out. They ran out of the hole and knocked down the tipi and broke the poles. Crow saw what was happening and waited above the hole for Coyote to come out. He was going to hit him on the head and kill him.

All the buffalo ran out but one slow one. As he came out Coyote ran out under his legs.

When Coyote got a little ways he said to Crow, "You lost your tipi. Now at night you can live in the brush and you can eat from the dead meat that's lying around. That is how you can make your living."

COYOTE TRICKS THE WHITE MAN

Coyote was walking down a road when he saw somebody riding toward him on horseback. When the rider came up Coyote saw that it was a white man. Coyote kept looking at him, already thinking up some way to cheat him.

The man pointed toward Coyote and said, "I'm looking for the cleverest coyote. Are you the one that tricks all the people; are you that clever one?"

Coyote said, "No, I am not that one."

But the white man insisted, "You are the man that cheats the people." Coyote kept denying that he was the clever one. "Hurry up," said the white man, "cheat me, perform some trick on me."

Coyote said, "Oh, I'm not that kind of man. They just call me that."

The white man said, "I know about you; let's have a match."

Finally Coyote said, "It's true, I'm that one, but my medicine for cheating the people is at home. I left it way back west and it would take me a long time to go get it."

The white man said, "Well, you go get it."

Coyote answered, "I'm pretty tired. I've traveled a long ways. If you want to have a match, you lend me your horse and I'll go get my medicine."

The man got off his horse and said, "All right, you go get your medicine."

Coyote picked up a little stick and went to the opposite side from the white man in order to get on the horse. Coyote then jabbed the horse as he pretended to try to get on him. The horse gave a snort and jumped away from him. "Your horse is afraid of me because I have no hat," Coyote said.

"All right, I'll give you my hat," the man said.

Coyote pretended to get on the horse, jabbing him again. "Your horse is afraid of me because I have no coat," Coyote explained. The white man gave Coyote his coat.

Coyote again caused the horse to snort and jump. "Your horse is afraid of me because I have no boots." The man gave Coyote his boots.

Again Coyote tried to get on the horse, but as usual the horse appeared to be afraid. "Your horse is scared of me because I have no pants." The man took off his pants and gave them to Coyote.

Coyote did the same thing to the horse and said, "I haven't any gun." The man strapped his gun on Coyote. This kept up until the white man did not have a stitch of clothes.

When Coyote got all the white man had, he got on the horse and rode away, leaving the man with nothing on. After riding a short distance he turned and said, "Say, white man, you know it now. I am a clever Coyote; this is how I cheat people." The white man called him to come back, but Coyote did not listen and rode off and left him there. He took everything the man had.

HOW THE POOR BOY GOT THE WIFE HE WANTED

Out on a hill a girl was crying for her brother who had been killed in a fight with the Comanches. "If I could just see my brother," she said. "If I could just see his bones. If somebody would just bring me one of his bones—any one—I'd marry him."

"What did you say?" someone asked. It was a poor boy who had quietly come upon the girl and heard her. She told him what she had said.

"I'm going to look for your brother's bones," he said. "You stand on this hill every day and look off in the distance. You watch for my return."

Poor Boy went off and prayed. *Hini*[1] said to him, "You see that bunch of horses in the distance? That is where you will find her brother." The Comanches were having a sun dance, and right in the center, at the lodge, was where he was to find that girl's brother. During the day everybody was taking part in the dance or watching, so he planned to sneak up there at night.

At night he came up on the north side of the arbor and sat very quiet. People were still around, but it was dark. As he sat there it sounded to him as if something up at the fork of the center pole was taking a breath and sighing, "Oh, I'm tired." It was the girl's brother, who was tied up there, cut through the wrists and ankles, but still alive. Poor Boy sat there wishing something would take pity on him and help him.

A spider said, "All right, I'll help. Go ahead, let's climb this pole." He climbed up and then across to the center pole. He had been turned into a spider.

The girl's brother said, "I sure am tired."

Poor Boy said to him, "Brother-in-law, I've come. Tonight I'm going to take you home." He and Spider cut the straps binding the man, and then he, too, was turned into a spider. There were three spiders now.

Spider said, "Before you get away from this sun dance the Comanches are going to chase you. You are going to turn into humans and they will find out who you are. You run into the chief's tipi. Only the chief and his wife are in there. Outside there will be many Comanches. The chief will announce that they will all smoke. He will offer you a black pipe and a red pipe. Be sure to take the black one, for if you take the red one they will kill you. The chief will also offer you red water and black water. Take the black water and drink it. When you get out of the tipi the people will chase you, but don't look back, for if you do, they will kill you. When they are chasing you, stop, but don't look back. They are going to holler and come up to you. The second time you stop, it is going to be

---

[1]The word *Hini* means "mind," "spirit." In this sense it means "something was telling him"; "in his mind he heard something saying." It does not refer to a being.

much worse. The third time it is going to sound as if they will run over you. But don't look back. The fourth time you will be free."

That was the way it happened. These two Apache boys who were being chased by the Comanches knew the rules and followed them. The Comanche leader told his men that if the boys went over the hill without looking back, his people were to let them go. The boys got away.

That night the traveling was good, for something was helping them. Near daylight they were getting near their camp. About daylight when the girl had finished eating she went up on the hill. She stood there looking off into the distance. She saw one fellow standing up. Then the other got up, and she saw two men standing there. She ran down the hill toward them. The camp saw her running and looked and saw the men. She threw her arms around her brother. Then she went through the camp hollering, "My brother has come back."

All the people said, "Yes, that is the fellow killed in battle; he has come back."

The old man said to his son, "Who brought you home?"

"That fellow."

"Oh, he is Poor Boy."

The old man announced that Poor Boy had brought his son back. The boy then told what had happened to him. He still had wound-marks on his wrists and ankles.

The old man said, "Son-in-law, come have a feast." The two boys who had come back sat together by the door. They began to eat. Visitors came in and asked the old man who brought his son back. "That's him. My son is sitting by his brother-in-law," he would say. They treated Poor Boy to the best of everything. He was married to the girl he had wanted.

THE WOMAN WHO MARRIED A STALLION

A young couple were just married. They went off on a hunt, hoping to get deer or other game. After a time they came to a place where they saw some deer and wild horses. The man told his wife, "You stay right here and don't leave this place." He got off his horse and started stalking the game on foot.

When he was out of sight this woman led his horse after her and started following the man. She came upon a pile of bones. They were nice looking bones, very greasy looking. The woman spoke to herself, "I wish these would turn into a young man. I would like to marry him."

This woman left these bones and went to where she could see her husband. She was standing there watching him stalk the game, when a nice looking young man came up from the creek. He was handsome with thick, bushy, black hair, braided nicely. He said, "What did you say when you saw those bones?"

"I didn't say anything," the woman replied.

The man insisted that she said something, but she denied it. He said, "I heard you say, 'I wish these bones would turn into a nice young man and steal me.'" She denied saying that. The man said, "I heard you say that," but she again denied it. The young man insisted that she had said that. Finally she admitted it. The young man said, "Those are my bones you were talking to. Tie that horse here and you come back with me where my mother is." She tied the horse.

They traveled a long way. It was a very hot day. After a while he said, "You lie down and rest, you are tired." She lay down and went to sleep. After some time she woke up. There standing over her was a great big thing. It had a big fat neck and a long mane. It was a large stallion. He was standing on the sunny side of her and she was lying in his shade. He told her that after she went to sleep he turned into a wild stallion. When she saw he was a stallion she began crying. She got up to run away, but he went behind her and forced her on. He would swing his head from side to side and push her along, sometimes biting her on the buttocks. They married.

The game fled from the husband and he didn't get any. He went back for his wife, but she was gone. The horse was tied to a tree. He got on his horse and started riding around. He went all over the territory, through the creek and up and down looking for his wife.

He went north. He heard some wild horses. He went over

toward them. He saw a large stallion standing alone; under him he could see a head. When he got near the horses ran, and he saw that there was a woman under the stallion. When she saw the man, she ran faster than the horses did. She was leading them and wherever she went they followed.

The man went back to camp. When he got to the camp he called, "Hurry up, hurry up everybody, a wild stallion has stolen my wife. She is living with him and she has married him."

They all began calling to each other, "Hurry up and get the fastest horses and get leather ropes."

The husband called, "Whoever has a fast horse hurry up and come with me."

They all got on fast horses.

The man took them back to where he had seen the wild horses. They trailed them and finally they found them. The stallion was with the woman and he would make the other horses stay away. The Indians made their plans. Some were to go this way and some were to go that way to surround the horses.

But the horses began running here and there. The woman was leading them. They would go wherever she went. When the Indians closed in and got pretty close, the stallion broke through, but the woman and the other horses were still in the ring. They got very close and some began to put their horses in among the wild ones. In that way they headed the woman off by herself. They didn't do anything to the horses; they wanted to capture the woman.

They tried to rope her, but every time they threw the rope she would throw up her hands and they could not get her. They kept trying to rope her but every time she would throw up her hands. They worked around for a long time, until their horses were tired and they wanted to rest.

About this time a young man rode up; his horse was fresh. He chased after the woman. She was fast but he was right over her. He made a feint at roping her and she threw up her arms. As she put them down, he quickly threw the rope and caught her. She bucked like a horse and whinnied like a wild mare. Finally they grabbed her. She would kick and bite like a wild horse. She had no clothes on, except a few rags around her neck and her wrists. Her other clothes had been torn off.

They led her back to camp, as they would a horse, and she sat back on her haunches as a horse would. They set up a pole in the center of the camp and tied her there. Every little while she would get all tangled up in the rope and fall down. The kids were having fun with her. They would throw blankets over her and she would buck.

At night they heard a wild horse around. It was her husband, the stallion. He ran around the edge of the tipis neighing. He had lost his wife.

Next morning the real husband fixed himself up and went to the woman's brother. He told him, "You see your sister out there. What she is doing is shameful. You can do whatever you like with her."

But the woman's brother said, "You do what you want to. You are boss of her. You can kill her there if you wish."

Maybe it was the man's father, but some old man cried, "Come over here and see this wild horse that is tied. We are all going to look at her."

When they heard this old man talking they all came out. The husband went to his tipi and got his arrows. This woman was running round and round wild. The man came up with his arrows. Her brother said, "She is acting in a shameful way. You, her husband, do as you wish."

Finally the woman got all tangled up in the rope. The man then took his arrows and killed her, his wife. The third arrow killed her. She had no clothes on and teeth marks all over her body showed where the stallion had bitten her. He took the rope off of her and the dogs ate her. That is what he did with his wife.

Alabama-Coushatta Tales

HOWARD N. MARTIN

THE CREATION OF THE EARTH

In the beginning everything was covered by water. The only living things were a few small animals floating on a raft. Nothing else could be seen.

One day the animals decided that they wanted to make the land appear; so they called for someone to try. Crawfish said he would and dived off the raft. The water was so deep that he was unable to reach bottom.

Three days later Crawfish tried again and failed. On the third trial, though, he reached the bottom. Using his tail to scoop up the mud, he began building a great mud chimney. He worked rapidly, building it higher and higher, until the top of the mud chimney stuck up above the surface of the water. The mud began spreading to all sides, forming a great mass of soft earth.

The animals looked in all directions. They agreed that Crawfish had done a good job, but they thought that the surface of the earth was too smooth. So Buzzard was sent out to shape it. Now Buzzard was a huge bird with long, powerful wings. He flew along just above the top of the soft earth, flapping his wings. When his wings swung down, they cut deep holes or valleys in the soft earth. When his wings swung up, they formed the hills and mountains. When Buzzard didn't flap his wings and just sailed along, he made the level country or plains. And so the surface of the earth is made up of plains, valleys, and mountains.

The Alabama-Coushatta Indians migrated into Texas to get away from the white settlements in the Old South. They found a wild and isolated hunting ground in the Big Thicket, where a reservation was later set aside for them. Though they are now Christianized, much of their mythology and legendary history survives in their native Creek dialects.

THE ORIGIN OF THE ALABAMA-COUSHATTA INDIANS

Indians were made from clay down in a big cave under the earth. In this cave they lived a long time before they decided to go up to the surface of the earth. After they started upward, they camped three times on the way. Finally, they reached the mouth of the cave.

There they found a large tree standing. The Alabamas and Coushattas went out of the cave on opposite sides of a root of this big tree. That is why they do not talk exactly the same way; but they have always lived near each other.

At first the Indians would stay outside only during the night, returning to the cave when day came. One night when they came out to play, they heard an owl hooting. Most of the Indians were so frightened that they ran back into the cave and never returned to the surface of the earth. That is why the Alabamas and Coushattas are so few. If the owl had not hooted, then all the Indians would have remained on the surface of the earth, and the Alabamas and Coushattas would have been more numerous.

One day a white man came to the cave and saw some tracks in the sand. He wanted to find out who had made the tracks, so he went to the place three times but did not see anyone. He finally decided to play a trick on these strange people. Early one morning he put a barrel of whiskey near the place where he found the footprints. When the Indians came out of the cave that night to play, they saw the barrel and wondered what was in it. One of them tasted the contents. Soon he began to feel good and sing and dance. Then the others drank also and became so drunk that the white man was able to catch them. After that the Alabamas and Coushattas had to stay on top of the earth and were not allowed to go near the big cave.

THE MAN WITH HORNS

Before the Alabamas came to Texas they were always fighting another tribe. For a long time the Alabamas had been

losing their battles. Often they had to run deep into the woods
and hide. One day they camped in some thick bushes near a
beautiful stream. Food was plentiful and the camp seemed to
be in a safe place, so the Alabamas stayed several days. On
the third day a woman went down to the stream to fill a pot
with water. There in a clay bowl near the bank of the stream
she saw an Indian baby. Although she wanted to pick up the
baby, she was afraid to wade into the stream since the enemy
might have used the baby to set a trap. The woman filled her
pot with water and then hurried to the camp to report what
she had seen.

On the chief's orders some of the men brought the baby to
the village. It was a very beautiful child. The chief said that he
thought this was an unusual child and would bring luck to
the tribe.

By the next morning the child had grown to the size of an
eight-year-old boy. The people marveled at this quick growth.
Everyone was convinced now that the boy was not just an
ordinary person.

On the next day he had grown to the size of a sixteen-year-
old boy, and on the third day he was fully grown and had large
horns sticking out of his head. Since the stranger did not have
any clothes large enough to fit him, the chief ordered the men
of the camp to bring clothes to the "Horned Man," as he was
called by the Alabamas.

Horned Man told the people that he had come to help them
but that they would also have to help themselves. Then he
called for the bravest men in the camp. He said he wanted the
head of the most vicious wolf they could find in the forest.

Three days later the warriors returned with the head of a
large wolf. Horned Man put the wolf's head on top of the
chief's tent, and immediately it began turning around and
around. It looked in all directions. Finally it stopped, pointing
to the east. Horned Man said that the wolf's head indicated
that enemies were approaching from the east, so he led all the
people to a hiding place in the south. The next day the wolf's
head pointed to the west, and this time Horned Man led the
Alabamas to some dense woods in the north.

"The wolf's head will always point to your enemies," said Horned Man, "but if the head should stop pointing and fall to the ground, this will indicate that you are completely surrounded."

By watching the wolf's head closely the Alabamas managed to slip away from their enemies for a long time. But one day the head became uncertain in its movements. It turned slowly without pointing very long in any one direction. Suddenly it fell to the ground. At this signal the Alabamas grasped their axes and placed themselves in readiness for battle. The enemy warriors rushed into the camp, and the fighting began. All of the enemy tribesmen were killed, while the Alabamas did not lose a man.

"Bring Horned Man to me," said the chief, "so I can thank him for helping us win this victory."

They looked all over the woods but could not find Horned Man. He had disappeared. And none of the Alabamas ever saw him again.

RABBIT OUTWITS FARMER

One warm summer day a farmer was hoeing in his field. The peas had just come up and were barely tall enough to be hoed. As the farmer finished one row and stood in the shade to rest, Rabbit came along and asked, "What are you doing in this field?"

The farmer answered, "I have been hoeing peas so that I will have something to eat when cold weather comes."

Then Rabbit said, "If you were like me, you wouldn't have to work at all but would always have a good time." Rabbit then went merrily on his way.

Some time later, when the peas were almost ripe, Rabbit returned to the field. The farmer was away, so Rabbit decided to play a trick on him. He cut down every plant in the field and went back into the forest.

When the farmer returned to the field, he found that his crop was ruined, and he suspected that Rabbit had done it. The next day the farmer, meeting Rabbit in the forest, asked him why he had destroyed the peas. Rabbit said, "I thought you told me that I could have the peas when they grew up." This reply made the farmer so angry that he threatened to kill Rabbit.

Rabbit said, "I will let you kill me if you will do it by chopping off my head." The farmer agreed, and Rabbit told him to get an ax. Rabbit then laid his head on a large stone. The farmer said to himself, "Now I will get revenge for the destruction of my crop. I will swing the ax so hard that it will go right through Rabbit's neck." He swung the ax with all his force, but before it came down Rabbit jumped out of the way. The sharp ax hit the stone and broke into many pieces. The farmer was so angry that he started to turn his dogs loose to kill Rabbit. But Rabbit said he would set the woods on fire if the farmer tried to kill him on land in any way beside the method they had agreed upon.

Rabbit then suggested another way in which the farmer could get revenge. Rabbit said that he could be killed only by drowning. So the farmer put him in a basket with a large stone, threw the basket upon his shoulder, and started toward the sea.

For a long time the farmer walked without stopping. Finally, Rabbit asked how much farther they would have to travel before they reached the sea. The farmer said the sea was now in sight. Rabbit then said, "You had better get a drink of water, because you have walked all day without drinking." The farmer decided that he was thirsty, so he laid the basket down and walked to a near-by spring for a drink.

While the farmer was away, another man came along, driving some cattle, and asked Rabbit why he was in the basket. Rabbit said that he was being taken to the home of the chief, who would give him his daughter to marry. He said that he was not to be seen until he was married to the chief's daughter. That was the reason he was being carried in a basket.

Now the stranger had seen the chief's daughter and he greatly admired her. So he asked to take Rabbit's place. No sooner was this done than Rabbit stepped out and drove the cattle away.

When the farmer returned from the spring, he carried the basket to the seashore. Without hesitating he threw the weighted basket into the water.

On the following day the farmer met Rabbit, who was driving a herd of cattle. To the farmer's question Rabbit replied, "When someone is thrown into the sea but swims ashore, that indicates that he will have good luck. That is why I have a herd of cattle."

The farmer asked, "If I were thrown into the sea, would I, too, have good luck when I came out of the water?"

"Certainly," said Rabbit, and to the farmer's mind came visions of good crops and an abundance of food. So, he got into a basket and asked Rabbit to carry him to the sea. From a high cliff Rabbit threw the farmer into the water.

WHIPPOORWILL

When the Indians came to the top of the earth, they made friends with the many kinds of birds and animals they found, and men and birds and beasts all lived together in one village.

The women of this village learned to make thread out of cotton. They also learned to use colors in preparing the thread. As a result, it wasn't long before they were weaving beautiful cotton clothes. One woman was especially good at weaving, and everyone liked the clothes she made. The reason she could weave so well was that she had learned to make a special thread. She kept this thread in a basket in her home.

One day this woman started to weave a coat. When she took down her thread basket, she saw that the basket was empty. She cried out, and the people of the village gathered around her. She told them what had happened and later repeated her story to the chief.

Everyone was surprised to hear that the thread had been stolen. The chief called a council meeting to discuss the theft. Then the other members of the tribe were called to the meeting. All the birds and animals came too.

The chief told what had happened. He said that the thief

must be punished. He concluded by saying that all the inhabitants of the village were present at the meeting and that someone in the crowd was a thief. Immediately all the Indians said, "We didn't steal the thread." All the animals said, "We didn't steal the thread." All the birds denied the theft, except Whippoorwill, who was sitting near the edge of the crowd with his head hanging to the ground.

The chief walked over to the bird and said, "Whippoorwill is the thief. He shows that he is guilty."

"Yes, you are right," said Whippoorwill, "I stole the thread. My heart will always feel sorry if I do not say I stole it."

It was necessary to punish Whippoorwill, so the chief said, "From now on Whippoorwill cannot talk in his own language. All he can say is 'I stole it' so people will know he is a thief."

Whippoorwill was so ashamed of himself that he left the village and made his home in the thick underbrush somewhere in the woods. He still lives in hidden places, and if you listen carefully near a creek or river you can hear him saying, "I stole it. I stole it."

MEXICAN TALES

Stories of My People

JOVITA GONZÁLEZ

THE PAISANO

Everyone knows that when the world was young all the creatures of Nature spoke a common language and understood each other. Social classes and distinctions also prevailed among them. The eagle was the proud king of the air and all flying things, and the mockingbird had the vain glory of being the lord of the singers. In this manner all the different families with a king at their head formed a world of their own; and quarrels, jealousies, and disputes were never lacking among the feathered people.

There was a bird, who, although of plebeian origin, was a distant relation of the pheasants. This made him vain, arrogant, and haughty. Every evening he went walking, his crest waving in the air and his tail switching from left to right with the pride of the peacock. He did not deign to speak to the humble sparrows and the modest dove who always mourned her misfortunes. But he was only too glad to greet the nobles and the lords of high position whenever the occasion presented itself. Forgetting his humble birth, he addressed them as cousins and *paisanos*.

"Good morning, *Paisano* Zenzontle,[1] how is your Lordship?" Or, "How are you, *Paisano?*" addressing the noble Sir Cardinal.

His lack of common sense and his excessive vanity blinded

[1]Mockingbird.

19

him in such a way that he never did notice the disdain and coldness with which he was tolerated. One day while the eagle was discussing important matters of state with the nobles of the kingdom — the cardinals, the scissortails, and the hawks — the foolish cousin of the pheasant family came into the chamber without announcing himself. He did not see the consternation on the faces of the nobles, who were shocked at his daring, but, bowing and smiling, said to the monarch:

"How fares your Majesty and my *paisanos*, the nobles here assembled?"

The eagle, furious at seeing the familiarity with which a plebeian treated him, cried out in a voice like the tempest of a July night:

"Out of my presence, creature of low birth! I banish you forever from my kingdom. From now on you forfeit the noble name of *Faisán*. You will forget to fly and will feed on the most unclean things of the earth, snakes, tarantulas, and poisonous insects."

The poor bird, blinded with shame and mortification, tried to fly from the courtroom but could not; his wings had lost their strength. To his greater dishonor, he was forced to run out of the room like a common beast. Since that time he has been the outcast—a pariah—of the birds. He hunts here and there among the chaparral and cactus in his endeavor to hide his shame and disgrace. When the heat of the desert plains is unbearable, something like a sob is heard. It is his voice harsh and melancholy mourning the loss of his caste.

Not only the birds mock him, but man, to remind him of his pride and vanity, calls him *paisano*.

THE MOCKINGBIRD

There was a time when all the creatures of Nature talked a common language. This language was Spanish. *El zenzontle*, the mockingbird, had the sweetest voice of all. The other birds stopped their flight to listen to him; the Indian lover ceased his words of love; even the talkative *arroyo* hushed. He foretold the spring, and when the days grew short and his song was no longer heard, the north winds came. Although he was not a foolish bird, *el zenzontle* was getting conceited.

"I am great, indeed," he said to his mate. "All Nature obeys me. When I sing, the blossoms hid in the trees come forth; the prairie flowers put on their gayest garments at my call and the birds begin to mate; even man, the all wise, heeds my voice and dances with joy, for the happy season draws near."

"Hush, you are foolish and conceited like all men," replied his wife. "They listen and wait for the voice of God, and when He calls, even you sing."

He did not answer his wife, for you must remember he was not foolish after all, but in his heart he knew that he was right.

That night after kissing his wife good night, he said to her, "Tomorrow I will give a concert to the flowers, and you shall see them sway and dance when they hear me."

"*Con el favor de Dios*," she replied. ("If God wills it.")

"Whether God wills it or not I shall sing," he replied angrily. "Have I not told you that the flowers obey me and not God?"

Early next morning *el zenzontle* could be seen perched on the highest limb of a huisache. He cleared his throat, coughed, and opened his bill to sing, but no sound came. For down with the force of a cyclone swooped a hawk and grabbed with his steel-like claws the slender body of the singer.

"*Con el favor de Dios, con el favor de Dios*," he cried in distress, while he thought of his wise little wife. As he was being carried up in the air, he realized his foolishness and repented of it, and said, "O God, it is you who make the flowers bloom and the birds sing, not I." As he thought thus, he felt himself slipping and falling, falling, falling. He fell on a ploughed field, and what a fall it was! A white dove who had her nest near by picked him up and comforted him.

"My wings," he mourned looking at them, "how tattered and torn they look! What shall I tell my wife?"

The dove took pity on him, and plucking three of her white feathers, mended his wings.

As a reminder of his foolish pride, the mockingbird to this day has the white feathers of the dove. And it is said by those who know that he never begins to sing without saying, "Con el favor de Dios."

THE DOVE

Do you know why the dove ever mourns? This is the story common among Mexican people.

All nature, the stars of the heavens, the beasts of the forest, and the birds of the air had been told that the Messiah was to be born. And when the Angel announced the birth of the Savior, all the creatures of the earth came to worship Him, all but one — the dove. She was so humble and unassuming that no one thought of telling her the wonderful news. Yet the sign that brought the birds and beasts to the manger itself was the form of a fluttering dove — assumed by the Holy Spirit.

But the dove herself never saw the Christ Child, and that is why her song is a sob. In the mellow warm mornings of spring, or when the evening star makes her appearance in the twilight, a soft, mournful cry is heard in the cañada. It is the dove.

THE CICADA

La Cigarra[2] was a gay person, in fact too gay to suit his wife. In spring when the huisache was in bloom he became intoxicated with the balmy perfumed air and the joy of living. It was then that, forgetting his duties of a faithful husband, he made love to the butterflies, which, like flying flowers, tempted him with their beauty, and the hummingbirds, the tenors of the fields.

His wife was jealous and when her erring husband returned home in the evening, satisfied with himself and life, you should have heard her garrulous voice rise above the stillness of night.

[2]The locust or cicada.

But he said nothing and merely sat heavy eyed with love and too happy to hear. As summer came on and the July heat made his life unbearable, his romantic adventurous habits were transformed into a languorous lassitude. Perched on the bark of a mesquite, he complained in his shrill voice of the cruelty of the sun. It was then that his wife, forgiving his past offenses, bathed his feverish forehead with the morning dew. The butterflies seeing him so domesticated flew to more venturesome lovers and the hummingbirds forgot him in disgust.

All was peaceful again until spring, when passions were stirred in his heart, and his roving disposition returned. At last his wife went to the eagle, the monarch of all flying beings, and presented her plea. After due deliberation the king replied:

"Only one thing can check his roaming ways and that is to make him ugly in the sight of the ladies. From now on his eyes will be popped and round, and his colored wings an ashy gray. If this does not stop him nothing else will."

And it did, for the butterflies laughed at his owl-like eyes and colorless wings. Chagrined and morose, he came home and for months refused to speak. His wife's wishes had gone beyond her expectations; she wanted him at home, it is true, but expected him to keep her company as in the days of their courtship. Realizing that she could never be happy with this ugly creature who did nothing but complain, she went to the king again and this time asked him to make her like her husband. And with her change she became fretful like him. So to this day the shrill voices of the cicadas are heard in the heat of summer, the male complaining and shrill, the female shrill but contented.

THE GUADALUPANA VINE

In South Texas there is a vine used for medicinal purposes known as the Guadalupana vine. It bears small gourdlike fruit. The seeds have a bright red covering, which on being removed shows the image of our Lady of Guadalupe. Everybody is acquainted with the story of the apparition of our Lady of Guadalupe in Mexico. The story of the vine in itself is equally interesting.

Two vaqueros were going to the nearest town for provisions. One of them was riding a very spirited *potro*. On coming to a creek the horse was frightened, and in spite of all that the rider could do the bronco threw him on the rocky banks. The other, terrified by the accident, did not know how to help his companion, who was slowly bleeding to death. As he sat there, a lovely lady came to him. She was dressed in blue, and he noticed that her mantle was sprinkled with stars. What astonished him more was to see that she floated, her feet not touching the ground. But he attributed this phenomenon to his bewildered condition. She approached, holding a small red fruit in her hand.

"Try this, my son," the lady said; "dip it in mescal and put it on the wound."

"But it will burn," stammered the surprised vaquero. The lovely lady smiled, shook her head, and whispered, "*No arde, no arde.*" ("It will not burn.")

The vaquero was cured immediately. The vaqueros consider this a miracle of the Virgin, and to verify this story they point to the fact that the Virgin left her image engraved on all the seed.[3]

▼▼▼▼▼▼▼▼▼▼

A Pack Load of Mexican Tales

RILEY AIKEN

THE THREE COUNSELS

This was a boy who ran away from home. Though at heart not bad, he had three habits that were by no means good, for

---

[3]On the border, the Mexican housewife puts up jars of the Guadalupana fruit in mescal. The people use no other remedy for cuts and wounds.

he would stick to no purpose, was always asking about people's affairs, and would not control his temper.

Sí señor, he ran away from home, but, do you know, he was hardly beyond the horizon when he left the highway for a trail, called to an old man to know his business, and flew into a rage when the latter did not answer.

Presently, however, the *viejito* spoke. "I am a peddler of advice," said he.

"What kind of advice?" asked the boy.

"It will cost you one peso to find out," was the answer.

The boy had only three pesos, but curiosity induced him to give one to the *viejito*.

"First," said the old man, "don't leave a highway for a trail."

"Is that what you call advice?" asked the boy. "You are a fraud."

"Don't you like that one?" asked the *viejito*. "Then give me another peso and lend an ear."

The boy reluctantly handed over the second of his three pesos and waited. "Second," said the *viejito*, "don't ask about things that don't pertain to you.

"*Mal ladrón*," shouted the boy, "for one peso I would kill you."

"Calm yourself, *hijito*," said the old man. "I have among my wares one more bit of advice you need. Will you buy it or not?"

The boy's curiosity was too much for him. He gave his last peso to the stranger and listened attentively for the third time.

"Don't lose your temper," laughed the old man, and before the boy could gather his wits, he had vanished into the chaparral.

Sad and empty of pocket, the youth continued on his way.

He took to the road again just as a stranger mounted on a large black horse galloped up.

"Where to, *joven?*" called he.

"To the city," said the boy.

"Then you need advice," responded the man. "Look, I will help you. One league up the road you will find a short cut.

You will recognize it by my horse's tracks. It will save you
many miles."

The boy thanked him and continued on his journey with the
purpose of leaving the highway for the path. However, never
being able to keep to a purpose, he disregarded the path.

At noon he came to a ranch house. A bandit sat beneath an
arbor in front of it.

"*Pase, joven,*" he called. "You are just in time for dinner."

The boy entered the house and took a chair at the table.
He had waited no time when a servant placed before him a
dish containing the head of a man. He was at the point of
asking a question when he remembered suddenly one of his
three costly bits of advice. "I had better ask no questions,"
thought he.

"Young man," said the bandit, "what do you think of this
head?"

"It is a good head," replied the boy.

"Have you no questions?" queried the bandit.

"No, señor, none."

"Would you like to see some of my keepsakes?" asked the
bandit.

"If it is your pleasure to show them," said the boy, "then it
will be my pleasure to see them."

A closet was opened and the boy was shown many skeletons
hanging by the neck.

"How do you like my men?" asked the host.

"They are good men," answered the boy.

"*Joven,*" said the bandit, "I kill all my guests. These men,
like you, each in his turn stepped across my threshold to have
dinner with me. Each was shown a head, but different from
you, they wanted to know all about it. Their curiosity brought
them to their present condition. You, however, have asked
nothing about things that do not concern you, and for that
reason my servants will conduct you safely from the ranch.
In my corral there are three mules and a horse. The mules will
be loaded with gold, and the horse will be saddled. These are
yours."

Six bags of gold were tied *mancornado* (in pairs) and placed on the mules. The boy mounted the horse and with the help of the servants was soon on the highway again. "Indeed," he said to himself, "it pays to keep to the main road and it pays to ask no questions about things that do not concern one. Now I am rich."

"Halt!" called a voice from the roadside.

There stood a bandit with his arms crossed.

"What have you in those sacks?" he asked.

The boy was on the point of cursing with rage when he recalled the third bit of advice.

"It is a secret I prefer not to tell," he answered calmly.

"Speak or I shall kill you," threatened the bandit.

"If you feel that is best," said the boy, "then follow your conscience."

"Ha!" said the man, "you are a wise boy. *Adiós;* may you have a pleasant journey."

This *joven* entered the city. Before many weeks had passed he had built and stocked the best store in town and was making barrels of money. Furthermore, he met and married a wealthy girl. However, the best of all was that she, too, did not leave the main road for a path, asked no questions about things that did not pertain to her, and always kept her temper.

JUAN IN HEAVEN

Juan de Toluca had been a good man. Therefore it was to the gates of Paradise that he directed his steps upon leaving this life.

"*Buenos días,* San Pedro," said he. "*Con su permiso* I wish to enter here."

But before St. Peter gave his permission, he began asking questions. He wanted to know how much money Juan had, his name and age, and his religion. At last he asked, "What is your race?"

"*Mexicano,*" answered Juan.

"That is too bad," said St. Peter. "We don't keep Mexicans here."

"Why?" asked Juan. "Isn't it enough that one has kept the commandments and attended church?"

"Generally speaking, that is true," said St. Peter, "but the Lord has asked me to keep to the letter of the law. It is nowhere written in our constitution that heaven was made for Mexicans; therefore, I must ask that you step out of line and go to the regions below."

Juan was insistent, however. It had never been his plan to live in the infernal regions. Besides, he had gone to considerable expense upon leaving the vale of tears and had paid sixty pesos for a new hat. This useless expense St. Peter regretted sincerely, but he maintained that he could do nothing about the matter.

"Well, if I must take the other trail, I shall go," said Juan. "However, San Pedro, please do me one and only one favor."

"And what favor is that, Juan?"

"Permit me, please, to take one little peep at the City of Paradise."

St. Peter refused, saying that the memory of the sight of heaven would make hell hotter for him.

"You had better run along," he continued. "You are blocking the line."

Juan fell upon his knees and pleaded so earnestly that St. Peter said, "Well, if that's all you want, have your way."

Thereupon he allowed the Mexican to stick his head through a small opening in the gate of pearls.

Juan saw all that he had ever imagined he would see and even more. He realized the bitter truth of St. Peter's remarks to the effect that he would regret one sight of heaven, and determined quickly to resort to cunning. He removed his hat, and at a moment when St. Peter's back was turned sent it rolling down the main street of heaven.

"My hat fell off!" he cried. "*Ay, ay, ay, sombrero de mis entrañas!* I will never leave this place without the sombrero so dear to my affections."

Peter was greatly perplexed. Some contend he had taken a liking to the Mexican. However this may be, the fact is he opened the gate and bade Juan get his hat and hurry back.

Once in Paradise, however, Juan found it convenient to lose himself in the great crowds of angels, and since St. Peter was having trouble at the gate, the illegal entrance to heaven was overlooked.

Everything had gone smoothly in God's kingdom until one day an angel asked to speak privately to the Lord.

"What do you want?" asked Nuestro Señor (Our Lord).

"No, nothing, Señor," replied the angel reverently, "except, Señor, I have lost a ring and I suspect someone of having . . ."

"Sh—," said the Lord. "Not so loud. Never mention the ring again."

The angel bowed, apologized, and left immediately.

Three days later another angel would speak privately with the Lord.

"What do you want?" asked the Lord.

"No, nothing," said the angel, "only, Señor, I have lost a diamond brooch, and I suspect someone of having . . ."

"Sh—," said the Lord. "Not so loud. It will ruin the reputation of my place. Go now and never mention the brooch again."

Three days passed and still another angel requested to speak to the Lord in private.

"What do you want?" asked Nuestro Señor.

"No, nothing," said the angel, "only, Señor, just this morning I lost my earbobs and . . ."

"I know," said the Lord; "I know."

Nuestro Señor looked sad and perplexed. At last, he said in a whisper, "Do you know, I believe there is a Mexican in heaven."

He went immediately to St. Peter. "Don't waste your breath, St. Peter," said He. "It isn't a question of denial. A Mexican is among us, and we must find some way to rid the place of him without a scandal. Look, the Texan is his neighbor. He knows the Mexican; go quickly to the devil and borrow him for a few moments."

Presently the Lord and St. Peter were asking all manner of questions.

"What are his weak points?" asked Nuestro Señor.

"Well, well," said the Texan.

"Ah, ah," said Nuestro Señor, "no spitting here."

"Well," continued the Texan, "first, I would say women."

"We won't bother about that," said the Lord. "Go on, go on."

"Second, I would say *tequila.*"

"Go on," insisted the Lord.

"Third, I would say *La Cucaracha* and his native land."

"Good," said the Lord, "you may go now. St. Peter, get François, the French fiddler."

"*Bueno, Señor,*" said St. Peter.

"François," said the Lord, "can you play *La Cucaracha?*"

"*Mais, oui, Monseigneur,*" said the Frenchman.

Immediately he tuned his instrument.

"Come out here on the balcony where the angels can hear you," said Nuestro Señor. "I'm anxious to know if they like the piece."

"*Très bien, Monseigneur,*" bowed François.

He put his instrument beneath his chin and, after tightening his bow and getting a long breath, he began:

> "*La cucaracha, la cucaracha,*
> *Ya no quiere caminar.*
> *Porque le falta, porque no tiene,*
> *Marijuana que fumar.*"

Suddenly away out in the crowd a hat went sailing into the air, and someone yelled, "*Viva México!*"

"There he is, St. Peter," said Nuestro Señor. "Get him."

And that is the true story, *amigo,* of the only Mexican who ever went to heaven, and you see why they kicked him out.

SISTER FOX AND BROTHER COYOTE

For weeks 'Mana Zorra had been stealing a chicken each night from a ranch not far from her abode when one night she found a small man standing near the opening she had made in the wire of the chicken house. The man was only a figure of wax put there by the *caporal* to frighten the thief. 'Mana Zorra, unaware of this, was afraid, but, being very hungry, she decided to speak to the little man and ask permission to borrow a chicken.

"*Buenas noches*," said 'Mana Zorra.

There was no answer.

"He is either too proud to speak or doesn't hear," said the fox to herself. "If he isn't *mal criado* (ill-bred), then he didn't hear. I will speak to him again."

Going nearer the wax man, she said, "*Buenas noches, Señor.*"

The little man made no response whatsoever, and the fox, after sizing him up from feet to head, decided that she had been insulted.

"Ay, the things I'm going to tell this *hombrecito*," said she. "He shall speak to me this time or I will slap his face."

She walked up to the figure and shouted at the top of her voice, "Step aside, please, and let me pass."

The wax man stubbornly stood his ground and refused to speak.

"'*Ora verás como yo te hago a un la'o* (Now you shall see how I make you move to one side)," said 'Mana Zorra.

She struck the little man in the face and much to her surprise her foot was caught and held fast.

"Let me go!" shouted 'Mana Zorra, "or I shall hit you again."

The wax man refused to let go and 'Mana Zorra hit him full in the face with a hard right swing. The result was that this foot too, like the other, was caught and held.

"*Ay, como eres abuzón,*"[4] grumbled 'Mana Zorra. "Listen, *amigo,* either you let me go or I shall give you a kicking you will never forget."

The wax man was not impressed by the threat and refused to let go. 'Mana Zorra made good her word as to the kicking, but the little man didn't seem to mind at all and added insult to injury by holding her hind feet too.

"I'll bite," she threatened; "I'll bite." And quickly she bit the neck of the wax figure only to find herself caught not only by four feet but by her mouth as well.

"You think you have me," she scolded. "All right, how do

[4] A provincialism meaning an abusive person.

you like this for a belly buster?" She pushed him so hard with her stomach that both of them fell rolling to the ground.

Just then who should appear on the scene but 'Mano Coyote? "What are you doing there, 'Mana Zorra?" he asked.

"No, nothing," she answered. "This Christian and I have come to blows over a chicken. I have a contract with the *ranchero* which provides me a hen a night, but this little fellow can't read and has made up his mind to interfere. Hold him for me, 'Mano Coyote, and I will get a hen for both of us."

The coyote, a gullible fellow, caught the wax man in a clinch and held him while the fox pulled loose, and continued to hold tight until she stole a hen and escaped into the chaparral. Then, much to his chagrin, he found that he had been tricked, and as a result would likely lose his life.

Dawn found 'Mano Coyote struggling with the wax man, and he was there and still fighting when the *caporal* arrived.

"*A' amiguito,*" said the *caporal*. "This is what I have been wanting to find out for a long time. So it is you, Señor Coyote? And I had always thought you my friend. If you wanted a hen to eat, why didn't you come to me like a gentleman and ask for her? However, though greatly disappointed in you, I will give you another chance."

The *caporal* freed the coyote from the wax man and placed him in a little room with one broken window.

"Don't jump through this window till I call you," said the ranch foreman to the coyote. "My dogs will catch and kill you. Wait until I tie them up and get us a snack to eat. Then when I call, jump through the window and come to the kitchen."

The *caporal* heated water and poured it into a large pot that he had placed beneath the window. Then he called, "Come out, Señor Coyote; breakfast is ready."

The coyote jumped through the window and fell into the pot of boiling water. It was surely a miracle that saved his life, but the scalding water took the hair from his body and several toenails from his feet.

"*Ay, ay,*" said 'Mano Coyote, as he crept with flinching feet and sore hide through the thicket. " 'Mana Zorra will pay for this. If I ever see her again I will kill her and eat her up."

Thus went 'Mano Coyote through the brush whining and swearing revenge until he reached a *laguna*. There, before him, lay the fox gazing at something in the water.

"Now I have you," cried the coyote. "Now you are to pay for your smart trick."

"Don't kill me, 'Mano Coyotito," pleaded the fox. "Look! I was placed here to watch this cheese."

"What cheese?" asked the coyote.

The moon was full and the reflection lay at the bottom of the *laguna*.

"There," said the fox, pointing at the reflection. "If you will watch it for me I will get us a chicken. However, be on guard lest the cheese slip beneath the bank."

"I'll watch it for you," said the coyote, "but don't be long. I'm dying for a chicken to eat."

'Mano Coyote had waited and watched several hours when he discovered the cheese slipping beneath the western bank of the *laguna*.

"Hey, Señor Cheese, don't go away," he called. "If you run away, I'll catch you and eat you up."

While 'Mano Coyote talked, the cheese continued to slip away. The coyote, fearing it would escape, sprang into the *laguna* and was soaked and chilled to the marrow before he reached the bank again.

"'Mana Zorra will pay for this," he howled. "Wherever I find her I shall kill her and eat her up."

The coyote had hunted the fox several days when at last he found her lying on her back in a small cave beneath a cropping of boulders. She was sound asleep.

"A' 'Mana Zorrita," hissed the coyote, "now I shall eat you up."

"Don't eat me, 'Mano Coyotito," begged the fox. "Look! When I went to get a hen, the *caporal* asked me to lie here and hold the world on my feet to keep it from falling down. He has gone to get more help and will be back soon to fix it. *Ay de mí*, 'Mano Coyote, I'm hungry. I know where there is a hen, but she will likely be gone when the *caporal* returns. *Ay de mí*, 'Mano Coyote, I'm hungry."

"I'm hungry, too," said the coyote. "Look, 'Mana Zorra; move over to one side. I'll hold the world on my feet if you will hurry and fetch us a hen."

"Good," said the fox, "but take care that the world doesn't fall and come to an end."

"I'll hold it," said the coyote, lying on his back and pushing up with all the strength of his four feet. "However, hurry; I'm hungry."

The fox escaped, and the coyote remained beneath the rock for several hours until he was almost paralyzed by the increasing weight of the world.

At last, being unable longer to stand the pain of his cramped position, he said, "If it is going to fall, then let it fall. I'm quitting this job."

He sprang from beneath the ledge and ran into the clearing. The rock didn't fall and the world showed no signs of coming to an end.

"*Ay, ay,*" said he, " 'Mana Zorra shall pay for this. If I ever catch her I shall kill her and eat her up."

At last the fox was found beneath a large bush near a *gicotera*.[5]

"A' 'Mana Zorra," he cried, "you have played your last trick, for now I'm going to eat you up."

"Don't eat me, 'Mano Coyotito," begged the fox. "Look! I was on my way to get the chicken when a schoolteacher offered me pay to watch a class of boys."

"Where are the boys?" asked the coyote.

"There, before us; it is their schoolroom."

"Where is the money?" asked the coyote further.

"In my pocket," said the fox, as she rattled some broken pieces of porcelain.

"*Pos,* that's good," said the coyote. "What are you going to do with it?"

"I'm going to buy you a pair of trousers and a skirt for myself."

---

[5]*Gicotera*, a rat's nest at the roots of a bush, but Santiago Garza told me that a kind of bee makes its nests in a *gicotera*.

"Your idea is good," observed the coyote. "However, you must leave some money with which to purchase food."

"Certainly," said the fox. "I shall buy us a chicken apiece. But why did you mention food, 'Mano Coyote? *Ay, ay de mí,* I'm dying of hunger."

"I'm hungry, too," said the coyote.

"Look!" said the fox. "Watch these boys for me and I'll fetch the hen right away."

"*Cómo no?*" said the coyote. "Only hurry, 'Mana Zorra."

The fox saved her hide again and the coyote was left with the devil to pay, for the schoolroom was a hornets' nest and the boys weren't pupils but a lively lot of hornets.

The coyote sat listening to the hum of pupils reading their lessons when he noticed that the sound had ceased. "They are loafing on me," he said. "I'll shake them up a bit."

He shook them up and this would have been his last adventure had he not found a *laguna* into which to dive and escape the swarm of hornets.

"*Ay, ay,*" wailed the coyote, " 'Mana Zorra shall pay for this. Wherever it is that I find her I shall eat her up, hide and hair."

At last 'Mana Zorra was found in a *carrizal*—a reed swamp. 'Mano Coyote had not forgotten the hornets' sting, the moon cheese, the world trick, and the wax man.

"Now there shall be no more foolishness," said he. " 'Mana Zorra must die."

"Don't eat me," pleaded the fox. "Don't eat me, 'Mano Coyotito. Look! I was on my way to get the hens when I met a bridegroom. He invited me to be godmother at his wedding. I felt it would look bad to refuse, and now that you are here you and I shall be *padrino* and *madrina*. You know how it is at these weddings. There is always plenty to eat and drink, and when it comes to chicken, there is none better in the world than that served at a wedding feast. *Ay, ay,* I'm hungry, 'Mano Coyotito."

"*Pos, sí,*" said the coyote; "I'm hungry, too. But where is the wedding party?"

"They are to pass at any time now," said the fox. "You stay

here and I'll see if they are coming. If you hear popping and cracking you will know it is the fireworks shot by the friends of the couple. I shall be back soon."

'Mana Zorra slipped around the canebrake and set fire to it in first one place and then another. 'Mano Coyote heard the popping and cracking and began to dance with joy.

"*Taco Talaco*," said he, "here they come. *Taco Talaco*, ay, *Taco Talaco*, what a hot time there will be."

He discovered his mistake too late. The fire had trapped him completely, and so ended the career of 'Mano Coyote the dupe, shouting "*Taco Talaco*" and dancing at his own funeral.

EL PÁJARO CÚ

It was when God made the world. When He created the birds, He first made them and then feathered them. This would have been wise except that a scarcity of feathers left one little creature completely unclothed. This was Pájaro Cú. Yet he, Pájaro Cú, didn't mind in the least, and went about from day to day as innocent as the dawn and as naked as the palm of your hand.

"What is to be done with him?" asked the owl.

"Poor thing," said the dove.

"Shocking," screamed the peafowl. And everyone agreed that it was shocking, a pity, and that something should be done.

"I move," said the owl, "that we each chip in a feather. None will miss so little, and yet all together will make him a splendid coat."

All agreed to this and were at the point of contributing when the peafowl began to wail. "No—, no—, no—," she screamed, "he would then be so vain we could never manage him; think of what you are doing; think of how beautiful he would be. His coat would contain red from the redbird, green from the parrot, black from the crow, white from the swan, gold from the canary, and silver from the guinea. No, no, it will never do, for he will burst with pride."

"We can't leave him this way," said the jackdaw. "He would disgrace the whole republic of birds."

"Yes," said the owl, "he must be clothed. If it is agreed, we will all give a feather, and I will go bond for him."

All the birds from the most common to the rarest contributed, and presently the Pájaro Cú was dressed beyond all description.

He walked to the fountain, gave one look at his magnificent self, and said, "Why do I associate with such birds? I will leave."

Thereupon he flew straight up into the blue of the heavens. Señor Owl followed but to no avail. He was too heavy, and Pájaro Cú was too light. He returned completely exhausted only to face an angry mob.

"So you were to go bond," said the rooster. "You have betrayed us."

"What do you plan to do, Señor Owl?" asked the crow.

"What do I propose to do? What can be done? May I ask?"

Thereupon the birds flew at him, and it was with many wounds he escaped to a small hole in the side of a hill.

Three days passed, and it seemed he would die of hunger. Then a visitor called at the cave.

"Crut, crut," said he.

"Come in, Señor Roadrunner," said the owl.

"I have brought you a lizard, Señor Owl."

"*Muchas gracias*, Señor Paisano. I am indeed glad that I have at least one friend. Tell me, Señor Paisano, what am I to do?"

"Stay here; don't leave. Señor Cuervo has sworn to kill you."

"But I can't stay here," said the owl. "I must leave this hole in the ground. Tonight, while Señor Crow is asleep, I shall go to the swamps, and I will never cease hunting until I shall have found the Pájaro Cú."

"I will help," said the paisano. "While you search the woods and swamps by night I will watch the roads by day."

And thus it has been ever since, that Señor Roadrunner keeps an eye on the roads and calls, "Cu-rut, cu-rut."

And in the woods at night the owl calls, "Cú, Cú, Cú, Cú, Cú."

KEEPING THE SHIRT-TAIL IN

Two men, famous in the art of lying, met one day at the crossroads.

"Where have you been, *amigo?*" asked one.

"*Amigo,*" responded the other, "I've been afar and have seen miracles and wonders."

"Yes?" responded the first. "Listen to me if you should care to learn about miracles and wonders. Just listen to me."

"Very well, what have you to say?" asked the first.

"Well, for instance, I saw a pumpkin that was so large a shepherd used its hollow in which to bed a thousand sheep at night."

"Wait," interrupted the first; "that reminds me. I, while traveling through Italy, saw an oven so large it took a thousand men to fire it."

"Why," gasped the other, "why such large ovens?"

"To cook your pumpkins in," answered the friend.

"You are good, *amigo,*" said the victim. "In fact, if truth weren't distasteful to me I'd swear you were my master. Let's combine our virtues and earn our living lying. You tell 'em and I'll swear to 'em. Yet, I warn you, if your exaggerations get top-heavy, I may find it hard to coöperate. Let's say, in such a case, I give your shirt-tail a jerk. That will be the sign to cut down a bit."

Having reached an agreement in all matters pertaining to their procedure, they continued on their way. Presently they came to a town and approached a group of men on the plaza.

"In my country," began the master, "rattlesnakes are a mile long."

His companion, fearing such audacity, jerked the other gently by the shirt-tail.

"They may not be a mile long at that," retracted the first, "but they are easily a half-mile in length."

The modest companion continued to tug at the shirt-tail.

"Of course, they could be shorter, but I'd swear that if their shirt-tails were out, they would be two yards long."

The people could stand no more.

"Kill the cowards," they cried. "Run them out of town."

"You see," said the master as he looked back upon the place, "people prefer lies straight. A diluted lie is a sin against art. Follow my advice: keep your own shirt-tail in and leave mine alone."

They chose to travel separately. The master was to lead and the friend was to follow.

Presently the first man entered a wretched little village. He told the people that in the last town he had passed through there was a newly-born baby with seven heads. This news caused much interest and the informant was given all the food he could eat.

Presently the next man arrived.

"Señor," the people asked, "is it true that in a town up the way a child was born with seven heads?"

"Why, señores," gasped the late arrival, "I . . . I couldn't exactly swear to that, but . . . but . . ."—he stuck his shirt-tail in and continued—"but on a *mecate* (a rope line) I saw hanging out to dry a little white shirt with seven collars on it."

This fellow, too, like the first, was treated with much consideration.

These liars are still lying, and you may be sure they both keep their shirt-tails in.

▼▼▼▼▼▼▼▼▼

The Little Animals

DAN STORM

THE COYOTE AND JUAN'S MAGUEY

This was a country fellow very poor named Juan. He had no other crops except one maguey plant. His *jacal* was the same size as the others in this same region; but, standing near this maguey plant, it looked like a child's house for dolls, because this maguey was the largest one in all the country. It held its blades curving over the roof in the manner of the branches of a tree.

Juan was very proud of this giant maguey, which gave him his living; he tended it with care and affection. He did not use a gourd and straw to suck out the *agua miel,* as this "honey water" is extracted from ordinary magueys. He bailed the honey water out from the hollow in the center of the great maguey with a gourd dipper and stored it in jars. The plant gave so much honey water that he had plenty to sell and plenty left over to make pulque to drink during the plant's period of resting.

And now after many mornings of good harvest from his great plant, came Juan just at sunup out of his house toward his maguey, gourd and jar in hand. He was singing a *cantina,* a barroom song, that he had composed out of his own head — about this maguey of his, the greatest in the world.

> Mi novia, mi maguey
> Nunca falla, nunca falla,
> Con su dulzura,
> Nunca falla
> Con el agua miel.

> My sweetheart, my maguey
> Never fails, never fails,
> With its sweetness,
> Never fails
> With its honey water.

Hardly looking at all into the hollow among the great leaves in the trunk of the plant where the sweet liquid always collected without fail, he dipped his gourd down and presently stopped his song and became somewhat sober. The hole was dry.

On his hands and knees Juan looked for tracks, and right away he saw them. They were of the little hands and feet of a Coyote.

"This thief must be caught," said Juan to himself. "He will continue this custom and tell all his *compadres* how sweet and delicious is this *agua miel.*"

So all day Juan cut long poles with his *machete* and sharpened them on the ends and drove them into the ground very close to each other around the great plant. By dusk he had build a round corral almost as high as his head about the maguey. Close to the ground he made a little door just large enough for the Coyote to enter. He filled the hollow up with *agua miel* and put a little pulque in there also and walked away past his house toward the hill just as darkness was dropping little by little from the sky. Juan did this so that if the Coyote were watching him, the animal would think the man was nowhere around because he could not smell him.

Before the dark could all come, the moon showed its rounded section above the near-by hilltop, and then the world got lighter and lighter until the whole round moon was very brilliant; and here in the moonlight came the Coyote trotting straight up to the maguey.

From the moon-shadows where he was hiding, Juan watched the Coyote stop in surprise when he saw the fence. But he must have been very thirsty for the *agua miel*, because he went around the corral till he saw the little door. Then he quickly entered.

And here came Juan, stooping low in a creeping run on his *guarache*-shod feet, fingering in his hand a stout stick. As he approached the corral, he could hear the coyote already saying, "Slup, slup; gulp, gulp."

"Drink well, my fearless devil," Juan whispered, as he stepped close against the corral, leaning directly over the little door. "Drink well, shameless one. For it is your last drink." So saying, he drew a deep breath and tore the air, shrill and loud, with a *vaquero's* Indian yell.

From outside the corral Juan saw the Coyote jump backwards out of the hollow straight up into the air into the moonlight and begin running with his feet while still in the air. Down he came and went flying around and around the inside wall of the corral so fast that he could neither stop nor see the little door. Juan thought that this was the funniest thing he had ever seen in his life and fell immediately into an insane fit of laughter: "Hua, hue, huee-haaa! What a fright I gave him! Hua, hua, haee!"

Finally, while Juan was laughing so loudly and bragging

about the terrible fright he had given the Coyote, this animal found the door and stuck his head through to come out.

In this moment Juan raised his club—still laughing—to bring it down upon the Coyote's head; but there he stood, holding his club aloft in the air like a statue, paralyzed with laughing while the Coyote came through the hole in the corral and escaped, running past Juan's front door. Juan tried to throw his club at the Coyote just as he turned the corner of his house, but, no. All he could do was stand there laughing and saying, "What a fright I gave him!" Not until the Coyote was out of danger in the night was Juan able to stop his laughing and begin cursing, in his frenzy stamping on his sombrero.

Juan, at that time, threw upon himself the blame for failing to kill the Coyote, but if he has any more sense now than he had then, he knows that the Coyote, through certain powers as a magician, simply chose this method of casting him under a spell of witchcraft.

SEÑOR COYOTE ACTS AS JUDGE

At the foot of a high mountain one day lay that bandit of the *animalitos*, Señor Rattlesnake, basking in the sun. While he lay sleeping, a great stone somehow came loose high upon the mountainside and came rolling down and finally settled right on top of Mr. Rattlesnake, pinning him fast to his bed.

After the snake had remained a writhing prisoner under the stone for some hours and had begun to fear that no one would ever come to his rescue except an enemy, here came jolly Señor Conejo.

"Greetings, Mr. Snake," said Mr. Rabbit. "I see you are trying to crawl under that stone."

"Do not taunt me, please, Brother Rabbit," begged the Rattlesnake in a pitiful voice. "I am in terrible pain. Only roll this stone off of me, and I will see that you are well rewarded."

Now Mr. Rabbit knew well that the Rattlesnake was no friend of his; but he was a friendly fellow and hated to see even his worst enemy in distress.

"*Pues*, that is the way you
will stay," said Señor Coyote.

"Very well," he said, and began immediately to push and dig his feet into the ground, first on one side of the big stone and then on the other. Finally, after much pushing and prying from the good Rabbit, the heavy stone rolled half over and Mr. Rattlesnake was free and there stood Señor Conejo very tired.

"Now," said the Rattlesnake, "in regard to your reward . . ."

"Oh, that will be all right," said the Rabbit.

"Yes," said the Snake, "I think it will be all right enough."

"What do you mean?" asked the Rabbit.

"I mean," said the Rattlesnake, "that as a reward for your help to me you are to have the privilege of being my dinner."

"No, no!" cried the Rabbit, beginning to walk backwards. "Do not eat me, Hermano Víbora!"

"Yes, yes," said the Snake, following the Rabbit and keeping his snake eyes fixed firmly upon him. "I must have my dinner."

In this very moment appeared Señor Coyote.

"What goes on here?" he demanded. Both the Rabbit and the Snake began talking at the same time. Each was willing for Señor Coyote to act as judge.

"Thus it is," the Rabbit said. "I came here and found Señor Rattlesnake helpless under this stone, and I pushed it off of him. He promised me a reward, but I ask none. All I want is my life. What a reward he wants to give me! He wants to eat me up. That is to be my reward. Now does it seem to you . . .?"

"Nonsense and foolishness," the Snake interrupted. "What Señor Conejo says is not the truth. I was under the stone, true enough, but I could have gotten out from under it any time. Señor Conejo was trying to roll the stone upon me so that it would crush me. Thus, I have the right to eat him."

Señor Coyote sat thinking with his chin in his hands, looking first to the Rabbit and then to the Snake. "Let us see," he said slowly. Then he said, "My friends, we must settle this matter very correctly. Now in the first place both of you are agreed that Señor Víbora was under the stone. Is it not so?"

"Yes," said the Rattlesnake, "that is true."

"Yes," said the Rabbit, "that is correct."

"Very well," went on Señor Coyote. "I must know now just

how everything was. Mr. Rattlesnake, will you please move over here next the stone and Señor Conejo and I will roll it back on top of you so that I may get an idea of just how everything was when Señor Rabbit arrived upon the scene. Then, you see, I can decide the thing correctly."

The Snake agreed, and the Rabbit and Señor Coyote rolled the stone back upon the snake's back.

"Now," said Señor Coyote, "is this the way you were, Brother Rattlesnake?"

"Yes," said the Rattlesnake, squirming in discomfort. "Yes, this is the way I was."

"*Pues*, that is the way you will stay," said Señor Coyote. "Now you have your reward for trying to eat Mr. Rabbit after he had treated you with kindness."

PAISANO SAVES RABBIT FROM RATTLESNAKE

Many are the tricks of the Paisano, called by the gringoes the chaparral bird or roadrunner. He has many ways of fighting his enemy the rattlesnake, such as building a corral of thorns around him and throwing prickly pear in his pathways. But the strangest thing of all that he ever did to the rattlesnake was the time he saved the rabbit's life.

The snake was *enborrachando*[6] the rabbit swaying his head from side to side and crawling closer and closer to the little helpless animal who could not move at all but stood there trembling unable to escape from the rattlesnake's spell.

Just when the big jaws of the rattlesnake were about to close down on the rabbit, out of the brush came this little *animalito*, the Paisano, running on his long legs. Up to the snake he ran, holding a long thorn in his beak; and while the snake's jaws were yawning wide, the Paisano, darting from the side, put the long thorn into the snake's mouth, straight up and down, propping his mouth open. Now the snake was helpless, and the little rabbit was free, and the Paisano was very happy.

[6]Literally, making the rabbit become drunk; charming.

To Whom God Wishes to Give
He Will Give

WILSON M. HUDSON

This was a lazy man who had an energetic man for his compadre.

One morning the energetic man, who owned a store, told his wife to carry a message to his compadre.

"Tell him," he said, "I want him to pay his account. It is long past due and I am tired of waiting. If he cannot pay, let him come over and help me haul some rocks, and I will give him credit for his work."

When he heard this message, the lazy man said, "I have no money and your rocks are too heavy for me. Tell my compadre not to worry about this little account. To whom God wishes to give He will give even if He has to put it in through the window."

It was the habit of this lazy man not to get up before ten o'clock in the morning. Usually his wife gave him breakfast in bed so that he would not have to make the effort of dressing himself at so early an hour.

One day the spring near his house dried up, and he was forced to go higher on the mountain to look for another one. While walking along a dim trail he heard hoofbeats rapidly coming nearer. As he stepped off the trail he saw a runaway horse mounted by a señor in elegant dress with a flowing white beard.

Without taking thought, he reached out and grasped the horse's bit and stopped him. The rider thanked him with dignity for his courage and presence of mind, saying that he would reward him by revealing the hiding place of a *tatema*.

A *tatema* is a buried treasure that can be found only by supernatural aid and that can be taken out of hiding only by the person to whom it is revealed or by others in his presence and with his permission.

Taking the lazy man to one side of the trail, the dignified stranger said, "Move that flat rock and underneath it you will find a treasure covered with oak leaves."

As the man was moving the stone, the rider and horse suddenly disappeared. The lazy man brushed the oak leaves aside with his hands and discovered six chests. He opened one and saw it was filled with silver coins. At this point his natural laziness began to overcome him. He put some coins into his pocket, only sixteen to be exact, because more would have been too heavy to carry along.

When he got home, he lay down on his bed to refresh himself with a good siesta. Late in the afternoon when he arose to eat supper he felt the weight of the coins in his pocket.

"Wife," he said, "take these to my compadre and pay my account."

The energetic compadre was greatly surprised to see the money because he could not imagine that the lazy compadre had worked to earn it. Being very curious, he decided to visit his compadre and learn whatever he could.

Early the next morning he went to his friend's house, but he had to wait until the lazy man awoke at his usual ten o'clock. When the energetic one asked about the money, the lazy compadre told him exactly what had happened the day before.

"But why," asked the energetic compadre, "didn't you bring more of the money?"

"It was too heavy, much too heavy," said the lazy man. "If you will pack it back for me on your mules, I will give you one half of everything in the boxes. To whom God wishes to give He will give even if He has to put it in through the window."

This proposal was eagerly accepted by the energetic compadre, and it was agreed that they should leave at eleven o'clock in order to reach the flat stone by the trail at midnight. They were to start from the house of the lazy man so that he would not have to walk.

In the meantime this lazy man lay down for a rest, asking his wife not to disturb him until eleven o'clock. At that time she woke him up and told him that his compadre had not come; yet he did not get up, saying that he supposed his friend would come later. At twelve o'clock the wife woke him again in a state of alarm. She tried to stir him up by telling him that his compadre might go alone and take all the treasure for himself.

"Lie down and go to sleep," said the lazy man. "I am tired and I will not get up at this time of night. To whom God wishes to give He will give even if He has to put it in through the window."

The wife had good reason to be afraid. The energetic man had asked himself why he should divide the treasure with his compadre, who had gained it by little if any exertion. He said to himself that he had been a hard worker all of his life and that for this reason he had mules and his lazy friend had none. Besides, how could such a lazy man make proper use of the great fortune?

So the energetic man went with his mules and his servants to the flat rock by the trail. The servants brushed aside the leaves and opened the chests; but instead of a multitude of coins they found a mass of foul-smelling mud.

The energetic man was so disappointed and angry that he decided to take vengeance on his lazy compadre. He ordered his drivers to load the chests on the backs of the mules.

At two in the morning he arrived with his cargo at his compadre's hut. He gave orders to empty the contents of the chests in front of the door and by the window. The lazy man and his wife were sound asleep and heard nothing.

In the morning the wife arose at her customary hour and tried to open the door. She could not—some great weight was holding it shut. Nor could she budge the window. She roused her husband and together they were able to push the wooden window ajar.

Immediately a shower of silver coins poured through the crack and into the room.

"See, wife," said the lazy man. "What did I tell you? To whom God wishes to give He will give even if He has to put it in through the window."

They opened the window a little more, and more coins came in. Finally they swung it open all the way. From the pile of coins inside, the wife pulled herself through the window onto another pile outside. At the door she saw a great heap of coins as high as the latch.

With encouragement from her husband and little real help, she carried all of the coins into the hut. Then she prepared a meal for him—he felt obliged to return to bed after all this disturbance. Here he was given breakfast by his wife. Then he told her to take some of the coins to his compadre's store and buy a good supply of food and some much-needed clothing.

When the energetic man was paid with the same kind of coins sent before by his lazy friend, he did not know what to think. He asked whether his compadre had made another trip to the hiding place of the treasure.

The wife told him that the door and the window had been blocked in the night with great piles of coins.

"My compadre was right," said the man, trying not to show his surprise. "To whom God wishes to give He will give even if He has to put it in through the window."

NEGRO TALES and JOKES

From the Brazos Bottom

OLE SIS GOOSE

Ole Sis Goose wus er-sailin' on de lake, and ole Br'er Fox wus hid in de weeds. By um by ole Sis Goose swum up close to der bank and ole Br'er Fox lept out an cotched her.

"O yes, ole Sis Goose, I'se got yer now, you'se been er-sailin' on mer lake er long time, en I'se got yer now. I'se gwine to break yer neck en pick yer bones."

"Hole on der', Br'er Fox, hold on, I'se got jes' as much right to swim in der lake as you has ter lie in der weeds. Hit's des' as much my lake es hit is yours, and we is gwine to take dis matter to der cotehouse and see if you has any right to break my neck and pick my bones."

And so dey went to cote, and when dey got dere, de sheriff, he wus er fox, en de judge, he wus er fox, and der tourneys, dey wus foxes, en all de jurrymen, dey was foxes, too.

En dey tried ole Sis Goose, en dey 'victed her and dey 'scuted her, and dey picked her bones.

Now, my chilluns, listen to me, when all de folks in de cotehouse is foxes, and you is des' er common goose, der ain't gwine to be much jestice for you pore nigger.

SHEER CROPS

Br'er Bear en Br'er Rabbit dey wuz farmers. Br'er Bear he

50

has acres en acres uf good bottom land, en Br'er Rabbit has des' er small sandy-land farm. Br'er Bear wuz allus er "raisin' Cain" wid his neighbors, but Br'er Rabbit was er most engenerally raisin' chillun.

Arter while Br'er Rabbit's boys 'gun to git grown, en Br'er Rabbit 'lows he's gwine to have to git more land if he makes buckle en tongue meet.

So he goes ober to Br'er Bear's house, he did, en he say, sez he, "Mo'nin', Br'er Bear. I craves ter rent yer bottom field nex' year."

Br'er Bear he hum en he haw, en den he sez, "I don't spec I kin 'commodate yer, Br'er Rabbit, but I moughten consider hit, bein's hit's yer."

"How does you rent yer land, Br'er Bear?"

"I kin onliest rent by der sheers."

"What is yer sheer, Br'er Bear?"

"Well," said Br'er Bear, "I takes der top of de crop fer my sheer, en yer takes de rest fer yer sheer."

Br'er Rabbit thinks erbout it rale hard, en he sez, "All right, Br'er Bear, I took it; we goes ter plowin' ober dare nex' week."

Den Br'er Bear goes back in der house des' er-laughin'. He sho is tickled ez to how he hez done put one by ole Br'er Rabbit dat time.

Well, 'long in May Br'er Rabbit done sont his oldest son to tell Br'er Bear to come down to the field to see erbout dat are sheer crop. Br'er Bear he comes er-pacin' down to de field en Br'er Rabbit wuz er-leanin' on de fence.

"Mo'nin', Br'er Bear. See what er fine crop we hez got. You is to hab de tops fer yer sheer. Whare is you gwine to put 'em? I wants ter git 'em off so I kin dig my 'taters."

Br'er Bear wuz sho hot. But he done made dat trade wid Br'er Rabbit, en he had to stick to hit. So he went off all huffed up, en didn't even tell Br'er Rabbit what to do wid de vines. But Br'er Rabbit perceeded to dig his 'taters.

'Long in de fall Br'er Rabbit lows he's gwine to see Br'er Bear ergin en try to rent der bottom field. So he goes down to Br'er Bear's house en after passin' de time of day en other pleasant sociabilities, he sez, sez he, "Br'er Bear, how erbout rentin' der bottom field nex' year? Is yer gwine ter rent hit to me ergin?"

Br'er Bear say, he did, "You cheat me out uf my eyes las' year, Br'er Rabbit. I don't think I kin let yer hab it dis year."

Den Br'er Rabbit scratch his head er long time, en he say, "Oh, now, Br'er Bear, yer know I ain't cheated yer. Yer jes' cheat yerself. Yer made de trade yerself en I done tuck yer at yer word. Yer sed yer wanted der tops fer yer sheer, en I gib um ter yer, didn't I? Now yer jes' think hit all ober ergin and see if yer can't make er new deal fer yerself."

Den Br'er Bear said, "Well, I rents to yer only on dese perditions: dat yer hab all de tops fer yer sheer en I hab all de rest fer my sheer."

Br'er Rabbit he twis' en he turn en he sez, "All right, Br'er Bear, I'se got ter hab more land fer my boys. I'll tuck hit. We go to plowin' in dare right erway."

Den Br'er Bear he amble back into de house. He wuz shore he'd made er good trade dat time.

Way 'long in nex' June Br'er Rabbit done sont his boy down to Br'er Bear's house ergin, to tell him to come down ter de field ter see erbout his rent. When he got dare, Br'er Rabbit say, he did:

"Mo'nin', Br'er Bear. See what er fine crop we hez got? I specks hit will make forty bushels to der acre. I'se gwine ter put my oats on der market. What duz yer want me ter do wid yer straw?"

Br'er Bear sho wuz mad, but hit wa'n't no use. He done saw whar Br'er Rabbit had 'im. So he lies low en 'lows to hisself how he's gwine to git eben wid Br'er Rabbit yit. So he smile en say, "Oh, der crop is all right, Br'er Rabbit. Jes' stack my straw enywheres eround dare. Dat's all right."

Den Br'er Bear smile en he say, "What erbout nex' year, Br'er Rabbit? Is yer cravin' ter rent dis field ergin?"

"I ain't er-doin nothin' else but wantin' ter rent hit, Br'er Bear," sez Br'er Rabbit.

"All right, all right, yer kin rent her ergin. But dis time I'se gwine ter hab der tops fer my sheer, en I'se gwine ter hab de bottoms fer my sheer too."

Br'er Rabbit wuz stumped. He didn't know what ter do nex'. But he finally managed to ask, "Br'er Bear, ef yer gits der tops en der bottoms fer yer sheer, what will I git fer my sheer?"

Den ole Br'er Bear laff en say, "Well yer would git de middles."

Br'er Rabbit he worry en he fret, he plead en he argy, but hit do no good.

Br'er Bear sez, "Take hit er leave hit," en jes' stand pat.

Br'er Rabbit took hit.

Way 'long nex' summer ole Br'er Bear 'cided he would go down to der bottom field en see erbout dat dare sheer crop he had wid Br'er Rabbit. While he wuz er-passin' through de woods on hiz way, he sez to himself, he did:

"De fust year I rents to de ole Rabbit, I makes de tops my sheer, en ole Rabbit planted 'taters; so I gits nothin' but vines. Den I rents ergin, en der Rabbit is to hab de tops, en I de bottoms, en ole Rabbit plants oats; so I gits nothin' but straw. But I sho is got dat ole Rabbit dis time. I gits both de tops en de bottoms, en de ole Rabbit gits only de middles. I'se bound ter git 'im dis time."

Jes' den de old Bear come ter de field. He stopped. He look at hit. He shet up his fist. He cuss en he say, "Dat derned little scoundrel! He done went en planted dat fiel' in corn."

ER DAID TURKLE

Two young Negroes fishing in the Sumpter Hole came upon a turtle which someone had recently caught and, in order to get the hook out of its mouth, had drawn its head out of the shell and cut it off, leaving the turtle on the ground. The turtle, of course, does not die until sundown, and so it was still floundering around when the Negroes passed by.

One of the Negroes said, "Dar's er daid turkle."

The other looked and replied, "Boy, you's foolish. Dat ar turkle ain't daid."

"Course he's daid. His haid's done cut off. Anything what's got hits haid cut off's bound ter be daid."

"No, he hain't daid. He's still er-crawlin'. Er daid thing cain't crawl."

"I'll bet yer er dime he's daid."

"You's faded. Er dime says he ain't daid."

So they argued, and finally decided to leave the matter to Uncle Toby, who was fishing farther down the river and who had the reputation of being a very good judge of small matters. Going down to where Uncle Toby sat on a log, the contestants argued their points at length. A dime was at stake and the decision was important.

The first boy said: "Now Uncle Toby, you knows dat turkle am daid. Hits haid is done cut off, en nothin' kin live wid hits haid off. He's bound ter be daid, en I wins dat dime."

Then the other spoke: "Uncle Toby, course dat turkle ain't daid. He's still er-crawlin' erround. Anything that can crawl cain't be daid. Dat's my dime, Uncle Toby, en when I wants hit I wants hit."

Uncle Toby smoked his pipe in silence a long time, while he carefully weighed all the facts in the case; then he gave his decision in slow and carefully chosen words. "Now, boys, hit's des' like dis. Dat ar turkle am daid but he don't know hit."

WHO DAT DARKEN DE HOLE?

Two cullud gentlemens wuz er-walkin' through de big woods er-huntin' rabbits, en dey seed er little cub bear run in de holler uv er great big tree. Dey tried to git 'em out, but couldn't.

Den one uv de hunters sed, "You keep er watch-out en I'll crawl up in de holler uv de tree en fotch 'em out."

De udder one sed all right, en de fust one got down on his han's and knees en crawled up inside de tree. Jes' den ole mammy bear seed 'em en made er break for her den. De watcher seed her jes' in time to grab her by de tail jes' ez she got her head in de hole, en he wuz er-holdin' on wid all his might while de ole bear wuz er-tryin' her bes' to git in de tree.

Der hunter inside wuz skeered by the racket en said, "Who dat darken de hole?"

De udder one holdin' wid all his might answered, "Ef dis tail holt slip, yer will find out who darken de hole."

HE HEARD THE BULLET TWICE

Negroes have always been closely connected with the courts, and many anecdotes concerning them have had their origin in the courtroom.

In the trial of a Negro for shooting at another a lawyer examining one of the parties interested began, "You say that when the defendant pulled his gun you began to run. How did you know that he was shooting at you?"

"I heard de gun fire, en I heard de bullet when hit passed me."

"Are you absolutely sure that you heard the bullet pass you?"

"Yassuh, I's shore I heard dat bullet pass me, 'cause I heard hit twice."

"You say you heard the bullet twice. How could that be possible?"

"Wall, sir, hit wuz jes' lack dis. I heard de bullet when hit passed me, en I heard hit ergin when I passed hit."

Juneteenth

J. MASON BREWER

ELIJAH'S LEAVING TIME

Master Dan Waller was a very sympathetic master. He visited all the cabins on his plantation every night to see how the slaves were getting along, and to find out whether anyone was sick. The slaves all liked Master Dan and generally left his chickens and hogs alone.

One Saturday evening, however, Elijah, one of the slaves who had a family, decided he would like to have some pork chops for Sunday. About nine o'clock that night Elijah went down to the master's hog pen and stole a pig. Just about the time he got back inside his cabin, the master, on his customary round of evening visits, knocked at the door. Elijah, the pig still under his arm, hurriedly put it in the baby cradle and covered it over with a quilt. He was rocking the cradle backwards and forwards when the master entered.

"What's the matter?" asked the master as he entered.

"Mah po' baby's sick," answered Elijah, "an' Ah's tryin' to rock 'im to sleep."

"Well, I'm sorry," said the master, starting over to the cradle. "Let me see him. He may need some medicine."

"No, sah, no, sah. Ef you pulls de kivver offen 'im, he gonna die, Massa."

"Well," answered the master, "I am not going to let him suffer. I am going to pull the cover off him and see what the trouble is."

"Aw right, Massa, aw right," answered Elijah, sidling towards the door. "You kin pull de kivver offen 'im ef yuh wants ter, but Ah ain't gwine stay hyeah and see 'im die."

SWAPPING DREAMS

Master Jim Turner, an unusually good-natured master, had a fondness for telling long stories woven out of what he claimed to be his dreams, and especially did he like to "swap" dreams with Ike, a witty slave who was a house servant. Every morning he would set Ike to telling about what he had dreamed the night before. It always seemed, however, that the master could tell the best dream tale, and Ike had to admit that he was beaten most of the time.

One morning, when Ike entered the master's room to clean it, he found the master just preparing to get out of bed. "Ike," he said, "I certainly did have a strange dream last night."

"Sez yuh did, Massa, sez yuh did?" answered Ike. "Lemme hyeah it."

"All right," replied the master. "It was like this: I dreamed

I went to Nigger Heaven last night, and saw there a lot of garbage, some old torn-down houses, a few old broken-down, rotten fences, the muddiest, sloppiest streets I ever saw, and a big bunch of ragged, dirty niggers walking around."

"Umph, umph, Massa," said Ike, "yuh sho' musta et de same t'ing Ah did las' night, 'case Ah dreamed Ah went up ter de white man's paradise, an' de streets wuz ob gol' an' silvah, and dey wuz lots o' milk an' honey dere, an' putty pearly gates; but dey wuzn't uh soul in de whole place."

DEY'S AUGANIZED

One day Ananias, tall black coachman of the Kaufmans, was driving his master down a long lane on the way to a neighboring plantation when a horse-fly alighted on the mane of one of the horses. "Massa," said Ananias, "you see dat hoss fly on dat hoss's mane? Watch me git 'im." Ananias had the reputation of being the most exact wielder of the coachwhip in the county, and his master always enjoyed watching him wield it. Ananias raised his whip and split the horse-fly into small pieces.

A little farther down the lane Ananias looked over and spied a bumblebee on a sunflower. "Massa," said Ananias, "yuh see dat bumblebee on dat sunflowah? Watch me git 'im." Ananias raised his whip again, and the bumblebee was torn to shreds by the snapper on the end of it.

After a little while the master noticed a hornets' nest hanging from the limb of a tree by the side of the road. "Look, Ananias," said he. "You see that hornets' nest hanging from the limb of that tree by the side of the road? You are such an expert with the coachwhip, let me see you cut that hornets' nest off the limb."

"No, sah, Massa," said Ananias, "Ah ain't gwine bothah dem hornets, 'case dey's auganized."

PRAY, BUT DON'T TRUST TOO MUCH

Uncle Bob Jordan was the out-prayingest Christian on the

Green plantation. He had long been known for his prayers, but now he was praying more than he had ever prayed. He was seventy-two years old and, as he could no longer work much, his master had promised him his freedom for twenty dollars. So Uncle Bob would go down into the woods near the big house every night about seven o'clock and get down on his knees and pray, asking God to please send him twenty dollars for his freedom.

He had been praying for about a month, when the master passed near the tree where Uncle Bob was praying one night and overheard the prayer. The master decided that the next night he would have some fun out of Uncle Bob. So just before dark he went down to the prayer tree and climbed up in it.

At dark Uncle Bob came under the tree, got down on his knees, and started praying as usual, "Oh, Lawd, sen' me twenty dollahs to buy mah freedom. Oh, Lawd, sen' me twenty dollahs to buy mah freedom."

"All right, Uncle Bob," came the master's voice from overhead, "look down at the foot of the tree and you will find a ten-dollar bill."

Sure enough, Uncle Bob looked and found a ten-dollar bill.

"Come back tomorrow night," said the voice, "and you will find a five-dollar bill."

"Sho', sho', Lawd," said Uncle Bob, taking the ten-dollar bill and sticking it in his pocket. "Thank Yuh, thank Yuh."

The next night the master beat Uncle Bob to the tree again and hid in its branches. At dark Uncle Bob came and prayed his accustomed prayer: "Oh, Lawd, please sen' me ten mo' dollahs to buy mah freedom."

"Uncle Bob," responded the voice from overhead, "look at the foot of the tree and you will find another five-dollar bill. Take the ten-dollar bill I gave you last night, and the five-dollar bill I gave you tonight, and bring them back tomorrow night. Put them underneath the tree so that I can get them, and the next night I will bring you a twenty-dollar bill."

"No, sah, no, sah, dat's aw right, Lawd," answered Uncle Bob. "Ah sho' thanks Yuh fuh de fifteen, but Ah'll git de udder five some place else."

BEAR MEETING AND PRAYER MEETING

One day Elder Sam Green asked Uncle Jack to go walking with him. While they were walking along, the question came up as to what one should do when in danger. Elder Sam said, "Allus w'en Ah'm in danja, Ah kneels down an' prays."

It happened that the path they were following led through a dense forest, and it was so narrow that the two men had to go single file. Just as Elder Sam finished telling how he always prayed when in danger, Uncle Jack, who was in the lead, saw a big black bear coming to meet them.

"Fo' de lan's sake, Eldah," cried Uncle Jack, "what'd yuh say you do w'en in danja?"

"Kneel down an' pray," said Elder Sam.

Uncle Jack got down on his knees and prayed. When he got up off his knees, the bear was closer to him than before.

"Eldah, Eldah," cried Uncle Jack, "Ah axed yuh what does yuh do w'en yuh's in danja?"

"Kneel down an' pray," said Elder Sam.

Uncle Jack kneeled down once more and prayed. When he got up this time the bear was within ten feet of him, and had his arms extended for a hug.

"Eldah! Oh, Eldah!" shouted Uncle Jack, "Ah says what does yuh do w'en yuh's in danja!"

"Kneel down an' pray," said Elder Sam.

"No, sah, no, sah, Eldah," yelled Uncle Jack, taking to his heels as fast as he could. "Prayah mought be aw right at prayah meetin', but 'tain't nuffin' at beah meetin'."

VOICES IN THE GRAVEYARD

One night two slaves on the Byars plantation entered the potato house of the master and stole a sack of sweet potatoes. They decided that the best place to divide them would be down in the graveyard, where they would not be disturbed. So they went down there and started dividing the potatoes.

Another slave, Isom, who had been visiting a neighboring

plantation, happened to be passing that way on the road home and, hearing voices in the graveyard, he decided to stop and listen to what was being said. It was too dark for him to see, but when he stopped he heard one of the thieves saying in a sing-song voice, "Ah'll take dis un, an' yuh take dat un. Ah'll take dis un, an' yuh take dat un."

"Lawd, ha' mercy," said Isom to himself, "Ah b'lieve dat Gawd an' de debbil am down hyeah dividin' up souls. Ah's gwine an' tell ol' Massa."

Isom ran as fast as he could up to the master's house and said, "Massa, Massa, Ah's passin' th'oo de graveya'd jes' now, an' what yuh reckon Ah heerd? Gawd an' de debbil's down dar dividin' up souls. Ah sho' b'lieves de Day ob Jedgment am come."

"You don't know what you are talking about," said the master. "That's foolish talk. You know you are not telling the truth."

"Yas, sah, Massa, yas, sah, Ah is. Ef yuh don' b'lieve hit, cum go down dar yo'se'f."

"All right," said the master, "and if you are lying to me I am going to whip you good tomorrow."

"Aw right, Massa," said Isom, " 'case Gawd an' de debbil sho' am down dere."

Sure enough, when Isom and the master got near the graveyard they heard the sing-song voice saying, "Yuh take dis un, an' Ah'll take dat un. Yuh take dis un, an' Ah'll take dat un."

"See dar, didn' Ah tell yuh, Massa?" said Isom.

In the meantime the two darkies had almost finished the division of the potatoes, but remembered they had dropped two over by the fence — where Isom and the master were standing out of sight. Finally when they had only two potatoes left, the one who was counting said, "Ah'll take dese two an' yuh take dem two over dere by de fence."

Upon hearing this, Isom and the master ran home as fast as they could go. After this the master never doubted Isom's word about what he saw or heard.

UNCLE JEFF'S GUIDING STAR

On some of the plantations near the Gulf of Mexico, the white folks on summer nights would have slaves row them out for a boat ride. Master Tom Travis liked to go boat riding on the Gulf two or three nights each week, and always he took Uncle Jeff along for his oarsman.

One night after a hard week's work, Master Tom and Uncle Jeff started out for a boat ride. Before long the master became very sleepy and decided to take a nap while Uncle Jeff rowed. Since Uncle Jeff knew no directions, Master Tom pointed out the Evening Star and told him to keep it in front of the boat.

Uncle Jeff carried out these instructions very well until he, too, became sleepy and dozed at intervals. After a while he awoke with a start and looked around at the heavens to find that the guiding Evening Star was behind the boat. He did not know that while he and the master slept the boat had changed ends and was drifting away from land. Very much excited, he woke his master up. "Massa, Massa," he called, "yuh better p'int me out anudder star. Ah done run by dat un yuh say to go to."

UNCLE JOHN'S PROPHETIC ERROR

On the Pleasant plantation, a slave known as Uncle John could tell his master every morning what the master was going to do all that day. The manner in which Uncle John found out about Master Tom Pleasant's plans was by hiding behind the chimney of the fireplace at the big house every evening. The master had a practice of telling his wife soon after supper each night what he planned to do the next day, and Uncle John had found this out.

After the evening eavesdropping, Uncle John was prepared the next morning to tell his master how many slaves were going to pick cotton, how many were going to chop cordwood, how many were going to husk corn, etc. He was often called upon to make such predictions, or rather, as it seemed, to read his master's mind. At length Master Tom Pleasant decided to make a thorough test of the darkey's fortune-telling abilities. The Civil War had commenced, and he considered it dangerous to have a fortune-teller among the slaves.

One Saturday night, shortly after Texas joined the Confederacy, the master told his wife that he was going to whip Uncle John good the next night, and find out whether he was fooling him or not. Uncle John was behind the chimney as usual and heard what the master had to say. The next morning the master called him and said, "John, what am I going to do today?"

"Wal," said John, "Boss, yuh's gonna whip ol' John ternight."

"Yes," said the master, "tonight at nine o'clock you meet me out at the stable and get your whipping."

"Aw right, Massa, aw right," said Uncle John.

The first thing Uncle John did was to go look for Uncle Jeremiah, his best friend. He asked him to get a lantern and an old bugle; to get high up in a tree near the stable shortly before nine o'clock that night, and wave the lantern and blow the trumpet every time he shouted to him to do so.

Uncle Jeremiah did as he was commanded and was in the tree at the hour appointed; Uncle John was at the back steps of the big house, where the master soon appeared.

"Don' whip me, Massa, don' whip me," pleaded Uncle John. "Ef yuh does, Ah's gwine call down Gab'ul f'om de heabens."

"Oh, yes," shouted the master, "I am going to beat you good. You know so much now, stop me from beating you."

"Flash yo' lightnin', Gab'ul, an' blow yo' trumpet!" shouted Uncle John. Uncle Jeremiah, hidden in the tree, started to waving the lantern and blowing the bugle.

"Stop! Stop!" shouted the master, seeing the light and hearing the trumpet. "I'll give you a thousand dollars if you don't have Gabriel come down."

"Naw suh, naw suh," shouted Uncle John. "Flash yo' lightnin', Gab'ul, an' blow yo' trumpet."

"Stop! Stop!" cried the master. "I'll give you your freedom if you don't have Gabriel come down."

"Naw suh, naw suh. Flash yo' lightnin', Gab'ul, an' blow yo' trumpet." Uncle Jeremiah waved the lantern again and blew the trumpet.

"Stop! Stop!" shouted the master. "I will give all of the slaves their freedom if you don't have Gabriel come down."

"Naw suh, naw suh. Flash yo' lightnin', Gab'ul, an' blow yo' trumpet."

Uncle Jeremiah, who had been very faithful up to this time, but who had just heard the master offer the freedom of all the slaves to Uncle John, now refused to flash the lantern. Instead he shouted from the branches of the tree to Uncle John: "Dat's ernuf. He done offahed yuh all ouah freedom. Whut mo' does yuh want?"

WHEN "WE" WASN'T "WE"

It was a very rainy, cold day on the Hornsby plantation, and consequently there was no outside work the slaves could do. Some of them remained at home telling tales, while others went hunting. Among those who went hunting were Clem and Jim. Clem had a gun and Jim had none. Jim went along just for company. They had not gone very far when Clem shot and killed a rabbit.

"We killed uh rabbit, didn't we?" said Jim.

"Yeah," said Clem, "we killed uh rabbit."

A little farther on Clem looked up in a tree, sighted a squirrel, and shot him down.

"We killed uh squirrel, didn't we?" said Jim.

"Yeah, we killed uh squirrel," said Clem.

On the way back home a fox crossed in front of them. Clem took aim with his gun and shot the fox.

"We killed uh fox, didn't we?" said Jim.

"Yeah," answered Clem, "we killed uh fox."

Just as they neared the edge of the woods leading to the big house, they saw a wild turkey perched on a rail fence. Clem raised his gun and fired, but the turkey flew away and the bullet that missed it killed a mule. The master, hearing the shot and seeing the mule fall, came up to the two slaves and angrily demanded, "Who killed my mule?"

"We did," answered Clem.

"We nuffin'," said Jim. "Yuh killed dat mule yo'se'f. Ah ain' got no gun."

THE HANDSHAKE OVER A FENCE

Zeke, who belonged on a farm in Caldwell County, was a most unruly slave. He was a good worker while he worked, but every once in a while he would hide out and be gone for weeks. Then, after he was well "rested," he would show up, take a whipping, and go to work again. Now he had been gone four months. It was cotton-chopping time. He was badly needed, and the master offered a big reward to whoever would catch Zeke.

One evening a simple slave named Ed, who was always placed on the outside row so that he could be watched and prevented from chopping out the cotton along with the weeds, spied Zeke in some bushes just over the fence.

"Hello dar, Ed," says Zeke. "How is yuh?"

"Ah's gittin' 'long putty good," says Ed. "How is yuh gittin' uh-long?"

"Ah's gittin' 'long de fines' kin'," says Zeke. "Ah ain't doin' no wo'k and Ah gits three hots uh day. 'Liza Jane brings 'em to me reg'lah ez dey cum."

"Dat's fine, dat's fine, Zeke," says Ed. "Ah sho' is glad yuh's doin' so fine. Why don' yuh shake han's wid me?"

"Sho', sho'," agreed Zeke, sticking his hand over the fence and catching Ed's.

As soon as Ed got a good grasp on Zeke's hand, he yelled, "Ah got 'im, Ah got 'im! Cum 'ere, cum 'ere!"

All the slaves came running to see Zeke. Ed got the reward, but not a slave in Caldwell County would shake hands over a fence after that.

JOHN'S LITTLE BOYS AND THE NEW PREACHER

John and Mariah were the most faithful members of the

little Baptist church down on the river. The preacher came once each month—every fourth Sunday—to preach to the hands on the Colonel's plantation, and the members had an agreement that he would always stay at John's cabin. He slept there and ate his meals there also.

John's wife, Mariah, was always tickled to have the honor of having the preacher stop with her on Saturday and Sunday. When he was there, Mariah cooked two or three chickens for dinner each day; so John's little boys, Joseph and David, were also glad when the preacher came, because they knew they were going to have chicken for dinner.

One fourth Sunday the regular preacher took sick and could not travel; so he sent a new preacher to preach in his place. Mariah treated him just as she treated the old preacher. She put a big dish of chicken on the table for him that Saturday just as she had always done when the old preacher came. She then sent the little boys out in the yard to play, while she, John, and the preacher ate. When Mariah called Joseph and David to dinner, the first thing the two boys did was to look at the chicken platter and see that it was empty.

"Where's de chicken?" they asked. The preacher, who had eaten up all the chicken and was still seated at the table, pointed to the gravy bowl and said, "Eat jayvee; jayvee's good."

After church services Sunday morning Mariah filled up the big dish with chicken again and placed it on the table. On the table was a long red oilcloth so long that a person could hide underneath it without being seen. So while Mariah was looking at a hoecake she had cooking in a skillet in the fireplace, Joseph and David took the chicken off the table, got under the table with it, and ate it all up.

When the bread was done Mariah called John and the new preacher in to dinner. They came in, sat down at the table, said the blessing, and got ready to eat. Then the preacher looked for the chicken platter, but it was nowhere to be seen. He said, "Where's de chicken?"

Joseph, the oldest boy, stuck his head out from under the table and yelled, "Eat jayvee; jayvee's good."

JOHN AND THE TWO WHITE MEN IN COURT

One year the boll weevils got into the cotton crop on Colonel Clemons' plantation and destroyed most of it. This made times very hard for the Colonel, and since he did not make any money, he did not provide sufficient food and clothing for the hands. So naturally they stole anything they could get away with.

Never a week passed that some of the hands were not arrested and carried to jail.

One day the sheriff came out to Colonel Clemons' farm and arrested John. With him were two white hands he had arrested on a neighboring plantation. John and the two white hands were all charged with stealing and they were to be tried on the same day at the same hour.

When John and the two white men were brought in to the courtroom and arraigned for trial, John was very nervous and was trembling. This was the first time in his life that he had not been able to think of an excuse. He knew, however, that they were going to try the white men first; so he decided to listen to their answers and imitate them when his turn came.

The first case called was that of one of the white hands who was accused of stealing a horse.

"Guilty or not guilty?" said the judge.

"Not guilty," replied the man. "I've owned that horse ever since he was a colt." The case was dismissed.

Then the judge called the second white man to the stand. He was accused of stealing a cow. "Guilty or not guilty?" asked the judge.

"Not guilty," replied the defendant. "I've owned that cow ever since she was a calf." The case was dismissed.

Then John was called to the stand. He was accused of stealing a wagon.

"Guilty or not guilty?" demanded the judge.

"Not guilty," replied John. "Ah's owned dat wagon ever since it was a wheelbarrow."

STORIES AND SONGS
FOR CHILDREN

From a Texas Household:
Mrs. Russell's Stories

BERTHA McKEE DOBIE

In 1847 Emeline Brightman married Charles Russell in
Goliad, and six years later they moved to Helena in Karnes
County. After the strenuous day of a frontierswoman was over
and the children were ready for bed, Mrs. Russell would tell
tales and sing songs that she had learned from her own mother.
When she was more than eighty years old she wrote down her
tales, ballads, and jingles at the suggestion of her son L. B.
Russell, who felt it was "a pity for so much folklore to die with
her." In 1927 Mr. Russell sent her manuscript to the Texas
Folklore Society. The nursery stories that follow have been
selected from those in her collection.

Mrs. Russell must have been an entrancing storyteller and
have possessed a lively sense of the dramatic. Her grandchildren remember her as a white-haired old lady, with a curl
bobbling on each side of her face. When she sat, she habitually
turned her feet in an exaggerated pigeon toe to keep the children who crowded about her from stepping on them. Even then,
when she was old, she acted out all the stories, as she talked
"in a long Texas drawl." But her son makes a distinction: "She
always talked slowly, with not exactly a drawl but with a
good deal of hesitancy and some interval between words."

Of her dramatic manner he writes thus: "Take, for instance, the story of the old cat spinning in the oven and the little mouse whose tail the cat 'jumped' at and bit off. When mother came to that 'jumped,' she would go through the motion of springing like a cat, and emphasize the word with capital letters, so to speak. And when she repeated the lingo,

> Away he went trittety trot;
> The faster he went the sooner he got,

she would make a song out of it, resembling somewhat the old-time hardshell preacher's sing-song sermon. All this singing and action captured us as children."

Her children and her children's children begged often for one "story" that was all action and in which the narrator's right hand served for stage and characters. The persons of the dialogue are an old lady, her little maid, and a friar. The old lady is represented by the thumb, the maid by the little finger, and the friar by the middle finger of a hand held vertically. The only property is a door formed by joining the first and third fingers at the tips. The friar is outside the door. Each speech is accompanied by a movement of the impersonating finger.

THE OLD LADY, THE MAID, AND THE FRIAR

An old lady sat rocking by the fire (*movement of thumb toward inside of hand and back, repeated while these words are spoken*) and her little maid was standing by (*similar movement of little finger*) when they heard a knock, knock, knocking at the door. (*Quick, repeated tapping of middle finger against the joined tips of first and third fingers.*)

Little Maid: Some one is at the door, ma'am. Some one is at the door. (*Agitated movement of the little finger toward "old lady"; so whenever the maid speaks.*)

Old Lady: See who it is; pray, see who it is. (*Calm and regular movement of thumb; so whenever the old lady speaks.*)

Little Maid: Who is it, sir? Who is it, sir?

Friar: A friar, ma'am; a friar, ma'am. *(Tapping of middle finger against joined tips of first and third finger; so in friar's next speech.)*

Little Maid: It's a friar, ma'am; it's a friar, ma'am.

Old Lady: Pray, what does he want? Pray, what does he want?

Little Maid: What do you want, sir? What do you want, sir?

Friar: To get warm, ma'am; to get warm, ma'am.

Little Maid: He wants to get warm, ma'am; he wants to get warm.

Old Lady: Then let him come in. Pray, let him come in.

Little Maid: Come in, kind sir. Come in.

Friar: Thank you, dame.

(The friar comes through the door: the middle finger is passed between joined fingers to inside of hand.)

Two of Mrs. Russell's grandchildren have told me that she could bring the friar into the parlor without unhinging the door. If anyone thinks that this is easy to do, let him try it for himself.

THE JOHNNYCAKE

Well, once there was an old man and an old woman who lived by themselves in a little log cabin in the woods. One morning they got up and put on a johnnycake to bake. After a while the old man says, "Old woman, it is time to turn that johnnycake."

And it says in a squeaking voice, "I can turn myself over," and over it flopped.

After a while the old man again says, "Old woman, that side of the johnnycake is done, and it is ready to turn."

The johnnycake says in the same squeaking voice, "I can turn myself over," and over it flopped.

After a while the old man says, "Old woman, that johnny-cake is done; you had better take it up."

The johnnycake squeaked out, "I can take myself up." So

it *flew* upon the table, flippity-flop, and out of the door flippity-flop, and the old man and the old woman went after it hippity-hop. But it could fly faster than they could run and soon got out of sight.

So it went flippity-flop till it came to some men thrashing out wheat, and they asked it, "Where are you going?"

It says, "Oh, just a little piece out yonder," and away it went flippity-flop till it came to a man boiling soap.

He says, "Where are you going?"

It says, "Oh, just a little piece out yonder," and away it went flippity-flop till it came to a miller grinding corn.

The miller says to it, "Where are you going?"

It says (squeaking), "Oh, just a little piece out yonder," and away it went flippity-flop till it came to a wolf.

And the wolf says, "Where are you going?"

It says, "Oh, just a little piece out yonder."

And the wolf says, "I'm deaf; I can't hear you; come a little closer."

So it went a little closer and says, "Oh, just a little piece out yonder."

The wolf says, "I can't hear you yet; come a little closer."

It went a little closer and says, "Oh, just a little piece out yonder."

And the wolf says, "I'm very deaf; come right close up to me."

And it came close up to the wolf and says, "Oh, just a little piece out yonder," and the wolf jumped at it and caught it and ate it up.

So the old man and old woman went after it hippity-hop till they came to the men thrashing out wheat, when they asked, "Have you seen a johnnycake going by here flippity-flop?"

"Yes."

"What did it say?"

"It said, 'Oh, I'm going just a little piece out yonder.'"

Then away they went hippity-hop after it till they came to the soap boiler. They asked, "Did you see a johnnycake go by here flippity-flop?"

He says, "Yes, and I asked, 'Where are you going?' It says, 'Oh, just a little piece out yonder.' "

And away went the old man and old woman hippity-hop, hippity-hop till they came to the miller grinding his corn, and they said, "Have you seen a johnnycake go by here flippity-flop?"

The miller says, "Yes; I asked it, 'Where are you going?' It says, 'Oh, just a little piece out yonder.' "

And away went the old man and old woman after it hippity-hop, hippity-hop till they came to the wolf. They said to the wolf, "Did you see a johnnycake going by here flippity-flop, flippity-flop?"

He says, "Yes. I asked it, 'Where are you going?' and it says, 'Oh, just a little piece out yonder.' "

And away went the old man and old woman after it, hippity-hop, hippity-hop, on and on into the woods, but they never saw anyone else who had seen their johnnycake. So they were very tired and went back home hippity-hop, hippity-hop.

THE LITTLE LONG TAIL

Once there was an old cat spinning in the oven, and a poor little mouse came creeping along, and the old cat *jumped* at it and bit off its tail, and the little mouse says to the cat, "Pray, give me my little long tail again."

The cat says, "Go to the cow and get me some milk."

> And away he went trittety trot;
> The faster he went the sooner he got.

He says, "P-r-a-y" (drawled out), "cow, give me some milk. I give cat milk; cat give me my little long t-a-i-l again."

The cow says, "Go to the barn and get me some hay."

> And away he went trittety trot;
> The faster he went the sooner he got.

He says, "P-r-a-y, barn, give me hay; I give cow hay; cow give me milk; I give cat milk; cat give me my little long t-a-i-l again."

The barn says, "Go to the smith and get me the key."

> And away he went trittety trot;
> The faster he went the sooner he got.

He says, "P-r-a-y, smith, give me key; I give barn key; barn give me hay; I give cow hay; cow give me milk; I give cat milk; cat give me my little long t-a-i-l again."
The smith says, "Go to the pit and get me some coal."

> And away he went trittety trot;
> The faster he went the sooner he got.

He says, "P-r-a-y, pit, give me coal; I give smith coal; smith give me key; I give barn key; barn give me hay; I give cow hay; cow give me milk; I give cat milk; cat give me my little long t-a-i-l again."
The pit says, "Go to the eagle and get me a feather."

> And away he went trittety trot;
> The faster he went the sooner he got.

He says, "P-r-a-y, eagle, give me feather; I give pit feather; pit give me coal; I give smith coal; smith give me key; I give barn key; barn give me hay; I give cow hay; cow give me milk; I give cat milk; cat give me my little long t-a-i-l again."
The eagle says, "Go to the sow and get me a pig."

> And away he went trittety trot;
> The faster he went the sooner he got.

And he says, "P-r-a-y, sow, give me pig; I give eagle pig; eagle give me feather; I give pit feather; pit give me coal; I give smith coal; smith give me key; I give barn key; barn give me hay; I give cow hay; cow give me milk; I give cat milk; cat give me my little long t-a-i-l again."
The old sow says, "Go to the crib and get me some corn."

> And away he went trittety trot;
> The faster he went the sooner he got.

He says, "P-r-a-y, crib, give me corn; I give sow corn; sow give me pig; I give eagle pig; eagle give me feather; I give pit feather; pit give me coal; I give smith coal; smith give me key; I give barn key; barn give me hay; I give cow hay; cow give me milk; I give cat milk; cat give me my little long t-a-i-l again."

The crib says, "Jump in the crack and help yourself."

So he jumped in the crack and got some corn, and took it to the old sow and got the pig, and took the pig to the eagle and got the feather, and took the feather to the pit and got the coal, and took the coal to the smith and got the key, and took the key to the barn and got the hay, and took the hay to the cow and got the milk, and took the milk to the old cat, and the cat licked and lapped and swallowed, and licked till it was all gone, and then she *jumped* at the little mouse and ate it up.

THE SILVER TOE

Once upon a time there was an old man and old woman working in their garden, digging potatoes. And the old woman found a silver toe. She took it in the house and put it under her pillow at the head of the bed. So that night something came and knocked at the door and said in a gruff, unearthly voice very slowly, "Give-me-my-silver-toe. Give-me-my-silver-toe. Give-me-my-silver-toe."

At last the old woman raised up mad and cross and says, "I've got no silver toe for you."

The coarse voice repeated slowly, "Give-me-my-silver-toe" (drawled out long).

The old woman again says, "I've got no silver toe for you."

It kept on saying, "Give-me-my-silver-toe. Give-me-my-silver-toe."

The old man says in a whisper, "You had better give him his silver toe."

But the old woman jumped up mad and opened the door a little bit, and there was something the like of which she had never seen in her life. She says, "What's them great long ears for?"

"To hear with."

"What's that great long hair for?"
"To sweep my grandmother's hall."
"What's that great long nose for?"
"To smell with."
"What's them great long nails for?"
"To scratch my grandmother's pots."
"What's them great big eyes for?"
"To see with."
"What's them great big teeth for?"
"To bite you, to bite you, to bite you."

THE BAD GAL AND THE GOOD GAL

Once there was an old woman who had two girls. They were called "the bad gal and good gal." One was very sweet and amiable, and the other was very cruel, ill-tempered, and mean.

One morning the good gal started to a celebrated spring some distance from her home, whose waters had a strange effect on those who took a wash and bath in them.

The first thing she came to in a narrow lane was some large, savage horses fighting. They were pawing and cutting each other all to pieces, and she did not know how she might pass them. After studying a minute, she says in a good, kind manner, "Part, horses, and let me through." And they parted and let her through.

She went on a piece farther, and came to two bulls fighting very savage. She says, "Part, bulls, and let me through." And they parted and let her through.

She went on a little farther and came to two old buck sheep fighting. She says, "Part, sheep, and let me through." So they parted and let her through.

She went on then till she came to a gate that was very heavy and hard to open. She says in a soft tone, "Open, gate, and let me through." So the gate opened and let her through.

She went on and came to the spring. She was washing and bathing and feeling very happy when all of a sudden up came a little thing and says, "Wash me and comb me and lay me down softly." And she washed it and combed it and laid it down softly.

Up came another little thing and says, "Wash me and comb me and lay me down softly." She washed it and combed it and laid it down softly.

Up came another little thing and says, "Pretty you are, and ten times prettier you shall be."

Up came another little thing and says, "Every time you comb, you shall comb out gold and silver."

Up came another little thing and says, "Every time you spit you shall spit a diamond."

So she went back home combing out gold and silver, spitting diamonds, and growing prettier and more lovely all the time.

The bad gal, seeing her sister's good fortune in her visit to the spring, thought she would go and try the effects it would have on her. One morning she put out and soon came to the narrow lane where the horses were fighting, and she says in a rough, savage voice, "Part, horses, and let me through." And they parted and let her in the middle, when they ran together and kicked her and hurt her considerably.

She went on and came to the two bulls fighting, and she says in as rough a voice as before, "Part, bulls, and let me through." They parted, and when she came between them they rushed together and she barely missed being killed by their horns.

So she went on till she came to the sheep fighting. She says in an angry voice, "Part, sheep, and let me through." So they parted and let her in the middle and then they butted her and butted her very much.

So she went on till she got to the gate, and she says in a more cross manner than ever, "Open, gate, and let me through." So it opened, and, as she passed, it slammed to and almost knocked her heel off.

So she went on to the spring and went to washing and bathing. And after a while up came a little thing and says, "Wash me and comb me and lay me down softly"; and slap! she took it on its poor little head and killed it.

And up came another little thing and says, "Wash me and

comb me and lay me down softly." Slap! she took it on its poor little head and killed it.

Up came another little thing and says, "Ugly you are and ten times uglier you shall be."

Up came another little thing and says, "Every time you comb, you shall comb out a peck of nits and lice."

Up came another little thing and says, "Every time you spit, you shall spit a toad."

So she went on home, combing out nits and lice, spitting toads, and getting uglier all the time.

THE CRICKET'S SUPPER[1]

One afternoon a little cricket came out of his hiding place to find something to eat, and all of a sudden, pow! came a lizard and caught him. The cricket says, "Oh, please let me go just this time, and I'll never come here any more."

"Oh, no, I can't do that. I have some young lizards at home, and they are very fond of crickets, and I promised to bring them one for their supper."

Pang! went a frog onto the lizard and says, "Oh, I've got you now, have I?"

"Oh, please let me go this one time, and I'll never come out here any more."

"Oh, no, I can't do that; I have a nest of little frogs at home, and they are very fond of lizards, and I promised to bring them home one for their supper."

Pang! went a snake onto the frog, and says, "Oh, I've got you now, have I?"

"Oh, please let me go, and I'll never come back here any more."

"Oh, I can't do that. I have some little snakes at home, and

[1]Below this story in Mrs. Russell's manuscript is written, "J. C. D.'s story." John C. Duval was a welcome visitor in the Russell home, where he sometimes stayed for weeks. For the young children he would spin "fairy" tales, chiefly out of his own imagination, so Mr. Russell believes.

they are very fond of frogs, and I promised to bring them one home for their supper."

Down came an eagle onto the snake and says, "Oh, I've got you now, have I?"

The snake says, "Oh, please let me go this time, and I'll never come back any more."

"Oh, I can't do that. I have a nest of young eagles at home, and they are very fond of snakes, and I promised to bring them one home for their supper."

Bang! went a gun, and down came the eagle, and down came the snake, and down came the frog, and down came the lizard, and down came the cricket, which ran to his hole; and the lizard ran to *his* hole, and the frog ran to *his* hole, and the snake ran to *his* hole, and the man with the gun took the eagle to *his* hole, and that ended all of their suppers.

Ratoncito Pérez

SOLEDAD PÉREZ

Once there was an ant. Like other ants she was very hard-working.

One day the ant found a real, and she said to herself, "What shall I buy? If I buy candy, I will eat it. If I buy a broom, it will wear out."

Finally she decided to buy a dress, some little boots, and a ribbon for her hair. So she did. Then she put on the dress, the little boots, and the ribbon and sat out in front of her house.

Soon a cat went by and said, "My, you are beautiful, little ant! Don't you want to marry me?"

The little ant replied, "How will you speak to me after we are married?"

"I will say mew, mew," answered the cat.

"No, you frighten me," said the little ant.

He said to the little ant, "My, you are beautiful,
little ant! Don't you want to marry me?"

In a little while a dog went by and said, "My, you are beautiful, little ant! Don't you want to marry me?"

The little ant answered, "How will you speak to me after we are married?"

"I will say bowwow, bowwow," answered the dog.

"No, you frighten me," said the little ant.

A bull came by and said, "My, you are beautiful, little ant! Don't you want to marry me?"

The little ant answered, "How will you speak to me after we are married?"

"I will say moo, moo," answered the bull.

"No, you frighten me," said the little ant.

A lamb came by and said, "My, you are beautiful, little ant! Don't you want to marry me?"

The little ant answered, "How will you speak to me after we are married?"

"I will say baa, baa," said the lamb.

"No, you frighten me," said the little ant.

Finally Ratoncito Pérez passed by. Ratoncito Pérez was very clean and well combed.

He said to the little ant, "My, you are beautiful, little ant! Don't you want to marry me?"

The little ant answered, "How will you speak to me after we are married?"

Ratoncito Pérez had a very sweet voice.

"I will say ee, ee, ee."

"I like that! You shall be my husband, Ratoncito Pérez," said the little ant. She was very happy.

The little ant and Ratoncito Pérez lived happily for a long time.

One day when the little ant went out, she told Ratoncito Pérez, "Take care of the soup until I come back."

Ratoncito Pérez peered down into the soup and fell in.

When the little ant returned she found Ratoncito Pérez dead. All the little animals came and tried to comfort her, but they could not. The little ant would not be comforted. Even to this day she grieves and mourns for Ratoncito Pérez and his sweet voice.

The Frog's Courting

L. W. PAYNE, JR.

One of the most widely known nursery songs in America is "The Frog's Courting," which has been in continuous use among Englishmen and Americans for practically four hundred years. In 1923 I became interested in the currency and distribution of this song in Texas. Within a few years I had collected some forty versions, mainly from my students in the University. The results of my study were published in the fifth annual volume of the Texas Folklore Society.

Two of the versions collected were notable for the byplay furnished by the singers. Professor W. J. Battle of the University of Texas sang "Frog Went A-Courting" and told how his father used to make a game of the song back in North Carolina. His custom was to gather a group of children about him and sing the song with great gusto and with improvised dramatic interpretations to suit the action.

Frog went a-courting, he did ride,
  Uhm-huhm;
Frog went a-courting, he did ride,
Sword and pistol by his side,   *(Jump up and down as if riding.)*
  Uhm-huhm.

He rode to Mistress Mouse's hall,   *(Knock on door and call.)*
Knocked at the door and loudly called.

"Miss Mousie, are you within?"   *(Make signs of spinning.)*
"O yes, kind sir, I sit and spin."

He took Miss Mousie on his knee,   *(Take one of children on knee.)*
"Miss Mousie, will you marry me?"

"Oh, no, kind sir, I can't say that,   *(Shake head.)*
Without the consent of Uncle Rat."

Old Uncle Rat came a-riding home,   *(Imitate riding. Imitate voice of rat.)*
"Who's been here since I've been gone?"

"A very fine gentleman has been here,   *(Imitate voice of mouse.)*
Who says he'll marry me if you don't care."

Old Uncle Rat laughed till he shook his fat side,   *(Laugh.)*
To think his niece would be a bride.

Where shall the wedding supper be?   *(Point far away.)*
Way down yonder in the old hollow tree.

What shall we have for the wedding supper,   *(Make signs of eating.)*
Black-eyed peas and bread and butter.

First came in was Captain Bed Bug.   *(Make signs of drinking.)*
And swore by all he had a rum jug.

Next came in was Colonel Flea,   *(Dance with one of children.)*
And danced the jig with the bumblebee.

The next to appear was old Sis Cow,   *(Guests improvised and*
Who tried to dance but didn't know how.   *imitated ad libitum.)*

And while they all were eating supper,   *(Great confusion: children*
In came the cat and made a great splutter.   *scatter pell-mell.)*

The first she pursued was old Uncle Rat,   *(Run after and strike*
Knocked him down and spoiled his fat.   *down a child, gently.)*

The next she pursued was Miss Mousie,   *(Run after another child.)*
But she ran up a hollow tree.

The frog he swam across the lake,   *(Imitate swimming.)*
And got swallowed up by a big black snake.

And this is the end of one, two, three,   *(Count on fingers, beginning with*
Frog and rat and Miss Mousie.   *thumb on one, throughout last*
    stanza, ending on thumb
    on the word Mousie.)

Another semi-dramatic version was supplied by Miss Rosalie Jameson of Granger, formerly of Waco. Her family came from Missouri about the middle of the nineteenth century and settled near Waco. Miss Jameson learned the song from her old white-haired Negro mammy named Mary. At sleepy time the old Negro would take the child and sing the frog song with dramatic sounds or gestures, such as a cluck or a knock; and at the close when the child was asleep, the old mammy would kiss her lightly three times before putting her to bed.

Mr. Froggy went a-courtin', and a-he did ride,

    Uhm-huhm;
Mr. Froggy went a-courtin', and a-he did ride,
With a sword and pistol by his side,
    Giddy-ap, giddy-ap, giddy-ap.
        (Cluck, cluck, cluck)

He rode up to Miss Mousie's hall,
And there he made a great long call,
   Howdy-do, howdy-do, howdy-do.
               (Knock, knock, knock)

He took Miss Mousie on his knee,
And he said, "Miss Mousie, will you marry me?"
   Ple-ease do, ple-ease do, ple-ease do.
               (Please, please, please)

Oh, where shall the wedding be?
Away down yonder in a holler tree:
   Lawdy-lawd, Lawdy-lawd, Lawdy-lawd.
               (Lawd, Lawd, Lawd)

The first to come was a big black snake,
And he made Mr. Froggy jump in the lake,
   Splinkity-splash, splinkity-splash, splinkity-splash.
               (Glub, glub, glub)

The next to come was a big black cat,
And he made Miss Mousie fly the track
   Bookity-book, bookity-book, bookity-book.
               (Book, book, book)

.   .   .   .   shelf,
And if you want to know any more, just sing it yo-self,
   Bye-ee bayby-eee, bye-ee bayby-eee.
               (Kiss, kiss, kiss)

LEGENDS

Treasure Legends of McMullen County

J. FRANK DOBIE

Texas is very rich in stories of lost or buried treasure. Here are some nine legends out of a comparatively small section of one county. They will illustrate the fertility in buried treasure legend of all that stretch of Texas, for the most part yet unplowed, lying towards the Rio Grande and populated by Mexicans and by Texans of frontier stock. McMullen County itself has as yet neither railroad nor bank. The people are as yet unhackneyed by the plow or commercial secretary. They still talk a language seasoned with Mexican idiom and honest with the soil's honesty; they have their old-time dances; they welcome heartily any decent stranger.

THE ROCK PENS

Excepting the Bowie Mine and the Nigger Gold Mine, no other purported lost treasure in Southwest Texas has caused so much discussion or enticed so many seekers as that of the "Rock Pens." These "Pens" are variously placed in Live Oak, La Salle, and McMullen counties, generally in McMullen. The "waybill" quoted below was given me by Mr. E. M. Dubose of Mathis, Texas, who has spent months, perhaps years, in trying to follow out its directions. Many of the details as I give them are also due to him, but the legend has been so familiar to me from my childhood up that I can hardly say to whom I owe it.

83

The story is that thirty-one mule loads of silver bullion, together with various fine images and other precious articles, were being brought from the mountains of Mexico by Texas bandits who had made a great robbery. They had crossed the Rio Grande in safety and were proceeding north to their rendezvous at San Antonio when they found that the Indians were closing in on them in the rough country west or south— for the river often changes its course—of the Nueces. They knew that an attack was imminent, and they picked the best place they could find in which to make their stand. It was by a small ravine in which was a spring of water, and here they threw up some crude breastworks in the form of two rock pens. In one of the pens they buried the bullion, and then, in order to hide all signs of their secret work, they ran the mules around and around over the disturbed earth. The fight soon followed, and in it all of the Texans but one are supposed to have been killed. He, Daniel Dunham, on his deathbed in Austin, dictated the following "waybill."

Austin, Texas
April 17th, 1873

About six or seven miles below the Laredo Crossing, on the west side of the Nueces River near the hills, there is or was a tree in the prairie. due west from that tree at the foot of the hills at the mouth of a ravine there is a large rock   under the rock, there was a small spring of water coming from under the rock, due east from that rock there is a rock pen or rocks laid around like a pen and due east a few yards there is another pen of rocks, in that pen is the spoils of thirty one mule loads

DANIEL DUNHAM

This remarkable document was in the possession of Matt Kivlin, an old Live Oak County settler, at the time of his death in the nineties. He had shown it to his sons a few times, but there was an accompanying paper that he had never shown. This accompanying paper he destroyed shortly before his death, or else his wife destroyed it immediately thereafter. One of his own sons conjectured, and certain circumstances have led others to conjecture, that Kivlin himself was one of the Texas bandits who invaded the Mexican mines and robbed a rich

Mexican church. It is known that Kivlin held the waybill as peculiarly veracious but that he had an overwhelming feeling against undertaking to follow out its directions.

Whether any attempts to find the Rock Pens were made before his death I do not know. A fact is that not long after his death an expedition, of which one of his sons was a member, set out to find the pens. Other "gold hunters" are known to have gone on the search. Therefore it must be that there were other directions in existence than those left by Kivlin. Men yet living claim to have seen the pens years and years ago before they knew that there was any significance to them, but though various old rock heaps have been found since, none has ever been found to answer to Daniel Dunham's description.

The Laredo Crossing mentioned in the waybill is supposed to be the Nueces Crossing on the old San Antonio-Laredo road. That is generally conceded to be on the Henry Shiner ranch in McMullen County. Nearly all the land in that part of the country is still in large pastures. Much of it is rough, the San Caja, Las Chuzas, and other so-called mountains being in the vicinity. Where it was once open, the country during the last fifty years has grown up in brush so that no man can be sure the pens do not exist until thousands and thousands of acres of uneven land covered with prickly pear, mesquite, black chaparral, "gran haney," and other thorned brush have been combed. The rocks were never piled high. They have been scattered, perhaps covered over with soil washed down from the hillside. In time of drouth it is a desolate country, and many a tale tells of early travelers perishing in it of thirst. Before the advent of the automobile one treasure-seeking expedition lived for days on jack rabbit meat, so remote were they in that region from supplies.

Sixty or seventy years ago Pate McNeill was coming from Tilden, or Dog Town as it was then called, down to Lagarto with his young wife. They were in a buggy, leading a horse, saddled. Somewhere in the Shiner country they saw a fine looking maverick cow. McNeill got out of the buggy, jumped on his horse, and took after her. When he had roped her and tied her, he looked around and saw that he was right in a kind of pen of rocks. At that time he did not know that great riches appertained to rock pens; so he calmly ran his famous brand of P A T E on the cow and went on down the country. Years later when the story of the Rock Pens came out, he went back and tried to locate the rocks, but the country had changed so much with brush and "washes" that he could never find anything.

"Uncle" Ben Adkins, a veteran of Beeville who guarded the western frontier during the Civil War days to keep cow thieves from driving cattle off to California, tells of a hunter who once stumbled into the pens and thought that he was in a deserted goat camp. Like others, he did not know at the time how close he was to millions.

Pete Staples, an old Negro trail driver, tells how, when he was once hunting wild turkeys with Judge Lowe of McMullen County, they stumbled into some curiously placed rocks. "Huh, what's this?" he said. "Looks mighty funny to me for rocks in this place. Where'd they all cum from and how cum this way? Ain't no other rocks like thesen for a mile."

"Natural rocks all right," said Judge Lowe, "but this is an old pen." (Judge Lowe died something like thirty years ago.) I have heard that he afterwards tried to find the pens, but failed. Pete, having a firm conviction that it is dangerous to "monkey" with money that some man now dead buried, has never been back to look for the pens, though he declares that men have tried to hire him as a guide and that he *could* find them, but "ain't a-guine to." The pens, according to Pete, are in the Guidan Pasture, which joins the Shiner and comprises some twenty or thirty thousand acres of land.

Another time, a good many years earlier, says Pete, a Mexican who was being chased by an Indian in the Las Chuzas country leaped over a spring of water and as he leaped saw a bar of silver shining in it. Later he went back and hunted for six months without ever finding the spring, much less the silver. It does look, as Pete expresses it, as if that money "ain't meant" for any of the people who have looked for it. When the man comes along for whom it is "meant," he will just naturally find it without even trying. Nevertheless, some people are still trying.

The cheering thing about looking for Rock Pens is that even though the search for them be fruitless, one may stumble upon some other treasure at almost any time, for the whole San Caja Mountain country is rich in lost and buried treasure. Some of the legends follow. For much of the material I am indebted to that interesting taleteller and onetime eager treasure-hunter, Mr. E. M. Dubose, of Mathis, already referred to. For material not derived from him I try to give specific sources. However, some of it is such common talk in the country and has for so long been a part of me that I cannot always cite exact sources.

A WEEK TOO LATE AT THE LAREDO-SAN ANTONIO CROSSING

Neal Russell was out with two other cowpunchers on the Nueces River. They had extra mounts and a pack outfit and were well supplied. One day while they were hunting cattle they came up on two very old Mexicans. The Mexicans looked scared and acted peculiarly, but they were so old and worn and thin that Russell paid little attention to their secret manner. Finding that they were out of something to eat, he told them where camp was and invited them up for a fill and a rest.

Well, after Russell and his men had come in and waited around a while, the Mexicans appeared. They ate and then, evidently feeling at ease with the Texans, who were talking Mexican like natives, they asked if anyone knew where the old San Antonio and Laredo crossing was.

"Why, yes," replied Russell, "it is not two hundred yards from here, right down the river. I'll show it to you in the morning."

The Mexicans now seemed to think that they had as well take the Texans into confidence, and what seemed the older of the two made this explanation. "I was through this country the last time in 1836. I was with a small detachment of the Mexican army taking a load of money to San Antonio to pay off General Cos's men. We had gotten a day's ride north of here when we heard by courier of Santa Anna's defeat. We knew that it was foolish to go on and so turned back, expecting at any hour to hear the Texans coming up on us. Just before we reached the east side of the Nueces, the front axle of our wagon broke square in two. There wasn't anything to do but to cut a tree down and from a post hew into shape another axle. We managed to pull out of the road a little way, and set to work.

"As I told you, we were expecting the Texans at any time. As a precaution against their coming we dug a hole right beside the wagon. Then we went off a way and cut two posts, in case one turned out bad. After we had got them back to the wagon and were at work, we all at once heard a galloping as if a whole troop of cavalry was coming down the hills. *Pronto, pronto,* we threw the new logs into the pit we had dug, spread a few skins down, piled the load of coin into them, covered the pit up, turned the wagon upside down over the fresh dirt, and set fire to it. It blazed up; we mounted our horses and rode westward. I don't know whether what we heard was Texas cavalry or not. I am inclined to think now that it must have been a herd of mustangs. Anyway, we left confident that signs of our digging would be wiped out by the fire and that the Texans would think we had burned our baggage to keep it from falling into their hands.

"So far as I know, I am the only survivor of that escort of Mexicans. I know that no Mexican has ever been back to get the money. I am come now with my old *compadre* to get it. You see how we are. We started out poorly prepared. Now we are afoot and without provisions. If you will help us, we will share with you."

The next morning, according to Russell, all five of the men started out with the camp ax and spade. They went to the old crossing, then out a few rods down the river. The old Mexican led them to a row of three little mounds—the knolls common in that country along the river valley. Beyond those three knolls was a stump, and beyond the stump was another knoll.

"That is the place," whispered the ancient Mexican. He was so eager that he was panting for every word.

The white men rode on slowly, for the Mexicans were on foot and the older was walking in a kind of stumble. When they got fairly around the mound, they saw a pile of fresh dirt. Pitched across it were two old logs. Mesquite lasts a long time, you know, when it is under ground. The men looked down into the hole. It was not very deep and apparently it had not been dug a week. The prints of the coins were yet plain on some of the dirt, and a few tags of rotted skins were about.

Russell said that the Mexicans did not say anything. They were a week too late. When he last saw them they were tottering back to Mexico with what provisions the cowboys could spare.

THE CHEST AT ROCK CROSSING ON THE NUECES

General Santa Anna was going from Laredo to Goliad.[1] While he was fording the Nueces at the old Rock Crossing in the Chalk Bluff Pasture, once a part of the George West Ranch, the Rock Crossing being about twelve miles below the Shiner Crossing, his "pay cart" broke down and a very heavy iron chest filled with gold fell into the river. The river was up; Santa Anna was in great haste to reach Goliad; there was little travel in the country. He decided to leave the chest in the river; so he had it chained to a tree, intending to get it on the way back, for he expected to make short work of subduing the insurgent Texans.

In after years, Pate McNeill, the same man that tied down the maverick heifer in one of the Rock Pens, found a piece of chain tied around an elm tree on the east bank of the river. Still later Dubose found the tree bearing the marks of a chain, but the chain itself was gone. Encouraged by the markings, he, with Stonewall Jackson Wright and Wright's brother-in-law, Albert Dinn, went to Beeville, about fifty miles distant,

[1]Santa Anna, according to Brown, did cross into Texas at Laredo, but he went to San Antonio, not Goliad. See Brown, John Henry, History of Texas, Vol. I, pp. 569 ff. Another Santa Anna chest is said to have been dropped off near Lockhart on the road to Nacogdoches. Of course, Santa Anna never went from San Antonio to Nacogdoches.

and got a four-horse load of tongue-and-groove lumber. They sank a shaft about eighteen feet deep in the middle of the river, a little below the crossing itself, accounting for the push of water. They were able to wall out the water but made poor way with the boiling quicksand.

The first night after the shaft had been started, Stonewall Jackson Wright and Dinn got to arguing as to what disposition should be made of the chest. Wright was in favor of taking it to his ranch, twenty or thirty miles down the country, before opening it. Dinn declared that he would open it at once and that the prize should be divided then and there. The argument waxed so hot that only Dubose's reminder that they had not yet found the chest prevented a collision.

There is a possibility, some claim, that a part of Santa Anna's army may have passed back over the same route and have taken the chest with them. However, there is in existence a Mexican waybill to the treasure. Mr. Whitley of McMullen County says that the chest was buried on the bank under a tree that had a limb straight out over the water, and that the chain around the tree trunk was a piece of log chain from an ox cart. But the tree caved in long ago, the water changed its course, and now there is no sign to go by, though doubtless the chest is somewhere in the vicinity of what is still known as Rock Crossing, a mere name, for it has been decades since a road ran that way.

SAN CAJA MOUNTAIN LEGENDS

The name "San Caja" is significant, though its meaning is in dispute. Some people who should know say that it means Holy, or Sainted, Box; that the word *caja*, meaning box, alludes to the chest, or chests, of treasure hid in the mountain. But a white man who is native to the San Caja country told me that a very old Mexican once told him that the name was originally Sin Caja, *sin* meaning without, and *caja* also meaning coffin; hence, Without Coffin.[2] According to the Mexican, the name

²This latter explanation is more probable. The feminine *Santa* is never apocopated in Spanish, and *Caja* is feminine.

was derived from the fact that a man had once been buried on or in the mountain without a coffin, perhaps not buried at all but left out in the open. Either interpretation is appropriate to the legends of the mountain.

Under the mountain is a cave, the entrance to which is on the west side halfway up the mountain. Mexican bandits who preyed on the wagon and mule trains that traveled the San Antonio-Laredo road were accustomed to ride their horses into that entrance. They had a great room underground that they used for a stable. Back of it was their treasure room, *"el aparto [apartado] del tesoro,"* in which were heaps of gold and silver coins, Spanish doubloons and old Mexican square dollars, golden candlesticks, silver-mounted and jewel-studded saddles, spurs and bits of precious workmanship, plated firearms, all manner of costly plunder meant for the grandees and the cathedrals, as well as the bullion of mines near at hand—for there were rich mines in that country in the old days of the Spanish.

According to Mexican tradition, after the *bandidos* had accumulated all this treasure, a terrible dragon came and killed some of them and ran the others away. The dragon had a spiked tail and two heads, and at night one might see fire flashing out of his nostrils. He came to be called *el celador del tesoro*—the warden of the treasure; and there are Mexicans today who would not think of violating the premises that he still guards.

An addition to the legend was told me by Mr. Whitley. Years ago, as he had heard the story, a certain white man who bore the marks of a borderer was visiting the penitentiary at Huntsville when he suddenly heard himself called in Mexican. He paused. At his side appeared a Mexican, begging to talk to him. The guard consented, and then in his own language the Mexican poured out his tale.[3] He was serving a life sentence

[3]A tale common to both legend and roguery. I have a copy of a letter written in 1911 by a prisoner in Madrid to an American at Aguas Calientes, Mexico, in which the prisoner offered to share $273,000 concealed on the American's land, provided the American would send funds for passage of the prisoner and his wife.

in the penitentiary, the sole survivor of a band of murdering brigands. All their booty was still in a cave to the south of the San Caja. If the white man would get it, he might have half, using the other half to free the prisoner. He gave directions about as follows: Go to the southeast side of the mountain; thence go about a mile to two little knobs, then on down a kind of ravine about the same distance, where an opening will be found that enters into the booty hall. The white man set out to follow directions, but he was already old, and death overtook him before he could search out the treasure.

"There are," says Mr. Whitley, "two knobs on the southeast side of the mountain, but two miles down instead of one, which shows that a Mexican has no sense of distance. In giving directions he always says *un pedacito*—a little piece—which may mean a half mile or five miles." Anyhow, the country does not seem to fit the Mexican's measurements.

To the northwest of the San Caja are the San Cajitas (Little San Cajas), where, according to Mr. Whitley, is another robbers' cave stored with fine saddles and other plunder left by Mexican *bandidos*. In it are ladders that were used to descend a hundred feet to the treasure floor. But no man has since the days of the bandits been down into this cave. It is said to be "alive" with rattlesnakes.

While Joe Newberry was bossing a ranch "down in the Sands" twenty-five years ago, an old Mexican who was headed west to hunt for the Rock Pens gave him a chart to nine jack loads of silver bullion buried on top of the San Caja, a certain number of *pasos* west of a *chapote*, or persimmon tree, and covered over with a great rock. The Mexicans who buried it were on their way to the City of Mexico from up the Nueces canyon, where the Spanish operated mines long since lost. It was during a terrible drouth; the Nueces had dried up, and the travelers had missed finding the lakes that they had vaguely heard of; they and their animals were perishing of thirst, and they realized that their nearest water was the Rio Grande, seventy miles away across a desert of rocks and sands. To reach it they must lighten their loads as much as possible. Their mistake was in not having buried the bullion earlier, for they were so exhausted and the way was so hard that all but one man perished in the attempt to reach the Great River. This solitary survivor for some reason did not return, but he made out a chart, which must have been fairly well circulated, for another Mexican coming north in search of the famed Casa Blanca cache also had directions to this San Caja treasure.

Dubose and his fellow explorers blasted a certain likely looking rock off and found under it a *tinaja* (rock hole) six feet deep, but no bullion in it.

According to "Uncle" Ben Adkins of Beeville, the San Caja treasure consists of money that was buried by Mexicans who were on their way to San Antonio. Just as they got to the Rock Crossing they heard that the Mexican army was being slaughtered in the Alamo and turned back in such haste that they left their precious freight on top of the loneliest "mountain" in Southwest Texas. A Mexican in Austin told me something like the same tale. He said that a detachment reached the river in winter time when a big rise was on, were unable to swim their treasure-laden mules across the flood, and while they were waiting for the waters to go down, heard that a band of Texans was close on their heels. They hastily took their freight to the mountain and left it there.

On the south side of the San Caja are said to be two cowhides of gold doubloons. Travelers out of the City of Mexico headed for the San Antonio missions lost their road and, perishing of thirst, began to look for water in the *tinajas* and crevices of the rocks. They found a little, enough for themselves, but not any for their poor beasts, which were in greater need than the men, for the men had had canteens of water for a day or two this side of their last watering. The party really had not traveled a great distance in coming from the Rio Grande, but they had been wandering lost over a rough country for days, keeping no general direction. The burros finally played out and the Spaniards hid their cowhides of doubloons in a crevice and placed over them a flat rock on which they marked with pear-apple juice a red cross. Over that they placed a second rock. Joe Newberry got the facts as to this treasure from a Mexican bandit on the Rio Grande who had come over on this side in hiding. Dubose actually found two flat rocks stacked up as if by hand, and under the first he found an Indian arrowhead, but nothing more.

THE MINES

Five or six miles to the southwest of the San Caja, the Spanish are believed to have operated a silver mine by the name of Las Chuzas, called so from its proximity to Las Chuzas Mountains. In later times Texas pioneers found that Indian bullets lodged in the spokes and felloes of their wagons were almost pure silver, and the Indians are supposed to have got their material for bullets from the Chuzas ore. The Indians would never tell where they got it. While Dubose and a man named Wallace McNeill were riding the country in quest of the Rock Pens they found the shaft of the mine at the foot of one of the Chuzas Mountains. That shaft is said to be lined with silver bars covered over with clay, but as the men were looking for the "thirty-one mule loads" and fully expected to find them, they did not investigate the shaft.

Some ten miles away, in the Guidan Pasture, and about six miles from the Nueces River, is what is known as the Devil's Water Hole, and there the smelter is supposed to have been located. Burnt rocks to this day evidence its existence. In the vicinity of White Creek, in the foothills below the Devil's Water Hole, were some other silver mines that used the same smelter.

Somewhere between the old Las Chuzas Mine and the Nueces River there is said to be a pile of silver bullion, crude, unformed, in the very hue and shape of the rocks around. How it came there or why, nobody knows. It just came there, so the Mexicans still say.

Fifteen or twenty miles beyond the San Caja in a westerly direction on what is now known as Los Picachos (The Peaks) Ranch, an early settler named Crier, according to John Murphy, a ranchman of the vicinity, actually used to operate a silver mine that yielded about twenty dollars to the ton of ore.

In the same general direction from the San Caja as Los Picachos is the Loma de Siete Piedras, or Seven Rocks Hill, on which the Mills Ranch is located. Near this hill, as I have the tale from Mr. Whitley, the Mills boys unearthed some human bones while digging post holes. They themselves had never dug for treasure, for though they had always heard that there was treasure stored away somewhere in their country, they had never been able to get the details that would guide them to it.

Naturally they talked of the rather unusual find, and not long after the event a gang of eleven or twelve Mexicans rode up to the Mills Ranch. Now, the San Caja country is in all ways a border country, and in many places one can cross the Rio Grande without meeting a river guard or seeing a customs officer; nowadays it is the rendezvous of *tequilleros* and *mescaleros* with their smuggled liquor from the other side. When the Mills boys saw the horses that the Mexican gang were riding, they knew at once from the brands that they were smuggled; and the saddles, ropes, bits, and other paraphernalia showed that the riders were fresh from old Mexico.

The spokesman of the band began by saying that one of their number was a descendant of a Mexican who, with his entire party, had been killed by Indians in that vicinity years ago. Their mutilated skeletons, scattered by the coyotes and buzzards, were known to have been buried months later by a Mexican freighter who came across them while he was hunting a mule that had broken away. The freighter had put a cross of mesquite sticks over the bones, but the cross was doubtless rotted away a long time ago, and now these men were come to put up another, if, by the will of God, they could find the place where the bones lay. Could anyone in the country give them the necessary information?

From the number, equipment, and general looks of the Mexicans, it appeared to the Mills boys that the mission of the gang might not be so altogether pious. They smelled a nigger in the woodpile, and told the Mexicans as much.

The Mexicans beat around the bush a while longer and consulted with each other for a few hours while their horses picked up mesquite beans down in the hollow. Then their leader came back to the Mills boys and let out that they were looking for the bones of men who had been killed while they were escorting seven jack loads of silver bullion from above— *de arriba*—to Mexico. If they could find the battle ground marked by the bones, they had a *plata* (chart) that would take them to the treasure.

At that the Mills brothers offered to show the bones provided they should get half the find. True to their nature, the Mexicans refused to go in on halves, and they left, trusting no doubt to come back some *mañana* and find the bones and bullion.

THE METATE ROCKS OF LOMA ALTA

Just west of the Hill of Seven Rocks towers in primeval roughness Loma Alta, the highest point of the whole country. John Murphy told me this story connected with it. An early settler named Drummond had a squat near the foot of the mountain. One time an old Mexican came to him looking for some bullion that he claimed had been buried in the vicinity by ancient *parientes* (kinsmen) in flight from the Indians. His *plata* called for a mesquite tree on the southeastern slope of Loma Alta marked by a certain sign. Murphy thinks that the sign was a cross but does not well remember. The *plata* called also for a line of smooth oblong rocks that bore a resemblance to the stones used for grinding corn on the *metate*. They had been culled from the hillside and laid to point to the hidden bullion. Drummond and the Mexican found the tree but rode around for days without being able to find the rocks. They finally decided that generations of horses and cattle had scattered them so that they could no longer be recognized as forming a line, and gave up the search.

The Mexican left, Drummond died, and years passed. Then one day while Murphy was holding down a wormy calf out in the pasture to doctor it, he raised his eyes and saw three or four of the *metate*-like rocks lined up in some thick chaparral. He was down on his knees, so that he could see under the brush. He thought of the tale that Drummond had told him, and looking about further, he found, badly scattered, yet preserving a kind of line, other such rocks. But he could never settle on a place to dig, and so far as he knows no one ever dug on that side of Loma Alta.

WHEN TWO PARALLEL LINES INTERSECTED

An old-timer of McMullen County, Kenney by name, tells of a fellow county-man, named Snowden, who was led by a Negro to believe that a certain boulder out on a plain ten or fifteen miles from the San Caja marked the site of buried money. In the first place, the boulder really did look to have been placed where it was by human agency, for there was not another rock of its kind within miles. Snowden went to San Antonio to consult a fortuneteller. The fortuneteller, without ever having seen the country, drew up a chart of the whole territory, marking down on it the position of the boulder. He told Snowden to draw two parallel lines from the northwest and southeast corners of the boulder, respectively, and to dig at the intersection of the lines. Snowden paid a nice fee for the information and came back to Tilden and organized an expedition.

When they came to draw the parallel lines, they found that they would not meet and sent back the chart for correction. But it was not returned, and becoming impatient for the treasure, the gold diggers twisted about the directions somehow so that the "parallel" lines would intersect. There they dug and dug. Finally, one of the party in disgust swore that he would sell out his interest "for two-bits' worth of Bull Durham tobacco." Snowden took him up. Presently all the other members had sold out on the same terms, leaving Snowden to pay the expenses of the whole work.

A LUCKY POST HOLE

Tilden (old Dog Town) is, remember, the county seat of
McMullen County. Not far from it is what is still known as the
"old Tolbert Ranch," though a man named Berry bought it
years ago. I have heard the following story so many times in so
many places that I have halfway come to believe it true.

Tolbert was a miser in early days when men kept their money
about them. It is said that he would never kill a maverick no
matter how hungry he was but would always brand it. He
never bought sugar or molasses; bacon was a rare luxury; he
and his men lived principally on jerked venison and javelina
meat. When he "worked" and had an outfit to feed, he always
told the *cocinero* to cook the bread early so that it would be
cold and hard before the hands got to it. When he died none
of his money could be found. So, even till this day, people dig
for it around the old ranch house. One man who was working
on the place fifteen years ago saw two men in a wagon go
down a ravine that runs near the ranch. He thought that they
were hunters; but when the strangers passed him on their way
out the next morning, he noted that one of them had a shotgun
across his knees. When the ranch hand rode down the ravine
a few days later, he found that the wagon tracks led from a
fresh hole under a live oak tree and that near the hole were
pieces of old steel hinges that looked as if they had been cut
off with a cold chisel. However, not many people think that
the two strangers got Tolbert's money.

Berry got that, and he never hunted for it either. He had
moved on to the ranch when he bought it and a number of
years had passed. One day when he had nothing else for his
Mexican to do, he told him to put some new posts in the old
corral fence, which was made of pickets that were rotting
down. The Mexican worked along digging post holes and
putting in new posts until about ten o'clock. Then at about the
third post from the south gate he struck something so hard that
it turned the edge of his spade. He was used to digging post
holes with a crowbar and a tin can, and so he went to a
mesquite tree where the tools were kept and got the crowbar.

But the crowbar would no more dig into the hard substance than the spade would. The sun was mighty hot, anyhow; so the Mexican went up to the house where *el señor* Berry was whittling sticks on his gallery, and told him that he couldn't dig any more, that at the third post hole from the south gate it looked as if the devil himself had humped up into a rock that nothing could get through. Berry snorted around considerably at first, but directly he seemed to think of something and told his man, very well, not to dig any more but to saddle up and go out and bring in the main *remuda*. Now, only the day before they had had the main *remuda* in the pen and had caught out fresh mounts to keep in the little horse pasture. By this time the other horses would be scattered clear away on the back side of the pasture. The Mexican wondered what the *patrón* wanted the *remuda* for again. But it was none of his business. Well, the ride would take him all the rest of the day, and at least he would not have to dig any more post holes before *mañana*.

After the Mexican had saddled his horse and drunk a *cafecita* for lunch and fooled away half an hour putting in new stirrup leather strings and finally got out of sight, Berry slouched down to the pens. He came back to his shade on the gallery and whittled for an hour or two longer until everything around the *jacal*, even the Mexican's wife, was taking a *siesta*. Then he pulled off his spurs, which always dragged with a big clink when he walked, and went down to the pen again. The spade and the crowbar were where the Mexican had let them fall. Berry punched the crowbar down into the half-made hole. It almost bounced out of his hand, and he heard a kind of metallic thud. No, it was not flint-rock that had stopped the digging.

Berry went around back of the water trough to the *huisache* where his horse was tied and led him into the pen. Then he started to work. He began digging two or three feet out to one side of the hole. The dry ground was packed from the tramp of thousands of cattle and horses. He had to use the crowbar to loosen the soil. But it was no great task to get out a patch of earth two or three feet square and eighteen or twenty inches deep. Berry knew what he was about, and as he

scraped the loosened earth out with his spade he could feel a
flat metal surface that seemed to have rivets in it. It was the
lid of a chest, and when he had uncovered it, Berry drew up
one of the firm, new posts to use as a fulcrum for the crowbar.
With that he levered up the end of the chest. As he suspected,
it was too heavy and too tightly wedged for him to lift out. He
kicked a chunk under the raised edge and then looped a stout
rope about the exposed end. He had dragged cows out of the
bog on his horse, and he knew that the chest was not so heavy
as a cow. He had but fifty yards to drag it, and that down grade,
before he was in the brush, where he could prize the lid off.

When the Mexican got back that night his *mujer* told him
that Señor Berry had gone to San Antonio in the buckboard,
and that he had left word for the *remuda* to be turned back
into the big pasture and for the repair of the corrals to be continued. "They say" that the deposit that Berry made at the
Frost National Bank was a clean $17,000, nearly all in silver.

Stampede Mesa

JOHN R. CRADDOCK

Among cattle folk no subject for anecdote and speculation is
more popular than the subject of stampedes. There has always
been a certain mystery surrounding the stampeding of cattle.
Sometimes they stampede without any man's having heard,
seen, or smelled a possible cause. The following account of
how Stampede Mesa got its name, together with the legend,
told in many variations, of the phantom stampede, is current
among the people of the Panhandle and New Mexico. I was a
mere child when I heard it first, and I have since heard it
many times.

Stampede Mesa is in Crosby County, Texas, about eighteen
miles from the cap rock of Blanco Canyon, wedged up between
the forks of Catfish (sometimes called White or Blanco) River.

The main stream skirts it on the west; to the south the bluffs of the mesa drop a sheer hundred feet down into McNeil Branch. The two hundred acre top of the mesa is underlaid with rocks that are scarcely covered by the soil, though grazing is nearly always good. Trail drivers all agree that a better place to hold a herd will never be found. A herd could be watered at the river late in the evening and then be driven up the gentle slope of the mesa and bedded down for the night. In the morning there was water at hand before the drive was resumed. The steep bluffs to the south made a natural barrier so that night guard could be reduced almost half. Nevertheless, few herd bosses of the West would now, if opportunity came, venture to hold their herds on Stampede Mesa. Yet it will never succumb to the plow. Scarred and high, it will stand forever, a monument to the days that are gone, a wild bit of the old West to keep green the legend that has given to it the name, "Stampede Mesa."

Early in the fall of '89 an old cowman named Sawyer came through with a trail herd of fifteen hundred head of steers, threes and fours. While he was driving across Dockum Flats one evening, some six or seven miles east of the mesa, about forty-odd head of nester cows came bawling into the herd. Closely flanking them came the nester, demanding that his cattle be cut out of the herd. Old Sawyer, who was "as hard as nails," was driving shorthanded; he had come far; his steers were thin and he did not want them "ginned" about any more. Accordingly, he bluntly told the nester to go to hell.

The nester was pretty nervy, and seeing that his little stock of cattle was being driven off, he flared up and told Sawyer that if he did not drop his cows out of the herd before dark he would stampede the whole bunch.

At this Sawyer gave a kind of dry laugh, drew out his six shooter, and squinting down it at the nester, told him to "vamoose."

Nightfall found the herd straggling up the east slope of what on the morrow would be christened by some cowboy Stampede Mesa. Midnight came, and with scarcely half the usual night guard on duty, the herd settled down in peace.

"There was phantom steers
in the herd that night."

But the peace was not to last. True to his threat, the nester, approaching from the north side, slipped through the watch, waved a blanket a few times, and shot his gun. He did his work well. All of the herd except about three hundred head stampeded over the bluff on the south side of the mesa, and two of the night herders, caught in front of the frantic cattle that they were trying to circle, went over with them.

Sawyer said little, but at sunup he gave orders to bring in the nester alive, horse and all. The orders were carried out, and when the men rode up on the mesa with their prisoner, Sawyer was waiting. He tied the nester on his horse with a rawhide lariat, blindfolded the horse, and then, seizing him by the bits, backed him off the cliff. There were plenty of hands to drive Sawyer's remnant now. Somewhere on the hillside they buried, in their simple way, the remains of their two comrades, but they left the nester to rot with the piles of dead steers in the canyon.

And now old cowpunchers will tell you that if you chance to be about Stampede Mesa at night, you can hear the nester calling his cattle, and many assert that they have seen his murdered ghost, astride a blindfolded horse, sweeping over the headland, behind a stampeding herd of phantom steers. Herd bosses are afraid of those phantom steers, and it is said that every herd that has been held on the mesa since that night has stampeded, always from some unaccountable cause.

I have a tale connected with two of these noted stampedes that I will relate here in the words of Poncho Burall, who told it to me.

"It was in the fall of 1900. This country was just beginning to settle. I was working for old man Jeff Keister's outfit then, taking a herd through to New Mexico. We'd been on the trail some ten days, I guess, when we came to a ranch in a valley down on the Salt Fork. Keister says a friend of his lives there, and he rides off. After a while two boys ride up and tell us that they will herd the cattle while the outfit goes down to the ranch to dinner.

"When we rode down to the house, Keister and an old man were sitting under a brush arbor that represented the front porch. First thing I noticed about the old man was that one of his arms is only about two-thirds as long as the other, and that he has to put it where he wants it with his other hand. We meets him and sets down to wait for dinner, not saying much but listening some.

" 'You'll find a-plenty good places to hold 'em nights, Jeff, but about the third night out you will be some'ers near Stampede Mesa. Don't you try to hold them thar.'

" 'I'm aimin' to hold them right there, Bill,' Keister says.

" 'Now, Jeff, you ain't forgot that stampede in '91, have you? Well, maybe you have, but I hain't. I carry a little souvaneer that won't let me forget. There was phantom steers in that herd that night. You recollect as how them steers went over the steep side of the mesa, Jeff? I must a been a sight when you found me. It's right nigh onto ten year now, and I ain't moved this old arm since.'

"Well, the wife called dinner just then, and the old man got strung out on something else, but that stampede business jest stuck to my mind.

"Along late one evenin' old Keister and I were riding the drag, when he puts the dogie he's been a-carryin' on his saddle down on the ground, and says, ' 'Tain't fer now, yuh kin walk. We are campin' on Stampede Mesa, as they call it.'

" 'I guess yuh noticed that feller's arm, back there in the valley,' says Keister, jerking his hand back toward the way we come.

" 'Yes,' I said, waiting for him to go on.

" 'Well, he got it up there on the south side of that mesa. Hoss went plumb crazy. Bill's allys said they wuz ghost steers in that herd that night. I think I seen 'em too. They jest came a-sailin' through the herd and right past your horse. I don't believe in hants, but it wuz scary.'

"Well, we drove 'em up on the mesa and let 'em graze. A feller and me took first guard that night. The herd settled down pretty soon, but I couldn't get that stampede tale out of my mind; every time a cow moved I thought something was going to happen. It was a mixed herd, and they lay as quiet as a bunch of dead sheep. It got so quiet that I could hear my pardner's saddle creak, away off to one side. The moon set, and it got darker. Just about then something passed me. It looked like a man on a horse, but it just seemed to float along. Then there was a roar, and the whole bunch stampeded straight for the bluffs. I rode in front of one critter like, and he jest passed right on, jest kinder floatin' past me. Then some old cow bellered and we milled 'em easy—but they wouldn't bed down again that night and it took every derned one of us to hold 'em."

There are some who say that the phantoms of this legend are tumbleweeds, blown by the wind. But there are many honest men who will tell you of the weird calls of the phantom nester and of the galloping phantom steers. Knowing the story, you cannot look at the mesa, branded by the white scar of the old trail, without a strange emotion.

The Deathless Pacing White Stallion

J. FRANK DOBIE

The great horse went under various names—the White Steed of the Prairies, the Pacing White Stallion, the White Mustang, the Ghost Horse of the Plains. There were, in fact, several extraordinary white mustang stallions scattered far apart, living at different times. In tradition they all blended into one, the stories about them combining to make the greatest horse legend of North America. The stallion's fire, grace, beauty, speed, endurance, intelligence were supernal, making him admired and sought by all men in an age when every man was a horseman. His passion for liberty was the passion that his admirers and pursuers idealized and were ready to die for. In body and in spirit he represented horse ranges stretching from far down in Mexico to the Bad Lands of Montana, and from the Brazos River in eastern Texas to the Rocky Mountains in Colorado.

In *Tales of the Mustangs* (published by the Book Club of

Texas in 1936) and elsewhere I have traced this super-equine over an empire of range lands and through more decades of time than nature has allotted to any other terrestrial horse. The earliest notice I have found of him is in Washington Irving's *A Tour on the Prairies,* which tells how in 1832 this mustang had for six or seven years been "setting at naught every attempt of the hunters to capture him" on his range in what is now Oklahoma.

When J. L. Rountree came to Texas and settled in Milam County on the Brazos River, in 1839, the White Pacer was ranging the prairie lands—much less extensive than those to the west — of that region.[4] It was not long before Rountree joined with two other men to run him down. The horse's circuit was well known. The mustangers placed three relays of horses along it and added three packs of hounds. On the third day an expert Mexican roper on the fastest horse in the country was brought into the chase, but the White Stallion could not be made to break his pace. He simply tired down everything after him. His hunters set snares for him under trees where he was accustomed to stand in the shade in the heat of the day, but no device known to man ever succeeded with the wary animal. He disappeared finally without anyone's knowing whether he had been killed, had died a natural death, or had left the country.

White Horse Plains, in Colorado, southward from Cheyenne, is said to have taken its name from a noted mustang stallion that roamed that region some time before 1890. "This horse was supposed never to have broken a pace, and at this gait was able to outdistance all pursuers, though many traps were placed for him and many a horse hunter gave chase."[5]

The White Steed came into fame, however, through the description by George W. Kendall in *Narrative of the Texan Santa Fé Expedition.* Kendall heard of the horse while, in 1841, he was on the Staked Plains of Texas, that vast land then being

[4]Information received in 1929 from L. S. Rountree, Austin, Texas, son of the original settler.

[5]Kupper, Winifred T., *Sheep and a Sheepman of the Southwest,* M. A. Thesis, University of Texas, 1938, p. 209.

the noble animal's home—and security. "As the camp stories ran," wrote Kendall, "he has never been known to gallop or to trot, but paces faster than any horse that has been sent out after him can run. Some of the hunters go so far as to say that the White Steed has been known to pace his mile in less than two minutes. Large sums have been offered for his capture and the attempt has often been made. But he still roams his native prairies in freedom."

But there is no point in reviewing what has already been written. It is all wrong anyhow. I have just learned the true history of the immortal white horse.

John R. Morgan, who lives near Wichita Falls and is past his eighty-sixth birthday, came to Travis County, Texas, from Kentucky in 1868. He was soon riding with his uncle, John W. Young, who had been a range man for going on a quarter of a century. From him and from other men who were then old-timers, Morgan learned the detailed history of the wonderful horse. I will try to give his story.

While mustangs were still plentiful in all the prairie country, there appeared among them in the vicinity of what is now called McKinney Falls, on Onion Creek in Travis County, an extraordinary stallion. This was in the early 1840's. The animal had the markings of a pure-bred Arabian. His form was perfect; his alertness and vitality were superb. He was pure white. His tail brushed the tall mesquite grass that carpeted the earth, and his tossing mane swept to his knees. His only gait out of a walk was a pace, and it was soon found that he never, no matter how hard pressed, broke that pace. His *manada*, or bunch of mares, normally numbered from fifty to sixty head—double the size of the ordinary mustang *manada*.

His favorite watering place was on Onion Creek near the McKinney Falls, but he led his *manada* over a great range, southwest across the Blanco, the San Marcos and to the Guadalupe. It was known that he even at times ranged down as far as the Nueces, though this was not on his accustomed round. He kept clear of the timbers, never crossed the Colorado to the east, and did not range into the rocky cedar hills to the west; he seemed to like the rich mesquite grass of rolling country edging the blacklands better than that on the blacklands themselves. His habits were closely studied. He was the most magnificent horse known between the Colorado River and the Rio Grande, and many men, alone and in parties, tried to trap or walk down or otherwise catch him.

It was observed that when persistently chased, the White Stallion usually moved southward. It was generally supposed that he had come up from that direction. There was some evidence that he had been imported to Mexico, had been brought up as far as the Texas border by one of the owners of the great horse ranches occupying that country, and then, after being established on this ranch, had quit it and the semi-domesticated horsestock to run with the mustangs. Many a good ranch stallion in those days answered the call of the wild mustangs, some of them never to be recovered.

The White Stallion, no matter how chased, always in time came back to the water of, and the mesquite grass along Onion Creek. The favorite point of view from which to see him and his *manada* was Pilot Knob, about four miles from McKinney Falls. From this eminence John W. Young himself saw the stallion and his *manada* several times. Any mustanging party that proposed a chase generally sent a scout to Pilot Knob to locate their quarry. The White Stallion's color, his alert movements, and the large size of his *manada* all made him and the bunch he led conspicuous. If started, he would lead out pacing —single-footing—the *manada* following at a dead run. In a mile's distance he would gain at least a hundred and fifty yards on anything behind him. Then he would stop and look back, and wait while his bunch approached. If pursuers were still following, he would pace on, gaining and gaining, but again would stop and look back, thus keeping out of shooting, as well as roping, distance.

The Indians had spotted him and they gave him a few chases, but the most persistent chasers were from San Antonio, then a horseback town. A certain doctor of San Antonio who was a horse fancier heard of the White Stallion, saw him in action, and offered five hundred dollars for him if delivered in "sound condition." Five hundred dollars in those days amounted to a small fortune.

A Spanish-born rancher named Santa Ana Cruz determined to win the prize. He had a ranch on Onion Creek, near McKinney Falls, and had numerous peon vaqueros under him. He was associated in a business way with Samuel A. Maverick, and in putting down desperados had led a desperate life; it is said that he kept as many as ten guards around his house every night. His men had chased the White Stallion numerous times. One day they ran him seventy-five miles south, and when they got back home two days later, found him grazing with his mares on the accustomed range.

Now, to win the five hundred dollars, Santa Ana Cruz picked twelve riders, furnished each of them with two horses selected for speed and endurance—particularly endurance—and disposed them in the direction that the White Stallion might be expected to run after he was started. A scout on Pilot Knob saw the *manada* go in to water. After they had drunk, the nearest of the twelve men began the chase. The White Pacer took out in the direction of San Antonio. That first day, however, he did not keep his direction and before the morning of the second day he had circled back into his favorite range. He was crowded harder, his mares lagged more, and on this day he crossed the Guadalupe, going southwest. For three days and three nights the Santa Ana Cruz men ceaselessly pursued him. The time picked for the chase was in the full of the moon in June, and the country covered was, in those days, nearly all open prairie.

Before the end of the third day, every animal in the *manada* following the White Stallion had been run down. He himself, however, had not once lagged, had not once broken his single-footing, except to change from right to left and left to right. Two of Santa Ana Cruz's relay men trailed him across the Frio River. Then they quit. The White Stallion was still pacing toward the Rio Grande.

He never returned to his old range. In time the Onion Creek country learned why.

Going on south, the Pacing Mustang no doubt drank at the Nueces River. Before modern ranchmen built tanks, drilled wells, and put up windmills, the wide country between the Nueces and the Rio Grande was very sparsely watered. In some places it is a level country, all brushed today; in other places it is crumpled into high, rough hills and cut by deep canyons. About three miles from a waterhole in one of these canyons there was in the forties a Mexican ranch called Chaparro Prieto. The low rock house, with portholes against Indian attacks, and the adjacent corrals were located in a wide draw matted with mesquite grass. Near by was a hand-dug well that supplied water for the ranch people and for the saddle horses. All stock loose on the range watered at the big hole in the canyon, the only watering within a radius of many miles.

The hole was boxed in by the canyon walls on both sides and by a high bluff above it, leaving only one entrance—from the north. One hot afternoon a vaquero from the Chaparro Prieto while riding near the waterhole saw a lone white horse approaching in a slow pace from the north. At the instant of observation he was hidden by some black chaparral and was considerably to one side of the trail the horse was traveling. The animal's behavior indicated that he had smelled the water. He was very gaunt, indicating that he had not drunk for a long while; he was evidently jaded, but his footing, though weary, yet seemed secure, and he maintained an alertness in ears, eyes, and nostrils. The wind was in the vaquero's favor. He cautiously slipped a hand over his mount's nostrils to prevent a possible whinny. As the horse passed nearer, he recognized him from descriptions he had often heard as the Pacing White Stallion of the Mustangs.

Here was a chance to rope what so many riders had tried and failed to capture. As has been said, there was but one entrance and exit to the boxed waterhole. The vaquero knew that the thirsty stallion would drink deep and come back up the bank loggy with water. After the mustang had gone down the trail out of sight, the vaquero placed himself in position for a sure throw when the animal should emerge. He was riding a fresh pony. He did not have long to wait. Within a few minutes the long-sought-for lover-of-freedom emerged, his ears working, his body refreshed, his senses more alert. He saw the trap and made a dash so cunning that he eluded the rope's throw. Quickly recoiling his riata for another cast, the vaquero spurred in pursuit. The Steed of the Prairies had come two hundred miles or more from his range on Onion Creek, besides pacing in great circles before he had finally headed straight for the Rio Grande. His marvelous endurance was at last wearing out; the water that had refreshed him now also loaded him down.

The second loop thrown by the fast-running vaquero went over his head. But he did not run full speed on the rope and jerk himself down. His response showed that he had been roped before. He wheeled just as the rope tightened and with wide open mouth rushed at his captor. He did not seem to see the horse ridden by the vaquero. He was after the man. He nearly seized him, but the agile cow pony had wheeled also. Fortunately for the vaquero's life, some scattered mesquite trees grew just ahead of him. Guiding his well-reined pony, he managed to get one of these mesquites between himself and the roped stallion. The mesquite served as a snubbing post for him to halt and then tie the magnificent horse. Magnificent, for, unlike many mustangs appearing magnificent at a distance, this one remained so at close quarters, even though worn by his long war of defense.

Tying him up as close as he could and leaving him to lunge at the rawhide-strong riata, the vaquero left in a long lope to get help at the Rancho Chaparro Prieto. He returned in less than an hour with two other vaqueros. With three ropes on the White Mustang now, thus checking his attempts to fight, they led and drove him to a spot on the prairie near the ranch corrals where the mesquite grass was particularly fine. There they threw the proud King of the Mustangs, tied ropes on him so that he could not choke himself to death, fixed a clog on one of his forefeet, and staked him. When night came, he was standing where they left him, not having taken a mouthful of grass.

The next day they carried a sawed-off barrel, used as a trough, within the horse's reach and filled it with water. He did not notice it. For ten days and ten nights he remained there, grass all about him, water at his nostril's tip, without taking one bite to eat or one swallow out of the trough. Then he lay down and died. He fulfilled the ringing cry of Patrick Henry, "Give me liberty or give me death." As he had lived, he died noble.

▼▼▼▼▼▼▼▼▼▼▼▼▼▼

The Legend of Sam Bass

WALTER PRESCOTT WEBB

Sam Bass was born in Indiana—that was his native home,
And at the age of seventeen young Sam began to roam.
He first came out to Texas, a teamster for to be;
A kinder hearted fellow you scarcely ever see.

This bit of biography of the Texas bandit was probably the first poem the writer learned outside the home circle. He learned it at the age when it was a great privilege to be permitted to pad along in the freshly plowed furrow at the heels of the hired man, Dave. Not only was Dave the hired man, he was a neighbor's boy, and such a good poker player that he developed later into a professional gambler. But at the time I write of, Dave was my tutor in Texas history, poetry, and music, all of which revolved around Sam Bass. To me and to Dave, Sam Bass was an admirable young man who raced horses, robbed banks, held up trains, and led a life filled with other strange adventure. At length, this hero came to an untimely end through a villain named Murphy, "who gave poor Sam away." It was a story calculated to capture the imagination of young men and small boys. All over Texas hired men were teaching small boys the legend of Sam Bass, a story which improved in the telling according to the ability of the teller.

Not only was the story thus told. Men of high station in life, the lawyers, judges, and old-timers, congregated around the courthouse of this western county and told of how Sam rode through the country at night after one of his daring robberies. Once a posse organized to go out and take Sam Bass. The leader of the posse was a lawyer, a smart man, and he knew exactly where Sam could be found and how he could be taken. He bravely placed himself at the head of a group of heavily armed men; he assured them that they would take the bandit and share the liberal reward that had been set on his head. They rode away into the night, they approached the lair of the fugitive; they *knew* they had him—at least the leader knew it. But that was the trouble. Sam did not run; therefore, the posse could not pursue. Sam seemed too willing to be approached; that willingness was ominous. Sam was such a good shot, so handy with a gun. The posse paused, it halted, consulted with the leader. The leader's voice had lost its assurance. The posse that had ridden up the hill now rode down again. Sam Bass *could not be found!* And until this day, when old-timers get together in that county some one is sure to tell the story of that hunt. The wag of the courthouse, a lawyer, reduced it to writing, and on such public occasions as picnics and barbecues, he will read the account of "How Bill Sebasco Took Sam Bass." It was cleverly done and made as great a hit with the public as did Dave's rendition of the song and story to the small boy. In both cases all sympathy was with Sam Bass, all opinion against Murphy and Bill Sebasco.

Thus in West Texas, from the judge in the courthouse to the small boy in the furrow behind the hired man, was the story of Sam Bass told. What was taking place in this county was occurring, with proper variations, in every other county in the state, especially in those of the north and west. The legend of Sam Bass was in the process of becoming. Today it would fill a volume.

Few are the facts known relative to Sam Bass, but some of them are these: Samuel Bass was from Indiana. He was born July 21, 1851, came to Texas, raced horses, made his headquarters in Denton County, participated in some bank robberies and train holdups. He became the recognized leader of his band and enjoyed a wide reputation, which he achieved before he was twenty-seven years old. In the summer of 1878 he left Denton County with the intention of robbing a bank or train. With him were Murphy, the man who had arranged to sell him out to the officers of the law, also Seaborn Barnes and Frank Jackson. The plan was made to rob the Round Rock bank on Saturday, July 20, 1878. En route to Round Rock, Murphy sent a note to Major John B. Jones, adjutant-general of Texas, giving their plan. The result was that when Bass reached Round Rock the town was full of Texas Rangers and other officers of the law. On Friday Bass with Jackson and Barnes went into Round Rock to look over the ground before their attempt to rob. While purchasing tobacco in a store adjoining the bank, they were accosted by officers of the law, and a battle ensued. Barnes was killed on the spot, along with an officer. Bass escaped with a mortal wound, was found next day in the woods, and died the following day, Sunday, July 21, 1878. On that day he was twenty-seven. Frank Jackson made good his escape and has never been heard from since.

From these facts, the legend of Sam Bass has grown. Legend and fact are inextricably mixed. I shall make no effort to separate the one from the other, but shall set all down, much as I heard it.

Bass died gamely, as he lived. He refused to give any of his comrades away, though he was rational until the end. "If a man knows any secrets," he said, "he should die and go to hell with them in him." Bass said that he had never killed a man, unless he killed the officer in Round Rock. Frank Jackson wanted to remain and help Bass, but the latter, knowing he was near the end, persuaded Jackson to leave him, and gave him his horse to ride.

Bass and his men had camped near some Negro cabins at Round Rock, not far from the cemetery. Bass had an old Negro woman, Aunt Mary Matson, to cook some biscuits for him and to grind some coffee. When she had done this, Bass gave her a dollar. He then asked, "Have you ever heard of Sam Bass?" She told him she had. "Well, you can tell them you saw Sam Bass," he said, and went away.

His generosity was well known. He always paid for what he

got from individuals. He was particularly considerate of poor people. He would give a poor woman a twenty-dollar gold piece for a dinner and take no change. He paid the farmers well for the horses he took from them, though sometimes he did not have time to see the farmer.

Sam Bass relics are scattered over the country, everywhere. Some say that he gave his gun to Frank Jackson. Others declare he surrendered it to the officers who found him. His belt with some cartridges in it is in the library of the University of Texas. A carpenter at Snyder has a horseshoe from Bass's best race horse nailed to the top of his tool chest. Near Belton are some live oak trees that Bass is said to have shot his initials in while riding at full speed. Horns of steers supposed to have been killed by Bass sell over the country at fancy prices. In Montague County there is a legend of $30,000 of loot buried by Sam Bass. Again, he is supposed to have left treasure in the Llano country. At McNeill, near Austin, there is a cave in which Sam Bass hid when he was in retirement. There he kept his horses and from there he made his forays.

Finally, when Sam was dead, legend wrote an epitaph on his monument which is not there. The legendary epitaph reads: "Would That He Were Good as He was Brave." No such inscription can be deciphered on Bass's monument. The monument has been badly mutilated by souvenir collectors, but the inscription remains.

SAMUEL BASS
BORN
JULY 21, 1851
DIED
JULY 21, 1878
AGED 27 YEARS

In the lower right hand corner of the block on which the inscription appears is the name of the maker, C. B. Pease, Mitchell, Indiana. The people of Round Rock say that the monument was erected by a member of his family about a year after Bass's death.

More interesting than Bass's rather pretentious monument is that of his comrade, Seaborn Barnes, who sleeps the long sleep by his side. A rough sandstone stands at the head of this grave. It has been chipped away until the name is gone. The inscription, however, remains along with the date of his death. Were there no legend of Sam Bass in Texas, this inscription would make one. It is written in language Bass would have loved; it has a certain impertinence to law-abiding people in the near-by graves, a certain pride in the leader at whose heels Barnes died. The epitaph contains seven words. The spirit of the person who wrote the seven words of that epitaph is the spirit that has created the legend of Sam Bass in Texas.

HE WAS RIGHT BOWER TO SAM BASS

GHOST STORIES

The Ghosts of Lake Jackson

BERTHA McKEE DOBIE

Old Alf ran his fingers vigorously through his hair in his characteristic gesture of reminiscence. I had asked whether he had ever heard that the old house at Lake Jackson Plantation, ten miles up the Brazos from Velasco, was haunted. He answered my question in his own oblique way.

"Le's see," he said, "it wus fo' year atter freedom dat Marse Sam done lef' t'ree hunderd bale ob cotton in de fiel' in Waller County, an' we all come postin' down to de Wha'ton Plantation to make sugar. Eve'y t'ing down heah wus sugar in dem days. Co'se de Wha'ton place all cut up now, but in dem days it run plum up ter Lake Jackson.

"Ol' Cunnel Jackson been dead long year befo' dat en de gran' ol' house seen trouble a-plenty. Oh, I dunno *how* big de Lake Jackson Plantation wus, but I knows dey wuk six er seben hunderd niggers dere atter Ward and Dewey tuk de place in 1873, an' I done go ter wuk fer 'em in '76 longer a lot er udder free niggers.[1] Dat wus atter Marse Sam done go out to Californey. I dunno how big it wus, but it wus awfu', awfu'. He wus a highty-tighty man, de Cunnel wus, en mighty proud er all his lan' en dat big, fine house. I dunno how many rooms it had, but dere wus a worril ob 'em, en de postes on de front gall'ry wus dat big aroun'. Oh, dey wus big an' fine, en de house look gran' eben dough when I see it it been gwine rack en ruin fer years. Dere wus a roun' tower, what some folks calls a cubola, on top, en it wus glass all roun', en dey say dat

---

[1]Ward and Dewey contracted with the state for convict labor, which they supplemented with "free niggers."

when de Cunnel was alibe he useter go up dere ev'y ev'nin
en look out ober his lan' fur's he could see. En dey say dat
eber since dat time he comes back ev' ev'nin' en look out ober
de lan'. I dunno 'bout dat. I ain't seed him. But da's w'at dey
say. De cubola had one o' dem weader fixin's on de tiptop of it.
It stayed dere untel de sto'm ob '75.

"Dat wus de wretchedes' fambly wid wunner nudder, allus
in a scrummage. You done year how Mr. George kill Mr. John,
ain't you? Ober de prob'ty, it wus. Mr. George wus arrange
fer to hab de place at Sandy Point, en he want Lake Jackson.
I's seed de spot where Mr. John fell mo'n once. You knows dat
if a man is pick up fum de place where he fall when he shot,
de rains wash out de blood an' de grass grow green, but if he
die where he fall it stay dark like blood to de end ob time en
no rain wash it out. Dat sho is de bressed truf, en da's de way
where Mr. John die atter Mr. George shoot him. Mr. George
lose his min' atter w'ile. Look like it gnaw on his min' w'at he
done. Dey wus allus in a perdiction, dose Jacksons. 'Pear like
dey jes' bawn dat away. Mr. Andrew kill hisse'f accidental
crawlin' t'rough a fence when he wus out huntin'. En all dat
calamity fambly ain't neber get no rest. One night I sleep in
de house on an ol' sofy. Dere wa'n't no win' stirrin' no way
you'd look. But de do's kep' op'nin' en shettin' en a-slammin'
en a-bangin' en I year all dat onres'less fambly walkin' up en
down all ober de house, jes' like I tell you. But I so tired dat
night I don' care 'bout nothin' no more 'cep'n' rest, en I rise
up on my elbow en say, 'It take a libe man t'row me out dis
night!'"

▼▼▼▼▼▼▼▼▼▼▼▼▼

Mexican Ghosts from El Paso

CHARLES L. SONNICHSEN

All up and down the valley near El Paso the ghosts are
walking. Almost any night at the proper time and place they

may be heard bewailing their sins of violence or greed, entreating the passer-by to get them out of Purgatory, or moaning over some hoard of buried gold. It is lucky for the nerves of most Americans that they are unaware of this condition; if their eyes should suddenly be opened, the Anglo-Saxon population of the valley would probably diminish rapidly. Fortunately, however, our ghosts are mostly Mexican, and as a rule they reveal themselves only to their own countrymen.

A GHOSTLY BABY SNATCHER

When Señor Zartuche was a baby, he was the victim of a malicious ghost who came every night at midnight and took him out of the house into the yard. There they would stay a few minutes; then the ghost would bring him back. Nobody knew why a spirit should behave in this eccentric manner, and nobody was able to do anything about it. The members of the family, of course, were completely terrorized, as who would not be to see a sight like this? But in spite of the cries and entreaties of the family and in spite of the kicks and squalls of the boy himself, the gloomy spectre carried out his nightly schedule.

Yes, it was hard on everybody, but particularly on the little boy. Every night he waited for the ghost, his little body shaking with terror. Day by day he grew thinner and paler, and it was quite obvious that soon there would not be any little boy for the ghost to carry out.

At last his mother was reminded of something she had once heard—that if one made himself into the shape of a cross on his bed, with arms flung out wide and face to heaven, he would be safe from witches. Perhaps the same treatment would make a ghost think twice about what he was doing. As a last resort, therefore, the mother got into bed with her child, and, as soon as she heard the ghost coming, assumed the required position.

The thing drew near, its fiery eyes fixed on the child, its claw-like hands extended to seize him. Then it saw the mother and drew back. "Now," she thought, "is the time to speak to it," for, as all Christian people know, a ghost cannot speak to a living person unless the person speaks first. She got out the right words with some difficulty:

"*En el nombre de Dios, diga lo que quiere?*"—In the name of God, what do you want?

The ghost began to talk. It told the woman of a buried treasure in that very house. She must dig in a particular spot and she would find first of all a saddle. Under the saddle were two earthen pots, one full of gold and the other of silver. Finally, pointing with a skinny forefinger, the ghost showed her where to dig.

By this time the señora was so frightened that she fainted away with a groan that would have wrung your heart. When she came to herself, the ghost was gone—to return no more.

Of course she wanted to find the treasure. She thought of starting to dig at once; but unfortunately, when she awoke from her fainting fit, she had forgotten in which corner the treasure was buried. She began to dig, nevertheless, and her family helped her, but none of them found either the saddle or the gold under it. At last they gave up in despair.

Some time later, a man who had heard the story decided to try his luck. He dug a little deeper than anybody else, and there was the saddle. He pulled the rotted relic out, and beneath it were the two earthenware pots. But do not suppose there was any gold or silver in them! Of course not! Everybody knows that the person to whom the ghost points out the location of buried treasure is the only one who can find it. In this case the two earthenware pots were full of charcoal.

Everyone in Socorro, downstream from El Paso, has heard this tale about Señor Zartuche—even his wife; but he will not talk about it. If he sees a stranger coming he will run. His wife says he is a little crazy, and it is a subject on which one hesitates to contradict her.

If one asks whether her husband's condition may possibly be due to his unfortunate experience in childhood she will reply, "*Quién sabe?*" and tell you about another ghost, well known in Socorro, which she has seen herself.

THE GENTLEMAN FROM SPAIN

This tale goes back many years to the time a strange Spaniard came up from Mexico hunting for buried treasure. He had a map which had been bequeathed to him, in the usual manner, by a dying friend, and he went to work in a certain adobe house which has been used as a store and which can still be recognized by the words GENERAL MERCANTILE painted on one wall.

The Spanish gentleman kept very much to himself. He was handsome, wore fine clothes, and should have displayed a social personality. But he chose not to make friends or to tell people about himself, and all they could find out was that he had a daughter in a convent in New York City to whom he frequently wrote letters.

He lived on mysteriously in Socorro for some time. Then one morning, very early, a goat herder on his way out of town with his flock heard the most horrible commotion coming from the adobe house. It sounded like a man frightened out of his wits or in terrible agony. The goat herder abandoned his flock and ran to see what the howling and roaring were about. What he saw was something to set one's hair on end. In a freshly dug hole lay the Spanish gentleman, stone dead; the marks of his struggle upon him; his pick and shovel at his side. On the table was a letter to his daughter in New York, telling her that he was near the end of his quest. The treasure was almost within his grasp. If the map proved to be reliable, he would be a rich man tomorrow.

The map! It should have been there along with the pick and shovel and the melancholy remains of the ambitious Spaniard. But, search as they might, the people of Socorro could not find so much as a scrap of it. Therefore, being constitutionally disposed to accept the inevitable without distressing themselves, they put the Spanish gentleman out of their minds and thought of other things.

This, however, did not suit the Spanish gentleman at all. The family which moved into the adobe house began to report the most peculiar disturbance. They would wake up in the night with the chill of fear running up and down their spines and hear in the darkness the clanking of iron. Something would rattle like a chain. Then would come the regular click and crunch of a spade digging in the earth. Then voices — babbling and unintelligible and far away, but human voices, none the less.

This went on without too much discomfort to the people of the house until the time when a woman who lived there awoke in the middle of the night to find someone shaking her. She awoke unwillingly, as one does at such an hour, but she sat up fast enough when she saw who was disturbing her.

"El Caballero de España!" she shrieked.

Hearing himself thus addressed, the vision spoke in reply. He told her of great wealth buried beneath the house—an enormous sum in a huge chest. He told her how he himself had located it and dug to where he could plainly see the carved lid. Then two hands reached up out of the hole and seized him by the ankles. He struggled and yelled like a madman, but in spite of all his effort those two hands drew him down—down into the hole. And that was the end of him.

Then he informed her why it had been necessary for him to disturb her rest. Before he had ever left Mexico City, he had promised to pray thirty souls out of Purgatory with the proceeds of his treasure hunting. He had been unable, of course, to keep his word. Now, said he, those thirty souls turned sixty cold and dismal eyes on him every time he passed that way in the other world. Something had to be done about it, and if the woman would dig up the treasure and get those souls through Purgatory, she could keep half the treasure. Was it any wonder, he asked her, that a spirit in his situation should find it impossible to rest? Then he showed her a map which he had in his hand. He unrolled it and began to explain the exact location of the buried gold. But by this time the woman was tried beyond her strength; she fainted away before the directions were complete.

The treasure has never been recovered, but many people in Socorro have heard the sounds of digging and seen ghostly

human forms in the old house. Mrs. Zartuche says she once
got a good look at the apparition and recognized him as the
Spanish gentleman.

THE AMOROUS GHOST

A few miles down the river from Socorro is San Elizario,
likewise ancient and likewise full of tales. Here is one.

Near the church in San Elizario is an old, rambling adobe
house of many rooms. It was once a mansion, the property of
a famous local character named Mauro Luján. Years ago this
house was the scene of many a gathering of plotting politicians.
During the Salt War of 1877, the bloodiest affair in Valley
history, Don Mauro's house is said to have been headquarters
for the leaders of the mob.

Since the old man's death, it has gone to ruin. No whitewash
has touched its walls for years and no one has bothered to
repair the places where the adobe has crumbled. Still Don
Mauro must love it, for he has often been seen wandering from
room to room saying his rosary.

Many people have lived in his house. To one pair of tenants,
María de Ramirez and her husband Alejo, he revealed the
location of a pot of money with which they were to have masses
said for his soul. They, however, were unfaithful to his trust.
They took the money across the river into Mexico, where they
set up for themselves in the grocery business. They did not
prosper, however, and María soon died, as one would expect.

Then an elderly pair named Maciel moved in, to whom Don
Mauro was only a name. Antonio worked until late at night,
leaving Bonifacia to go to bed by herself. At last the old lady
went to her friend Doña Tomasa Giron and told her a strange
tale.

"Every night," she said, "I go to bed by myself, because my
husband is working and comes home late. And every night
the ghost of an old man with a long, white beard comes and
gets in bed with me. When my husband comes home and wishes

to go to sleep, he has to say, '*Con su permiso*,'—'with your permission'—before the old man will let him get in bed."

"Hm," said Doña Tomasa, "does he get out of bed when your husband gets in?"

"Oh, no! He just moves over."

"It sounds like Don Mauro," remarked Doña Tomasa, thoughtfully, as her mind traveled back over Don Mauro's record. "He used to be fond of the ladies," she added—"*era muy enamorado.*"

"*Y todavía es*," said Bonifacia de Maciel, looking very wise, "*y todavía es. Me hace cariños.*"—He still is; he caresses me.

The Ghost Nun

RUTH DODSON

In the spring of 1942 Ramona Vasquez, while in my kitchen, mentioned a *troquero* who picked up a nun on the highway only to find that he had picked up a ghost. I began making inquiries to find out if other people had heard about the nun.

Mrs. Lowther, of Mathis, told me that a man had told a similar story to her husband. A man was coming from the Valley when he picked up a nun and took her as far as she wanted to go on the highway. He later found that no such nun belonged in any convent in that part of the country.

The next time I had Ramona with me I asked her for her story and this is what she told me:

A Mexican man was driving from Corpus Christi to Alice, where he had work with the W P A. At a place between Banquete and Agua Dulce he was stopped by a nun who was walking along the road. She asked for a ride to Alice. As they went along she asked the man when he would be returning from Alice. He told her that he was working for the W P A, and that he would return to Corpus Christi after work hours that day. The nun, who gave the man her name, told him that she, too, was working for the W P A in the office in Alice, and would like to catch a ride with him that afternoon. She told him that she would meet him at a certain garage on the edge of town.

When the man failed to find the nun at the garage that afternoon, he went to the office of the W P A, thinking that she had been detained. When he inquired at the office, he was told that no nun was employed there. The man then decided to go to the convent to see if she was there. The head Sister, when the man explained, told him that the nun by the name he gave had been dead eight years.

Ramona said that the man was now afraid to pick up anyone on the highway.

A Mexican woman in Corpus Christi told my sister this story:

A friend of hers who lives in Laredo wrote her that she was returning home on a bus. When the bus passed through Goliad a nun got on. There were also a good many soldiers coming from Houston to Laredo. The nun talked to the soldiers and told them that the war would end in 1942. After traveling for some time, a soldier noticed that the nun was no longer on the bus. He called this fact to the attention of the driver, who stopped to investigate. No one had seen the nun fall from the bus, which had not stopped since she was last seen. Strange to say, her baggage was gone, too.

When the driver reached Laredo, he went at once to the convent to see if a nun was expected and to report the case. The Sisters told him that they were expecting no one. Finally they placed pictures before him to see if he could identify any one of them. He selected one as the picture of the missing passenger. But this was the picture of a nun who had been dead for several years.

Some time later I went to see a young Mexican boy who was sick. He and a young woman, his cousin, were sitting on a platform that connects two parts of the house. It was a pleasant place to sit, and I joined them. After inquiring about the boy's health and getting a discouraging report, I decided to stay for some conversation, something that I thought the sick, lonely boy needed.

Finally, I remarked about the beauty of the crape myrtle
bush in full bloom near by. "Now," I said, "I must take a flower
off it or I might make it *ojo*,[2] mightn't I?" Both the seventeen-
year-old boy and the woman nodded their heads in agreement.
I told them that a woman had told me that she had had a lovely
gardenia growing within sight of the street. When it bloomed,
the passers-by admired it so much that they "did it harm" and
it died. "Yes," my audience assured me, "that could have been
done."

This gave me an opportunity to introduce the subject of the
supernatural. I told the story of the nun on the highway. I
sensed that the story was not new to them, so when I had
finished I asked them if they had heard anything in regard to
it. They had. This is what the woman told me:

Two soldiers were going from Sinton to Corpus Christi.
Somewhere on the road they were stopped by a nun who asked
for a ride. As they traveled along, the soldiers talked of war.
The nun, who was riding on the back seat, spoke and told
them that the war was going to end before the year was out
(1942).

When they reached Corpus Christi, the nun asked to be
taken to the cemetery and left there. The soldiers supposed that
she was going to visit a grave, and asked if they should stop
and pick her up on their way back. She told them no, but
she added that they might give the priest at Sinton a post card
which she handed them.

When the priest read the card, he asked the soldiers if they
would recognize a picture of the nun if they saw it; they said
they would. Then the priest brought out a large book in which
were many pictures of nuns. He turned the leaves until the
soldiers stopped him: "There is the picture of the nun," they
said, pointing to one. It was the picture of a nun who had
been dead several years.

[2]Cast an evil eye upon it.

▼▼▼▼▼▼▼▼▼▼▼▼▼

The Weeping Woman

SOLEDAD PÉREZ

The tale of the Weeping Woman (La Llorona) is not new. It is essentially a Mexican tale that has existed since Aztec times. According to Thomas A. Janvier[3] and Luis González Obregón,[4] the tale is based on Aztec mythology.

Both Janvier and Obregón refer to Bernardino de Sahagún[5] to point out the connection existing between the Weeping Woman and the Aztec goddess named Civacoatl, Cihuacohuatl, or Tonantzin who appeared dressed in white and bearing a cradle on her shoulders as though she were carrying a child. The goddess mixed among the Aztec women and left the cradle abandoned. When the women looked into the cradle, they always found an arrowhead shaped like the Aztec sacrificial knife. At night the goddess went through the cities and towns shrieking and weeping and disappeared in the waters of lakes or rivers.

Later, the myth became merged with the story of real tragedy, usually a story involving a crime, such as infanticide. Vicente Riva Palacio and Juan de Dios Peza retell a 16th-century tale of Luisa, a beautiful peasant girl who fell in love with Don Muño Montes Claros and bore him three sons.[6] When Don Muño abandoned Luisa to marry a woman of his own class, Luisa murdered the children and then went through the streets shrieking and sobbing. Don Muño committed suicide.

Today, the tale of the Weeping Woman is current throughout Mexico. In the United States it is known in Texas, California, Arizona, and possibly other states. Betty Leddy has listed forty-two versions in her study, "La Llorona in Southern Arizona," published in *Western Folklore*, VII (1948), 272-77. No similiar study has been made for Texas or California.

---

[3]*Legends of the City of Mexico* (New York, 1910), pp. 134-38, 162-65.
[4]*Las Calles de México* (7th ed.; México, D. F., 1947), vol. I, pp. 37-40.
[5]*Historia de Nueva España* (México, D. F., 1890), vol. I, bk. I, pp. 32-33.
[6]*Tradiciones y Leyendas Méxicanas* (México, n.d.), pp. 127-49.

During 1948 and 1949 I gathered a number of Llorona stories in Austin. Most of my informants had come from Mexico and had known it before leaving there. In some instances the tale has become localized. The Weeping Woman is often said to be someone who lived in Austin many years ago; she killed her children, and now her spirit wanders about.

Four Austin versions are given below. It will be seen that the Llorona story is easily adapted to narrative in which the teller is a participant.

I

A long time ago there was a woman who had two children. She did not love them; so she mistreated and neglected them. The children were always hungry and cold because their mother was too busy going to parties and dances to take care of them.

Finally one of the children died and later the other died too. The woman felt no remorse. She continued to lead a very gay life. When she died, she had not confessed her sins or repented of her ill-treatment of the children. Now she appears in the east and southeast parts of Austin grieving for her children. Her soul is doing penance for her sins.

II

Do you know why La Llorona appears near the Colorado River? Well, La Llorona was a woman who lived here in Austin. She had two children, but she didn't love them. One day she took them to the river and drowned them. She never repented, and that is why she appears there and cries for her children.

My son, Rodolfo, was ten or eleven years old when he and some other boys decided to spend the night out near the river. They went in a little cart and took some blankets.

At night they spread the blankets out on the ground and went to sleep. He says that after midnight all of them woke up at the same time and saw a shadow flit across them. Then they heard the piercing wail of La Llorona. They got up and came home immediately. My son was very frightened when he got home.

She had the face of a horse.

III

My brother had a very good friend who was a shoemaker. The two were heavy drinkers, and they liked to go out together to eat and drink.

Well, one night my brother went to see his friend about twelve-thirty and prevailed on him to go out to drink with him.

Shortly after the two had started out for their favorite saloon, they noticed that a very attractive woman was walking just ahead of them. They decided to follow her. The two followed for a long time, but they couldn't catch up with her. When it seemed that they were coming up even with the woman, she suddenly seemed to get about half a block ahead of them. Finally, my brother and his friend decided to turn back, but as a parting gesture they said, "Good-by, my dear!"

At the same time that the two said, "Good-by, my dear!" the attractive woman whom they had followed turned around. She had the face of a horse, her fingernails were shiny and tin-like, and she gave a long, piercing cry. It was La Llorona.

My brother would have run, but his friend had fainted, and he had to revive him. The two reformed after that encounter with La Llorona.

IV

My father was a missionary, and on one occasion he held a religious service in Atoyac, Michoacán. We lived in the neighboring town of Coyoacán, and after the service we left for home. It was rather late at night, but there was a full moon.

Some friends, my father, and I were traveling along, carefree, when we heard a scream. The dog that was with us growled and tried to hide. We saw a shadow flit by, and a moment later we heard another scream in front of us. My hair stood on end. It was La Llorona.

BALLADS AND SONGS

Songs the Cowboys Sing

JOHN R. CRADDOCK

These songs were for the most part obtained at the foot of the Plains, in Dickens County, Texas, where I was reared. They are songs that furnished entertainment to the people of that country before the phonograph and the radio came in; in those days the people used to meet for "singings," at which they would both sing and dance. They are the songs also that cowboys of the Swenson, Matador, and other ranches of the region used to sing—and sometimes yet sing—to pass the time along in camp or on the range or in entertaining each other. Like the old darkey songs, they are often hard to set to music. The cowboys and cow people in general sang them with a nasal twang that easily lengthened out short beats and as easily shortened down extra syllables. Nearly all regular cowboys still sing more or less, and wherever a few of them gather together one or two can be found that are noted for their memory and their ability to carry tunes. These troubadours of the range often improvise songs. The most popular songs, like "Utah Carl," "The Z Bar Dun," "Little Joe the Wrangler," etc., have been so often printed, in Lomax's *Cowboy Songs* and in other places, that they are not here reproduced.

THREE GAY PUNCHERS

The first song is still popular among punchers throughout Dickens, Kent, and Stonewall counties. From the brands used, I judge that the originators of the ballad worked from New

Mexico back to the Three A's of Stonewall County; however,
I have not been able to trail down the improviser of the lines.

> We are three gay punchers from Yellowstone Flat;
> We wear the high heels, also the white hat.
> We are noted in Texas and on the Staked Plains,
> And also in Montana, on the Yellowstone Range.

> We ride the Frazier saddle,[1] our chaps are the best,
> Our boots, spurs, and bits can't be beat in the West.
> We ride to the wagon, we ride in pursuit,
> We hear the cook holler, "Chuck-away, grab-a-root."

> We make a bed down on the ground frozen hard,
> For, boys, we'll soon be called to our guard.
> We ride up the cow trail, take down the rawhide;
> There is never a bronco but what we will ride.

> We rope 'em, ride, brand 'em, as in the days of old,
> And on the left shoulder we stamp the Shoe Sole.[2]
> We work the J Q, also the Bar S,
> But as for the Three A's we like 'em the best.

> We steal out their horses, to the dances we go,
> And if we get boozy, we pull off a show.
> It's now for cowpunching I have no more use,
> I'll hang up my saddle and coil up my noose.

> I am tired of cowpunching, the work is so rough;
> I'll do like my pardner, go east and play tough.
> For saddle and bridle I have no more use;
> I'll ride back to Three A's and turn Grey Walt a-loose.

> So hang saddle and bridle where they will keep dry,
> For, boys, we will need 'em in the sweet by and by.

THE WILD BOY

"The Wild Boy,"[3] like "Three Gay Punchers," is common to
New Mexico and West Texas. It seems to have originated in

[1] A brand of saddles manufactured at Pueblo, Colorado, still well-known all
over the cattle world.

[2] A ranch brand made in the form of a half-sole.

[3] The first stanza of this song is almost identical with the first two lines of
"My Parents Reared Me Tenderly" (Cox, No. 85, p. 300) and with the first two
lines of the second stanza of "Lackey Bill" (Lomax, 1929 reprint, p. 83), but
the narrative is entirely different.

the vicinity of the Rocky Mountains. All singers of the ballad
stick closely to the words as given.

My parents reared me ten-der-lee,
   They had no child but me,
But I was bent on rambling—
   With them I couldn't agree.

I started up the cow trail
   To see some Western land.
I met up with a wild bunch,
   And likewise killed a man.

I stole a many a fat horse,
   Stole him from the poor,
And over the Rocky Mountains
   I made his iron hoofs roar.

One morning, one morning,
   I think it was in May,
The sheriff rode up to me,
   Says, "I'm a-looking for you today."

He took me down to the new jail,
   And there I walked in.

My parents all deserted me,
   As likewise did my kin.

Except one old rich uncle,
   Far out in the West;
A-hearing of my trouble,
   They say he could not rest.

He went my bail at the Ute jail,
   He paid my debts by scores.
It's once I've been a wild boy,
   I won't be any more.

There's Agnes and there's Mabel,
   There's Mary likewise;
My deeds and desperation
   Brought tears into their eyes.

I've stolen many a fat horse,
   Stolen him from the poor.
It's once I've been a wild boy,
   I won't be any more.

THE YOUNG COMPANIONS

For "The Young Companions"[4] I am indebted to "Buddie"
Grubbs, of the Red Mud community; however, the ballad is
common both east and west of the New Mexico line. The
doleful tune to which it is sung is well fitted to the downfall
of the hero.

    Come, all my young companions, wherever you may be,
    And I'll tell you all a story,—to shun bad compan-ee.
    My home's in Arizona, among those desert hills;
    My childhood and my fireside are in my memory still.

    I had a darling old mother, she always prayed for me;
    The very last words she uttered were a prayer to God for me.
    Says, "Oh, keep my boy from evil. May God direct his ways;
    My blessings are upon you throughout your manhood days."

[4]An interesting variant to Lomax's "Young Companions," p. 81, and to me
preferable.

Well, I bid adieu to loved ones, to kind friends bid farewell,
I landed in Chicago—the very depths of hell.
It was there I took to drinking, I sinned both night and day,
And ever in my bosom those feeble words would say:

"God, keep my boy from evil. May God direct his ways;
My blessings are upon you throughout your manhood days."
Well, I courted a fair young damsel; her name I will not tell,
For why should I disgrace her since I am doomed for hell?

It was on a moonlit evening, the stars were shining bright,
When I drew my ugly dagger and bade her spirit take flight.
The justice overtook me, and, as well you now may see,
My soul is doomed forever, throughout eter-ni-tee.

And ever in my bosom, those dying words do say,
"God, keep my boy from evil throughout his manhood's day."
I am standing on the scaffold, my moments are not long;
You may forget this singer, but don't forget this song.

TONIGHT MY HEART'S IN TEXAS

A favorite song with a girl in our country used to be "Tonight
My Heart's in Texas," but I secured my version from a fiddler
at a cowboy dance on Red Mud Creek.

In the Lone Star State of Texas
   By the silvery Rio Grande,
A couple strolled one evening,
   Lingering hand in hand.

'Twas a ranchman's pretty daughter
   And the lad she loved so dear;
On the morrow they must part
   For many and many a year.

To Europe she was going
   To become a lady grand,
And she went away next morning
   From the silvery Rio Grande.

Her father hoped some earl
   Or else a count she'd wed,
But her heart was true to Jack.
   One day a letter came and thus it
      read:

Chorus: Tonight my heart's in Texas
             Though I'm far across the sea,
          For the band is playing Dixie
             And in Dixie I long to be.

          Dad says some earl I'll marry,
             But you have my heart and hand.
          Tonight my heart's in Texas
             By the silvery Rio Grande.

At a stately hall in England
Stood a Texas lass one night.
The scene was one of splendor
And the lamps were dazzling bright.

An earl knelt there before her,
Begging her to take his hand;
But her thoughts were far away
By the silvery Rio Grande.

"I can't say, 'Yes,'" she answered.
"Your title I cannot take.
There's a lad away in Texas—
They call him Texas Jack.

"Long ago I promised
That Texas lad to wed.
'Twas only yesterday I wrote,
And this the letter said:

Chorus

Old Tom Harkey, "a stove-up cowpuncher," used to play the fiddle and sing in the wagon yard at Spur. One evening I heard him sing this snatch[5] of song:

My lover is a cowboy;
He's honest, kind, and true.
He rides a Spanish pony,
And he totes tobacco to-o.

And when he comes to see me,
He rides a many a mile
Over the lonely prairie
To greet me with a smile.

I do not know when or where I learned the remaining songs. I've heard them all my life. The first is a kind of chant well punctuated with yells. To understand it you will have to understand the cowboy's innocent way of dramatizing himself. It is not at all expressive of the bad man. Probably it originated as a satire on the would-be bad man.

O I'm wild and wooly
And full of fleas.
Ain't never been curried
Below the knees.

I'm a wild she wolf
From Bitter Creek,
And it's my night
to ho-o-o-wl.

The next song[6] sounds like a garbled version of "Sing Polly Wolly Doodle All Day."

Oh, I came to the river
And I couldn't get across;
I paid five dollars
For an old grey horse.

I put him in the river
And he couldn't swim;

So I gave him hell
With a hick'ry limb.

I spurred him in the shoulder,
I spurred him in the flank,
And you oughter seen the sucker fish,
A-swimming for the bank.

[5]See Lomax, "The Jolly Cowboy," p. 284; Thorp, 86. Charles A. Siringo, *Riata and Spurs* (Boston, 1927), pp. 242-43, has a very interesting comment on the song.

[6]Compare with "The Old Gray Horse," Perrow, "Songs and Rhymes from the South," JAFL, XXVI, 124.

The next two stanzas might be a part of the three preceding, for all the sense they make, but I've always heard them separately.

O I just kept a-running
    Till I got tired,
And then I went
    To the wagon yard.

I stuck my head
    In a woodpecker hole,
And I couldn't get it out
    To save my soul.

The last snatch is on the theme that all cowboys — all "boys," let us say — like to dwell on: the theme of love and a girl.

I got a little girl,
A purty little girl.
She won't go back on me.

She can dance and sing
And cut the pigeon wing,
But she won't go back on me.

THE WANDERING COWBOY

One spring a few years ago, while we were working cattle on our ranch, I made up a song that I called "The Wandering Cowboy" and imparted it to the cow crowd. Six months later in a camp on the S M S Ranch, I heard a cowboy named Floyd Cain singing it; I am told that it is still sung in the S M S country.

I am a wandering cowboy,
    From ranch to ranch I roam;
At every ranch when welcome,
    I make myself at home.

Two years I worked for the Double L,
    And one for the O Bar O;
Then drifted west from Texas,
    To the plains of Mexico.

There I met up with a rancher
    Who was looking for a hand;
So when springtime greened the valleys,
    I was burning the Bar S brand.

I worked on through the summer;
    Then early in the fall,
Over the distant ranges,
    There came the old, old call.

So I drifted to Arizona,
    To work for Uncle Bob,

A-tailing up the weak ones
    On a winter feeding job.

But the ranch camp grew too lonely,
    With never rest or change;
So I saddled up one morning,
    And struck for a distant range.

One night in wild Wyoming,
    When the stars hung bright and low,
I lay in my tarp a dreaming
    Of the far off home ranch-o.

Where the cottonwood leaves
    are whispering,
In the evening soft and low;
'Tis there my heart's a-turning,
    And homeward I must go.

It is now I'm tired of rambling.
    No longer will I roam
When my pony I've unsaddled
    In the old corral at home.

Some Texas Folk Songs

WILLIAM A. OWENS

HOW COME THAT BLOOD ON YOUR SHIRT SLEEVE

This ballad came to me first as a fragment from Mrs. T. H. Burke of Silsbee. Mr. and Mrs. Irvin Thompson had arranged for me to record at their home. When I had the recording machine set up they sent for Mrs. Burke, only to be told that she had gone to the woods to pray, as she did every morning. After a while she came to the house and, though it was against her religion, sang a dozen or so songs, among them "The Boston Burglar" and "Little Mohea." She finally told me that she knew one more song, but that it was too old for me to want. She sang enough of it, however, for me to recognize it as "Edward."

It was several years before I located a complete version of the song. This time the singer was Mrs. Ben Dryden of the Sandy Creek settlement. Since then I have found several more versions, but none as full as Mrs. Dryden's. I heard all of these in Southeast Texas and was unable to find the song elsewhere in the state. Collectors from other parts of the United States have reported it only a few times.

The version printed by Percy is a story of patricide, with a suggestion of incest as the motive. In the versions I have found the crime is invariably fratricide, and there is no hint of incest. The murder always grows out of an argument over cutting down a juniper tree.

How come that blood on your shirt sleeve,
My son, come tell to me?
How come that blood on your shirt sleeve,
My son, come tell to me?

That blood's too red for that,
My son, come tell to me,
How come that blood on your shirt sleeve,
My son, come tell to me?

It is the blood of the old grey mare
That pulled the plow for me;
It is the blood of the old grey mare
That pulled the plow for me.

It is the blood of the old grey goose
That flew by the side of me;
It is the blood of the old grey goose
That flew by the side of me.

137

That blood's too red for that,
My son, come tell to me,
How come that blood on your shirt
    sleeve,
My son, come tell to me?

It is the blood of my own dear brother
That plowed by the side of me;
It is the blood of my own dear brother
That plowed by the side of me.

What did you and your brother fall
    out about,
My son, come tell to me?
We fell out about that little juniper
    tree
That grows under yander tree.

What you gonna do when your father
    comes home,
My son, come tell to me?

I'll set my foot in a sailing boat
And I'll sail across the sea.

What you gonna do with your
    pretty little wife,
My son, come tell to me?
I'll set her foot by the side of my side,
To sail across the sea.

What you gonna do with your pretty
    little children,
My son, come tell to me?
I'll leave them here in youry care
Till I return to thee.

When you coming back
My son, come tell to me?
I'm coming back when the sun goes
    east and west
And that shall never be.

SAM BASS

The ballad of "Sam Bass," though sometimes sung by members of my family when I was a child, was never as popular as "Jesse James." The subject of the latter seemed much nearer to us, and a more colorful and admirable person. The ballad about Jesse James was also more singable.

The facts out of which the Sam Bass legend grew have been set down briefly by Walter Prescott Webb in *Legends of Texas* ["The Legend of Sam Bass," to be found in this book on pp. 112-16]. Sam Bass was born in Indiana on July 21, 1851. At seventeen he began the roaming that led to the adventures told in the ballad. In Denton County, Texas, he raced horses and participated in some train robberies, becoming the leader of a robber band. In the summer of 1878 he left Denton County with Jim Murphy, Seaborn Barnes, and Frank Jackson, planning to rob the Round Rock bank. But Murphy had arranged to betray Bass, and passed the word to Major John B. Jones, adjutant-general of Texas. When Bass and his men reached Round Rock, the town was full of Texas Rangers. On Friday, July 19, Bass, Jackson, and Barnes went into town to see the lay of the land. In a store they were approached by officers and a battle took place. Barnes and an officer were killed; Bass escaped, but he was mortally wounded. He was found in the woods the next day and died the day after—Sunday, July 21, 1878—on his twenty-seventh birthday. Jackson escaped and was never heard from again.

In his book on Sam Bass Wayne Gard prints a version of the ballad similar to the one given here. He says the ballad has been attributed to a John Denton of Gainesville, Texas, but he is of the opinion that it is the work of more than one person.

Sam Bass was born in Indiana, it was his native home;
And at the age of seventeen young Sam began to roam;
He first came out to Texas, a cowboy to be,
A kinder-hearted fellow you'll seldom ever see.

Young Sam he dealt in race stock, one called the Denton mare;
He matched her at scrub races and carried her to the fair;
Sam always coined the money and spent it very free,
He always drank good whiskey, wherever he might be.

Sam left the Collins ranch in the merry month of May
With a herd of Texas cattle the Black Hills for to see;
Sold out in Custer City and all went on a spree,
A harder set of cowboys you'll seldom ever see.

On their way back to Texas they robbed the U. P. train,
They busted up in couples and started out again;
Joe Collins and his partner was overtaken soon;
With all their hard-earned money they had to meet their doom.

Sam Bass come back to Texas, all right side up with care,
Rode in the town of Denton with all his friends to share;
Sam's life was short in Texas, three robberies did he do;
He robbed from all the passengers and mail and express too.

Sam Bass had four partners, all bold and daring lads;
There was Richardson and Jackson, Joe Collins and Old Dad,
As bold and daring cowboys as Texas ever knew;
They whipped the Texas Rangers and run the boys in blue.

Sam had another partner, called Arkansaw for short;
He was shot by a Texas Ranger by the name of Thomas Floyd;
Floyd is a big six-footer, and thinks he's mighty fly;
But some can tell you his racket, he's a dead-beat on the sly.

Jim Murphy was arrested and then let out on bail;
He jumped his bond at Tyler and took the train for Terrell;
Old Major Jones was in with Jim and it was all a stall;
It was a job to catch poor Sam before the coming fall.

Sam met his fate at Round Rock, July the twenty-first;
They dropped him down with bullets, then emptied out his purse;
Poor Sam he is dead now, and six feet under clay,
And Jackson's in the bushes, trying to get away.

Jim Murphy borrowed Sam's money and did not want to pay;
He thought the only way to win was to give poor Sam away;
He sold out Sam Bass and Barnes and left their friends to mourn.
Oh, what a scorching he will get when Gabriel blows his horn!

GREEN CORN

In my community guitar pickers first learned chords and a few simple melodies. Those who progressed beyond that usually tried to learn "Green Corn" and "The Spanish Fandango." About the highest praise for a guitar-player was, "He can play 'Green Corn' good." J. D. Dillingham of Austin, who recorded the version printed here, insists that the only instrument suitable for "Green Corn" is the five-stringed banjo. When he heard I meant to include the tune, he wrote, "The music is well adapted to and for the banjo and is not worth a cent on any other instrument, but there isn't any other tune that can take its place on the banjo."

Oh, the ape chased the monkey,
And the monkey chased the devil;
He run him up the hill-side
And caught him on the level.

Chorus:
Oh, bring along oh bring along
Oh bring along your green corn;
Oh, my little yaller gal,
Don't forget the demijohn.

The world was made in six days
And rested on the seventh,
But according to the contract
It ought a been the eleventh.

Chorus:
Oh, bring along oh bring along
Oh bring along the hot corn;
Oh, my little yaller gal,
Don't forget the demijohn.

Oh, my little yaller gal,
I'll meet you in the morning —
Two forty on the shell road,
The omnibus a-coming.
Chorus

Oh, stand still, stand still,
There's no time for running;
If you'll look up on the hill-side
You'll see old massa coming.
Chorus

One hand full of switches,
Going to lead you on the level,
And I'll tell you, boys, if you don't
   mind
You're going to catch the devil.
Chorus

Oh, the best meat I ever eat
I bought it on the market street —
Oh, my little yaller gal,
Throw me down a chunk of meat.
Chorus

Here's the cat that chased the rat
From the table to the stack,
A sack of meal upon his back,
A yaller gal on top of that.

Chorus:

Hot corn, green corn,
Bring along your hot corn;
Oh, my little yaller gal,
Don't forget the demijohn.

THE SHERMAN CYCLONE

This account of the Sherman cyclone of May 15, 1896, was popular in Lamar County during my childhood. But recently when I tried to get the words, no one could remember more than the first stanza. Fortunately I was able to set Mrs. Nelle McCune Dowd of Denison on the trail of the song. The following is quoted from her article in the Denison *Herald*, July 25, 1948:

Many persons in Denison remembered hearing the words of the ballad . . . but none could furnish all the lines. . . . Someone remembered that a Mrs. Mattie East of Bells was the author. . . .

On a trip to Bells a *Herald* reporter was referred to Mrs. D. B. Proctor, a lifelong resident, who remembers many of the pioneers of the Grayson County community and who furnished the story of Mrs. East, whom she remembered as a minstrel. . . .

Mattie Carter East, the daughter of Parson and Mrs. East, was blinded in one eye as the result of whooping cough in infancy and lost the sight of the other eye as the result of a fall in childhood. With the blind's talent for music, she was a popular singer, in demand at all the picnics and all-day religious meetings, so much a part of the social life of the pioneers. As a young woman she developed the talent of putting to words the catastrophic events of the day and she would sing them to the tunes of well-known hymns or folk songs of the period. Printed copies of the favorites would be passed out around the crowd for ten cents apiece.

Mrs. Proctor recalls that Mrs. East would sit on a revolving swing pulled around and around by a team of horses, with a portable organ on her lap, singing her ballads while the older folks listened and the children played. The horses would tire and be replaced by a fresh team but Mrs. East's voice and energy seemed inexhaustible.

After her marriage, Mrs. East and her husband, who was also blind, and their son traveled through Oklahoma, Arkansas and Texas giving programs in churches and school houses to make their living. A covered wagon furnished living quarters and adventuresome young men from the surrounding country would volunteer as drivers for the sightless couple.

Kind friends, if you will listen,
A story I will tell;
'Tis of a great tornado
You all remember well;
It reached the town of Sherman
The fifteenth day of May,
And a portion of our city
Was completely swept away.

The people gay and happy
In their cozy little rooms,
They little thought so shortly
They'd be forced to meet their doom.
But, alas, their days were ended,
Their lives were snatched away —
Now beneath the sod they're sleeping
Till the final judgment day.

We saw the storm approaching,
The clouds looked deathly black,
And through our little city
It made its dreadful track.
We saw the lightning streaming,
We heard the thunder roll,
It was but the shortest moment
And the story soon was told.

We heard the crash of timbers,
Of buildings tumbling down,
Distressing screams of victims —
Oh, what a dreadful sound.
It would melt the hardest hearted
To hear them loudly cry,
"Oh, God, have mercy on me,
Is this my time to die?"

Some sought for homes of refuge,
Their lives to rescue there;
While others were dashed to cinders,
And whirled into despair.
The rain it fell in torrents,
The storm was quickly o'er,
The like of dead and wounded
Was never here before.

The loss of life and ruins
Are hard to estimate,
The happiest of families
There had to separate.
God help the broken-hearted,
That yet are left behind,
To make their preparation,
For soon may be their time.

Soon the storm was over,
The people gathered round;
And there the dead and dying
Lay prostrate on the ground.
To render their assistance
So quickly they begin
To remove them from their struggle,
Soon all were taken in.

By aid of kind physicians,
We dressed their ghastly wounds.
Our town has never witnessed
Such a horrid afternoon.
The good people of our city,
You may safely be assured
Will nurse the sad afflicted
Till health may be restored.

CORRIDOS

▼▼▼

Versos de los Bandidos

J. FRANK DOBIE

The ballad called *Versos de los Bandidos* deals with the raid by Mexican *bandidos* (bandits) into the lower Rio Grande country in August, 1916. For going on a hundred years now these raids of varying proportions and at irregular intervals have been made into the Nueces River and Rio Grande territory;[1] the raid of 1916 was the last of any size, however, and now that the once open lands on the Texas side of the Rio Bravo are being settled with cabbage growers and lettuce producers, it is not likely that there will ever be such another raid. *Versos* of local composition no doubt celebrated those "border forays" of the past, but, so far as I know, the ballad I am about to record is the first of its kind that has passed from lips to paper. Therefore, though it lacks the immortal vividness and spirit of those ballads that sing of raids by mosstroopers and the doughty Douglas on the Scotch border centuries ago, this ballad seems to me, on account of its historical and social background, to have an unusual interest.

Sometimes the Mexicans refer to it as *Versos del Rancho de Las Norias,* and to understand it, it is necessary to know something of the geography of the immense King Ranch, nearly a million acres in extent. The King Ranch is divided into three

---

[1]One of the most memorable of these raids was that of 1875. For accounts of it see "The Mexican Raid of 1875 on Corpus Christi," by Leopold Morris, in the *Quarterly* of the Texas State Historical Association, Vol. IV, No. 2, July, 1900, pp. 128 ff. Another account of the same raid was printed in the April, 1925, number of *Frontier Times,* Bandera, Texas, Vol. II, No. 7, pp. 44-47.

parts: the Santa Gertrudis (Saint Gertrude), Los Laureles (The Laurels, so called from the laurel leaf brand once famed as that of Captain Kennedy, partner to Captain King), and Las Norias (The Wells), the last named lying nearest the Rio Grande. In turn, Las Norias has three divisions: El Nopal (The Prickly Pear), El Sauce (The Willow), and the San José (Saint Joseph).

When early in August, 1916, the Mexican bandits crossed the Rio Grande, they were joined by a number of other bandits who had for several weeks been quietly camping and exploring on the Texas side. The objective of the band seems to have been Kingsville, which is on the King Ranch. The raid was expected, and on August 8 a few Texas Rangers arrived at Las Norias Ranch. About 3 P.M., August 9, while most of the rangers were out on scout, seventy of the *bandidos* attacked Las Norias headquarters; at dark they retreated. Early next morning seven rangers and eight King Ranch men, some of them "special rangers," started in pursuit. At a watering sixteen miles from Las Norias, they found where the Mexicans had made night camp. The Texans followed the trail all day. On the morning of the eleventh they met Manuel Lopez, a King Ranch Mexican who, after having been held captive by the bandits for several days, had been released only a few hours before. He reported that the bandits were killing their own men who were wounded in the Las Norias fight. This report accounted for various dead Mexicans that the trailers had found along the route.

About three o'clock in the afternoon of August 11, the Texans surrounded the *bandidos* in a *mogote* (thicket) only one mile from the Rio Grande. The Mexicans would have been across and in safety, but they had been intercepted by A. Y. Baker (a famous ranger and sheriff of the border country) and his party and turned up the river. It is generally said that not a single Mexican lived to ford the river. The pursuit covered a distance of ninety miles from Las Norias. During the whole raid the bandits shot only "one soldier and one white man, and never killed either."

Domingo, ocho de agosto
—¡Qué presente tengo yo!—
Que en el Rancho de Las Norias
Un combate se efectó.[2]

It was Sunday, the eighth of August — what a remembrance I have of that date! — that a battle took place on the Norias Ranch.

El tren, ese que viene de Brunsvile,
Viene dando de pitadas,[3]
En que llegaron los rinches
A buscar a los bandidos.

The train, the one coming from Brownsville, came whistling, and on it were rangers to hunt the bandits.

Por las tres de la tarde
Estaban todos bien montados.[4]
Les decía Tomás Mosley[5] —
"Estamos muy bien preparados."

By three o'clock in the afternoon, the rangers were well mounted. Tom Mosley said to them, "We are well prepared."

Él que compuso esos versos
No sabía lo que decía.
Esos versos van compuestos
Por los rinches y bandidos.[6]

The man that made those verses did not know what he was saying. Those verses have been composed by the rangers and the bandits.

Bandidos de Tamaulipas[7]
Que se mantienen con leña
—¡A qué susto les han dao[8]
Los rinches de la Kineña![9]

They were nothing but bandits from Tamaulipas who made a living by carrying wood. What a scare the King Ranch rangers gave them!

Dicen que Aniceto Pizaña[10]
Es un hombre muy valiente,
Pero no ha llegao a Las Norias
A calarse con su gente.

They say that Aniceto Pizaña is a very valiant man, but he has not arrived at the Norias to make himself familiar with his own people.

[2]*Efectó*, a corruption of *efectuó*.

[3]At Las Norias the train stopped only on signal or to discharge passengers. The signal indicating the intention of stopping was always remarkable to the few men who heard it.

[4]The rangers brought their saddles, of course, and they got horses from Las Norias.

[5]Tom Mosley was at one time cattle inspector for the Texas Cattle Raisers' Association. At this time he was special ranger on the King Ranch; later he became sheriff of Kleberg County.

[6]This stanza is entirely conventional.

[7]As a matter of fact, it was claimed that a number of the *bandidos* were from Mazatlán in the State of Sinaloa. According to popular belief, a German emissary had fitted them out for the raid, promising to give each man $100 upon return from Texas and assuring them that while north of the Rio Grande they should have *uñas libres* (free fingers). In the song, however, the *bandidos* are contemptuously referred to as wretched *leñeros* of Tamaulipas, who eke out their existence by carrying in bundles of wood on their donkeys.

[8]*Dao* is a common form of apocopation for *dado*.

[9]The King Ranch had several men deputized as "special rangers." *Kineña* may mean either the King country or anyone who lives on the King Ranch.

[10]This Aniceto Pizaña was a rather noted leader of the bandits. The point of the mockery lies in the fact that he was born and reared on the King Ranch.

Andará por San Benito,
Harlingen o Raymondvile,[11]
Pero a Las Norias no ha llegao
Porque él teme morir.

Perhaps he may go by San Benito,
Harlingen, or Raymondville. He has
not come near the Norias because he
is afraid to die.

Domingo ocho de agosto
—¡Qué fecha tan cabal!
Llegaron a Las Tenerias[12]
Con el fin de remudar.

On Sunday, the eighth of August —
what a significant date! — the bandits
arrived at Las Tenerias, where they
expected to catch fresh horses.

Salieron de las Tenerias
Muy alegres todititos.
—¡Qué susto dieron a Osavio[13]
Para quitarle la silla!

They left Las Tenerias very happy,
all of them. What a scare they gave
to Osavio when they took his saddle
away from him!

Pasaron por Las Canteras[14]
Bien armados todititos;
Iban a domir
Al punto de Los Cerritos.

They passed by Las Canteras, all of
them well armed. Their plan was to
sleep at Los Cerritos.

Salieron de Los Cerritos
Con el fin de caminar
Al punto de Las Norias
Que se iban a robar.

They left Los Cerritos with the
purpose of traveling to Las Norias,
which they were going to rob.

Vuela, vuela, palomita,[15]
Anda para el cuartel,[16]
Anda, dice a Maestro Cesar[17]
Que volearon el hotel.[18]

Fly away, fly away, little dove; go
to the barracks at Kingsville and tell
Mr. Caesar that they are firing on the
ranch house.

[11]San Benito, Harlingen, and Raymondville are all towns in the lower Rio
Grande Valley.

[12]Las Tenerias is the name of a big watering place in one of the pastures
of the King Ranch. The bandits knew their country well, for the pasture watered
by Las Tenerias was used largely for grazing horses.

[13]Osavio, a King Ranch Mexican, happened to be at Las Tenerias when the
bandits rode up. They took his saddle away from him but allowed him to go
unharmed. He went on in to a ranch afoot, arriving "as white as a ghost."

[14]Las Canteras is the name of another watering, a sulphur well. The bandits
were traveling "up the country" in a northwest direction. Los Cerritos is the
last watering place between the Sauce Ranch and Las Norias. Here the bandits
would camp and spend the night. Cerro, the diminutive of which is cerrito, in
the Southwest usually means rock hill, but there are no rocks within miles of
these Cerritos.

[15]The injunction to the little dove to fly somewhere and tell somebody something is one of the commonest of all conventions in Mexican folk songs.

[16]The cuartel refers to the temporary barracks at Kingsville, where some
United States troops were then quartered.

[17]Maestro Cesar is Mr. Caesar Kleberg, general manager of the King Ranch,
who lived at Kingsville.

[18]Mexicans commonly refer to the two-storied house that serves as headquarters for Las Norias as el hotel.

The song as here concluded does not complete the story of the siege, retreat, and annihilation of the raiders, but I am assured by my brother that this is the entire song, as it was sung by the *Kineñas*.

El Toro Moro

FRANK GOODWYN

The *corridos* that have been composed by the King Ranch hands about their experiences and sung are many, many, and some of them are almost interminable. The great thickets of brush on the ranch have harbored many *ladinos* (outlaw cattle), and no horseback work in the world is more exciting, strenuous, daring, and dangerous than the pursuit of these cattle. *El Toro Moro*—the account of how a notorious *moro* (blue, or purple) bull defied the vaqueros and was finally roped, necked to a lead-ox, and shipped away—may be regarded as representative of these corridos and also of the work of the vaqueros that inspires such song. Euvence García, *caporal* of the Norias "cow crowd," which caught the Toro Moro, is credited with having roped and handled more wild cattle than any other man in Texas, and he deserves the credit. Las Norias is the southernmost and largest division of the King Ranch. While living there I learned "El Toro Moro."

Aquí me siento a cantar
Con la voluntad de Dios.
Estos versos son compuestos
Por la corrida del dos.

I'll sit down here and sing
by the will of God. These
verses are composed by cow-
camp Number Two.

Señores, voy a cantar
Con muchísimo decoro.
Estos versos son compuestos
Al mentado Toro Moro.

Sirs, I'm going to sing
with a lot of decorum.
These verses are composed
about the famous Purple Bull.

Es un torito moro,
Tiene el espinazo bayo.
No lo han podido lazar,
Y hechan la culpa al caballo.

He is a little purple bull.
He has a dun (tan) back.
They have not been able to rope him,
and they blame it on the horse.

Buenos pollos lo han corrido,
Queriendose aprovechar,
Pero en eso no han podido
Porque les entra al barral.

Expert birds have chased him,
attempting to win favor. But in
this they've not succeeded, for
they are led into the thicket.

De becerro lo conocen.
Desde que tenia tres años
Ahí anda en la Marcelina,
Completando los siete años.

Since he was a calf they have known
him. Since he was a three-year-old he
has been in the Marcelina pasture,
and now he's completing his 7th year.

Se lo halló Euvence García,
Se lo enseño a su compadre;
Se pusieron a pensar
Y se les hizo muy tarde.

Euvence García found him, and
showed him to his companion. They set
themselves to planning, and this
made them too late.

Y le decía su compadre
Con un cariño a lo bueno,
"Lo hecharemos por la brecha
Y por ahí esta Eugenio."

Euvence's companion said, with
a most true affection: "We will chase
him by the opening, and there Eugenio
is waiting."

Eugenio como un territo,
Ya estaba en su agostadero,
Y al oir el primer grito
Fué y se hizo al corredero.

Eugenio, like a little terror, was
there in his place. Upon hearing the
first yell, he broke and made for
the running place.

Cuando Eugenio lo vido
Al brincar la nopalera,
Desde ahí se lo fué entrando
Con su yegua tesonera.

When Eugenio saw the bull jumping the prickly pear, he went after
him on his tireless mare.

El toro se le fué
En el punto de Placetitas,
Fué y les dijo a los demás
Que le truenan las pesuñitas.

The bull got away from him at
the point known as Placetitas. He went
and told the other hands that its hoofs
were making the ground thunder.

Decía Manuel Rosas
En su caballo Cupido,
"Ojalá que se topara
Este torito conmigo."

Then Manuel Rosas, on his horse
Cupido, said: "Oh, that this little
bull would meet up with me!"

Otro día se lo topó
En ese Plan del Jardín.
El toro, al brincar la brecha,
Ahí le pintó un violín.

On another day Manuel did meet
him on the Plain of the Garden.
When the bull jumped past the opening, he gave him the slip.

Manuel Rosas lo corrió,
Diciendo, "Ora si lo laso."
Pero jamás le tocó
El polvo del espinazo.

Manuel Rosas chased him, saying,
"Now I'll rope him!" But the dust
on the bull's back wasn't even
brushed off.

Manuel Rosas lo corrió
Por todo el Plan del Jardín;
El caballo se voltió,
Y no lo pudo seguir.

Manuel se arrendó a la brecha
Y topo con su tocayo.
"Se me fué por hay ansina
Porque se voltió el caballo."

Decía Manuel la Changa,
Que era un hombre de valor,
"Héchenmelo por aquí
Para hacerles un favor."

Por toditia la brecha
Se veia una polvadera;
Era la Changa diciendo,
"Yo ya perdí esta carrera."

Más allá iba Chon Cortinas,
Corriendo y moviendo un brazo,
"Ese toro tiene espinas;
Por eso yo no lo laso."

Dijo Macario Mayorgua,
Viéndolo tan apurado,
"Voy a ver a mi compadre
Ya tendrá el rodeo dado."

Cuando Euvence lo vido
Ya venía muy ajilado,
Con sonrisas nos decía,
"El torito está amarrado."

Decía Eugenio Cantú
En la orilla de un mogote,
"Héchenmelo por aquí
Pa doblarle un calabrote."

Eugenio se lo lasó
Por no verlos batallar,
Fué y les dijo a los demás
Que lo fueran a llevar.

Decía Euvence García
En el tordillo grandote,

Manuel Rosas chased him all
along the Plain of the Garden.
His horse turned a somersault,
and he couldn't follow farther.

Manuel went back to the opening,
and there he met his namesake.[19]
"The bull got away from me over
yonder because my horse turned over."

Then said Manuel the Monkey,
who was a man of valor: "Just
chase him around this way that I
may do you a favor."

All along through the opening
was raised a cloud of dust. It was
the Monkey saying, "This is a race
I have lost."

Farther on Chon Cortinas entered
the chase, running and waving his arm.
"This bull has thorns; that's why
I don't rope him."

Then said Macario Mayorgua, seeing
him so played-out, "I'm going back
to my partner. By now he has a
round-up made."

When Euvence saw him (Macario)
coming to the round-up with such
speed, he said to us, smiling, "The
little bull is now roped and tied."

Then said Eugenio Cantú, who was
at the edge of a thicket, "Chase
him to me around this way that I
may dab a loop on him."

Eugenio roped him so as to prevent
the other hands from bothering
themselves. Then he went and told
them to go and bring the bull out.

Then Euvence García on his big
gray horse said: "Neck him to the

---

[19]His namesake was Manuel la Changa, Manuel the Monkey, so called on
account of his comic pranks.

"Mancuérnenmelo con los bueyes,　　oxen and take him to the Tecolote
Llévenlo pa'l Tecolote."　　　　　　Trap."20

Por todo lo de la brecha　　　　　　All along the opening the game
El fuego está cerrado.　　　　　　　is now closed. The men told the
Le dijeron al patrón　　　　　　　　boss [the *patrón* is over the
Que el toro estaba amarrado.　　　　*caporal*] that the bull was roped.

Lo llevamos para Norias;　　　　　　We took the bull to Norias;
Lo embarcamos pa' For Wes.　　　　we shipped him to Fort Worth. Now
Ya se fué el Torito Moro;　　　　　the Purple Bull is gone. He'll
Ya no volverá otra vez.　　　　　　never come back.

Y con esta me despido　　　　　　　And now I beg dismissal without
Y sin dilación ninguna.　　　　　　further delay. He who composes
El que compuso estos versos　　　　these verses is named
Se llama Miguel de la Luna.　　　　Miguel de la Luna.

Corrido de Kansas

BROWNIE McNEILL

On the King Ranch in South Texas lives a group of people of Mexican descent who work on the ranch tending the cattle and performing all the tasks incident to the cattle business. These Mexicans fill a variety of occupations; they are the lowly ranch hands, the fence menders, the fence riders and guards to keep out poachers, the cowboys, and even the foremen. They enjoy a certain amount of security in their jobs; many of them were born and reared on the same ranch, and in return for this security they possess an undying loyalty to their employers which is maintained within themselves by a rigid code. These people are happy in their work and for this reason, when they sing, they sing ballads about cowboys and rounding up cattle.

Much has been written and said about the Chisholm Trail and the great contribution made to American literature by the cowboy who drove cattle up that trail. Little mention, however, is given the Texas-Mexican *vaquero*, who definitely had

20Oxen, trained to lead and kept for such purposes, are used to bring in outlaw animals that have been roped and tied out in the brush. Tie a wild animal by the neck to one of these "neck oxen," and he will bring it in.

a place in that chapter of life in the Southwest. The *vaqueros* also had their *Little Joe the Wrangler* and their *Zebra Dun* and stampedes which scared them just as much as they did the Anglo-Americans.

The *Corrido de Kansas* is what José Gómez, former cowboy on the King Ranch, remembers of a long ballad describing the adventures of a group of Mexicans on a drive from South Texas to Kansas that probably took place in the 1880's.

Cuando salimos pa' Kansas	When we left for Kansas
Con una grande partida,	With a large party,
Nos decía el caporal:	The foreman said to us:
—No cuento ni con mi vida.—	"I don't even count on my life."
Quinientos novillos eran	There were five hundred steers
Pero todos muy livianos,	And they were all very wild,
No los podíamos reparar	We could not keep them herded
Siendo treinta mexicanos.	Being only thirty Mexicans.
Cuando llegamos a Kansas	When we arrived in Kansas
Un torito se peló,	A young steer took out (of the herd),
Fué a atajarle un mozo joven	A young boy went to cut him off
Y el cavallo se voltió.	And his horse fell down.
Cuando dimos visto a Kansas	When we came in sight of Kansas
Se vino un fuerte aguacero,	There came a heavy rain-shower,
No los podíamos reparar	We could not keep them herded
Ni formar un tiroteo.[21]	Nor get a shooting started.
Cuando dimos visto a Kansas	When we came in sight of Kansas
Era puritito correr,	It was nothing but running,
Eran los caminos largos,	The roads were long,
Y pensaba yo en volver.	And I thought about turning back.
La madre de un aventurero[22]	The mother of a driver
Le pregunta al caporal:	Asks the foreman:
—Oiga, déme razón de mi hijo,	"Listen, give me news of my son,
Que no lo he visto llegar.—	As I have not seen him arrive."

[21]Sudden showers and thunderstorms were a frequent cause of cattle stampedes. When they did stampede, the cowboys would ride to the front of the herd and try to turn the lead steer and thus start the cattle to circling. This was a difficult and dangerous job, but one means of accomplishing it was to shoot a gun near the lead steer; or if he failed to turn from the noise, the cowboy would actually shoot the lead steer and turn those behind.

[22]José Gómez could not remember all the verses and hence there is quite a skip in the story at this point; the group has delivered its cattle in Kansas and has returned home.

—Señora, le voy a decir
Pero no vaya a llorar,
A su hijo le mató un novillo
En la puerta de un corral.

"Lady, I will tell you
But don't go and cry,
A steer killed your son
On the gate of a corral.

Treinta pesos alcanzó
Pero todo limitado,
Y trescientos puse yo
Pa' haberlo sepultado.

Thirty *pesos* were left over
But it was all owed,
And I put in three hundred
To have him buried.

Todos los aventureros
Lo fueron a acompañar,
Con sus sombreros en las manos,
A verlo sepultar. —

All the drivers
Went to accompany him,
With their hats in their hands,
To see him buried."

▼▼▼▼▼▼▼▼▼▼▼▼▼▼▼

El Contrabando del Paso

BROWNIE McNEIL

Of the thousands of miles of border between the United States and its two neighbors, probably no spot gave as much trouble to the officials of the United States government during prohibition as El Paso, Texas. A permanent garrison of troops of the United States Army in El Paso, where a great many men had a great deal of leisure time, provided an irresistible market to the *mexicanos* on the other side who were daring enough to risk a possible hail of bullets to supply that market with liquor. Every conceivable method of slipping a little firewater across the border was employed by the boys who preferred *la bulegueda* to more stable and honest means of earning the *frijol,* some bringing it across the bridge concealed in automobiles, some floating it across at a lonely spot along the river on a dark night, and some trying the *charco seco.*

Some years ago the Rio Grande changed its course just below the city of El Paso and sliced off a part of Mexico, a strip of land approximately one-half mile long and a quarter of a mile wide, leaving it within the boundaries of the United States. The United States government, however, has never recognized the territory as a part of our country, and hence it has become a no-man's-land. The Border Patrol maintains a constant look-out from a series of towers along the bank of the old channel for anyone attempting to smuggle in contraband merchandise. Although El Pasoans refer to the place as Cordova's Island, it is known to the Spanish-speaking folk on both sides of the river as *el charco seco* (the dry marsh). The term marsh refers to the dense patches of reeds with intermittent canebrakes which separate the island from the United States border. It is said that the ghost of many a *contrabando* (smuggler) walks the dry marsh on nights when there is no moon, for the area was a favorite crossing spot for smugglers during prohibition days, and many a gun battle has taken place there between the smugglers and the United States officers. It is no wonder that the phrase *andar en el charco seco* (to walk the dry marsh) has become a grim synonym for smuggling.

The ballad of *El Contrabando del Paso* is the lament of a youthful smuggler who fell in with bad company and met the inevitable end of all smugglers—Leavenworth.

El diecisiete de Agosto	The seventeenth of August
Estábamos desperados,	We were in despair,
Y nos sacaron del Paso	And they took us from El Paso
Para Kansas mancornados.	Handcuffed on the way to Kansas.
Nos sacaron de la cárcel	They put us out of the jail
A las ocho de la noche,	At eight o'clock at night,
Nos llevaron por el dipo,	They took us through the depot,
Nos montaron en un coche.	They put us aboard a coach.
Yo dirijo mi mirada	I direct my glances
Por todita la estación,	All around the station,
A ver mi madre idolatrada	To look for my beloved mother
Que me dé su bendición.	So that she might give me her blessing.
Ni mi madre me esperaba,	Neither my mother was waiting for me
Ni mi señora, mi mujer,	Nor my lady, my wife,
Adiós, todos mis amigos,	Goodbye, all my friends,
¿Cuándo les volveré a ver?	When shall I see you again?
Allí viene silbando el tren,	There comes the train whistling,
Ya no tardará en llegar,	It won't be long in arriving,
Yo les digo a mis amigos	I tell all my friends
Que no vayan a llorar.	Not to cry.

Ya voy a tomar el tren,
Me encomiendo al Santo Fuerte,
Ya no vuelvo al contrabando
Porque tengo mala suerte.

El contrabando es muy bueno,
Se gana muy buen dinero
Pero lo que no me gusto
Es que me lleven prisionero.

Ya comienza a andar el tren
Ya repicar las campanas
Yo le digo a mister Gil
Que si vamos a Louisiana.

Mister Gil con su risita
Me contesta:—No, señor,
Pasaremos la Louisiana
Derechito a Livenvor.—

Corre, corre, maquinita,
Suéltale todo el vapor,
Anda a llevar este gaviota
Hasta el plan de Livenvor.

Les encargo a mis amigos
Que salgan a experimentar,
Que le entren al contrabando
A ver donde van a dar.

Les encargo a mis paisanos
Que brinquen el charco seco,
No se crean a los amigos,
Esos cabezas de puerco.

Que, por cumplir la palabra,
Amigos, es la verdad,
Cuando uno se halla en la corte
Se olvidan de la amistad.

Pero de eso no hay cuidado,
Ya, lo que pasó, voló,
Algun día se han de encontrar
Como me encontraba yo.

Vísperas de San Lorenzo
Eran las once del día
Que pisamos los umbrales
De la penitenciaría.

I'm going to take the train,
I commit myself to the strong saint,
I shall never go back to smuggling
Because I have bad luck.

Smuggling is very good,
One makes good money,
But what I don't like
Is that they take me prisoner.

Now the train begins to move
And the bells to ring,
I ask Mister Hill
If we are going to Louisiana.

Mister Hill with his little laugh
Answers me: "No, sir,
We'll pass through Louisiana
Right straight to Leavenworth."

Run, run, little machine,
Turn loose all the steam,
Hurry and take this sea gull
To the plain of Leavenworth.

I recommend to my friends
That they go give it a try,
That they get into smuggling
And see where they will land.

I recommend to my countrymen
Who may skip on the dry marsh,
Don't believe those friends,
Those pig heads.

Who, as for sticking by their word,
Friends, it's the truth,
When a person finds himself in court
They forget friendship.

But as for that there's no remedy,
Now, what's happened is past,
Some day they are bound to find
    themselves
In the same situation as I.

On the eve of St. Lawrence
It was eleven in the morning
When we stepped on the threshold
Of the penitentiary.

El que cuenta estos versos
Le ha pedido el perdón,
Si no estan incorregibles
Pues, estando tu opinión.

Allí te mando, mamacita,
Un suspiro y un abrazo,
Aquí dan fin las mañanitas
Del contrabando del Paso.

He who recites these verses
Has asked your pardon,
If they are not incorrigible
Well, that being your opinion.

I send you there, dear mother,
A sigh and an embrace,
Here the verses about the smuggler
 of El Paso
Have come to an end.

▼▼▼▼▼▼▼▼▼▼▼▼▼

Deportados

PAUL S. TAYLOR

This *corrido* tells the story of a Mexican who goes by train to Texas looking for work only to be turned back at the border. He parts from his tearful mother at the station. When he gets to Chihuahua he must pass through the confusion of Mexican customs inspection. At Juarez (or El Paso) the American immigration officials say he hasn't enough money to enter and make him take a bath. The *gringo* inspectors treat all of the Mexicans without "compassion," many of whom they round up like cattle and put back across the frontier. The would-be migrant cries out that his people are not bandits—they have come to *camellar*, to work hard with their backs humped over like a camel's. The deportees, he says, will be well received in their own beautiful land. A *corrido* like this one makes you see why thousands of Mexicans have preferred to swim the Rio Grande and enter the United States as *espaldas mojadas*— wetbacks.

Voy á contarles, señores,
voy á contarles, señores,
todo lo que yo sufrí,
cuando dejé yo á mi patria,
cuando dejé yo á mi patria,
por venir á ese país.

I am going to sing to you, señores,
I am going to tell you, señores,
all about my sufferings
when I left my native land,
when I left my native land,
in order to go to that country.

Serían las diez de la noche,
serían las diez de la noche
comenzó un tren á silbar;
oí que dijo mi madre:
—Hay viene ese tren ingrato
que á mi hijo se va á llevar.—

It must have been ten at night,
it must have been ten at night,
when a train began to whistle;
I heard my mother say,
"Here comes that hateful train
to take my son away."

Por fin sonó la campana,
por fin sonó la campana.
—Vámonos de la estación,
no quiero ver á mi madre
llorar por su hijo querido,
por su hijo del corazón.—

Finally they rang the bell,
finally they rang the bell.
"Let's go on out of the station;
I'd rather not see my mother
weeping for her dear son,
the darling of her heart."

Cuando á Chihuahua llegamos,
cuando á Chihuahua llegamos,
se notó gran confusión,
los empleados de la aduana,
los empleados de la aduana,
que pasaban revisión.

When we reached Chihuahua,
when we reached Chihuahua,
there was great confusion:
the customs house employees,
the customs house employees,
were having an inspection.

Llegamos por fin á Juárez,
llegamos por fin á Juárez
ahí fué mi apuración:
—¿Que dónde va, que dónde viene,
cuánto dinero tiene
para entrar á esta nación?—

We finally arrived at Juárez,
we finally arrived at Juárez,
where I had my inspection:
"Where are you going, where are you from,
how much money have you
in order to enter this country?"

—Señores, traigo dinero,
señores, traigo dinero
para poder emigrar. —
—Su dinero nada vale,
su dinero nada vale,
te tenemos que bañar.—

"Gentlemen, I have money,
gentlemen, I have money
enough to be able to emigrate."
"Your money is worthless,
your money is worthless;
we'll have to give you a bath."

Los güeros son muy maloras,
los gringos son muy maloras,
se valen de la ocasión,
y á todos los mexicanos,
y á todos los mexicanos,
nos tratan sin compasión.

The "blondes" are very unkind;
the gringos are very unkind.
They take advantage of the chance
to treat all the Mexicans,
to treat all the Mexicans,
without compassion.

Hoy traen la gran polvadera,
hoy traen la gran polvadera
y sin consideración,
mujeres, niños y ancianos,
los echan de esa nación.
los llevan á la frontera,

Today they are rounding them up,
today they are rounding them up;
and without consideration
women, children, and old folks
are taken to the frontier
and expelled from that country.

Adiós, paisanos queridos,	So farewell, dear countrymen,
adiós, paisanos queridos,	so farewell, dear countrymen;
ya nos van á deportar	they are going to deport us now,
pero no somos bandidos	but we are not bandits,
pero no somos bandidos	but we are not bandits,
venimos á camellar.	we came to *camellar.*

Los espero allá en mi tierra,	I'll wait for you there in my country,
los espero allá en mi tierra,	I'll wait for you there in my country
ya no hay más revolución;	now that there is no revolution;
vamonos cuates queridos	let us go, brothers dear,
seremos bien recibidos	we will be well received
en nuestra bella nación.	in our own beautiful land.

▼▼▼▼▼▼▼▼▼▼▼▼▼

Corrido de Texas

PAUL S. TAYLOR

This *corrido* is a song of the laborer under contract, leaving his woman behind in Texas as he goes to the industrial North to avoid picking cotton. It seems that in the first two stanzas the farewell speeches of husband and wife have been collapsed by the singer into a single speech attributed to the wife.

Mi chinita me decía:	My woman used to tell me,
—Ya me voy para la agencia	"I am going to the agency—
á pasearme por el norte	I'll roam around the north
y para hacerle su asistencia.	and take care of you.

De la parte donde estés	"Wherever you may be,
me escribes, no seas ingrato	write to me, don't be forgetful;
y en contestación te mando	and in reply I'll send you
de recuerdos mi retrato.—	my picture as a forget-me-not."

Adiós estado de Texas	Goodbye, state of Texas,
con toda tu plantación,	with all your growing crops;
me retiro de tus tierras	I am leaving your fields
por no pizcar algodón.	so I won't have to pick cotton.

| Esos trenes del Tipí | These trains of the T & P[23] |
| que cruzan por la Lusiana | that cross Louisiana |

[23]Texas and Pacific Railroad.

se llevan los mejicanos
para el estado de Indiana.

El día 22 de abril
á las dos de la mañana
salimos en un renganche
para el estado de Lusiana.

Adiós estado de Texas
con toda tu plantación,
me despido de tus tierras
por no pizcar algodón.

Adiós Fort Worth y Dallas,
poblaciones sin un lago,
nos veremos cuando vuelva
de por Indiana y Chicago.

El enganchista nos dice
que no llevemos mujer
para no pasar trabajos
y poder pronto volver.

carry the Mexicans
to the state of Indiana.

On the 22nd of April
at two o'clock in the morning
we left in a *renganche*[24]
for the state of Louisiana.

Goodbye, state of Texas,
with all your growing crops;
I bid farewell to your fields
so I won't have to pick cotton.

Goodbye, Fort Worth and Dallas,
cities without a lake;
we'll see each other when I return
from Indiana and Chicago.

The contractor tells us
not to take a woman along,
so as to avoid difficulties
and so as to return soon.[25]

[24]A gang of laborers shipped under contract by an employment agency.
[25]The third and fourth stanzas are repeated at the end.

NEGRO SONGS

▼▼▼

Follow the Drinking Gourd

H. B. PARKS

The following account is a compilation of three incidents and an attempt to explain them. A number of years ago while a resident of Alaska I became much interested in folklore and consequently anything of this nature came to attract my attention quickly. I was a resident of Hot Springs, North Carolina, during the year of 1912 and had charge of the agricultural work of a large industrial school. This school owned a considerable herd of cattle, which were kept in the meadows on the tops of the Big Rich Mountains on the boundary between North Carolina and Tennessee. One day while riding through the mountains looking after this stock, I heard the following stanza sung by a little Negro boy, who was picking up dry sticks of wood near a Negro cabin:

> Foller the drinkin' gou'd,
> Foller the drinkin' gou'd;
> No one know, the wise man say,
> "Foller the drinkin' gou'd."

It is very doubtful if this part of the song would have attracted anyone's attention had not the old grandfather, who had been sitting on a block of wood in front of the cabin, slowly got up and, taking his cane, given the boy a sound lick across the back with the admonition not to sing that song again. This excited my curiosity and I asked the old man why he did not want the boy to sing the song. The only answer I could get was that it was bad luck.

About a year later I was in the city of Louisville and, having considerable time to wait for a train, I went walking about the city. My journey brought me to the river front, and while standing there watching the wharf activities I was very much surprised to hear a Negro fisherman, who was seated on the edge of the wharf, singing the same stanza on the same tune. The fisherman sang the same stanza over and over again without any variation. While I am unable to write the music that goes with this stanza, I can say that it is a jerky chant with the accented syllables very much prolonged. When I asked the fisherman what he knew about the song, he replied that he knew nothing about it; he would not even converse with me. This seemed to be very peculiar, but because of the story of bad luck told by the grandfather in North Carolina I did not question the Negro further.

In 1918 I was standing on the platform of the depot at Waller, Texas, waiting for a train, when, much to my surprise, I heard the familiar tune being picked on a violin and banjo and two voices singing the following words:

> Foller the Risen Lawd,
> Foller the Risen Lawd;
> The bes' thing the Wise Man say,
> "Foller the Risen Lawd."

The singers proved to be two Negro boys about sixteen years of age. When they were asked as to where they learned the song, they gave the following explanation. They said that they were musicians traveling with a colored revivalist and that he had composed this song and that they played it and used it in their revival meetings. They also said the revivalist wrote new stanzas to fit the meetings.

These three incidents led me to inquire into the subject, and I was very fortunate in meeting an old Negro at College Station, Texas, who had known a great many slaves in his boyhood days. After I had gained his confidence, this man told the following story and gave the following verses of the song.

He said that just before the Civil War, somewhere in the South, he was not just sure where, there came a sailor who had lost one leg and had the missing member replaced by a peg-leg. He would appear very suddenly at some plantation and ask for work as a painter or carpenter. This he was able to get at almost every place. He made friends with the slaves and soon all of the young colored men were singing the song that is herein mentioned. The peg-leg sailor would stay for a week or two at a place and then disappear. The following spring nearly all the young men among the slaves disappeared and made their way to the North and finally to Canada by following a trail that had been made by the peg-leg sailor and was held in memory by the Negroes in this peculiar song.

When the sun come back,
When the firs' quail call,
Then the time is come
Foller the drinkin' gou'd.

Chorus:
Foller the drinkin' gou'd,
Foller the drinkin' gou'd;
For the ole man say,
"Foller the drinkin' gou'd."

The riva's bank am a very good road,
The dead trees show the way,

Lef' foot, peg foot goin' on,
Foller the drinkin' gou'd.
Chorus

The riva ends a-tween two hills,
Foller the drinkin' gou'd;
'Nuther riva on the other side
Follers the drinkin' gou'd.
Chorus

Wha the little riva
Meet the grea' big un,
The ole man waits—
Foller the drinkin' gou'd.

Now my birthplace is in the North and I also belong to a family that took considerable part in the underground railroad movement; so I wrote about this story to the older members of the family in the North. One of my great-uncles, who was connected with the railroad movement, remembered that in the records of the Anti-Slavery Society there was a story of a peg-legged sailor, known as Peg Leg Joe, who made a number of trips through the South and induced young Negroes to run away and escape through the North to Canada. The main scene of his activities was in the country immediately north of Mobile, and the trail described in the song followed northward to the head waters of the Tombigbee River, thence over the divide and down the Tennessee River to the Ohio. It seems that the peg-legged sailor would go through the country north of Mobile and teach this song to the young slaves and show them a mark of his natural left foot and the round spot made by the peg-leg. He would then go ahead of them northward and on every dead tree or other conspicuous object he would leave a print made with charcoal or mud of the outline of a human left foot and a round spot in place of the right foot. As nearly as could be found out the last trip was made in 1859. Nothing more could be found relative to this man.

The Negro at College Station said that the song had many verses which he could not remember. He quoted a number which, either by fault of memory or secret meaning, are unintelligible and are omitted. The ones given are in the phonetic form used by the College Station Negro and become rather simple when one is told that the "drinkin' gou'd" is the Great Dipper, that the "wise man" was the peg-leg sailor, and that the admonition is to go ever north, following the trail of the left foot and the peg-leg until "the grea' big un" (the Ohio) is reached, where the runaways would be met by the old sailor.

The revivalist realized the power of this sing-song and made it serve his purpose by changing a few words, and in so doing pointed his followers to a far different liberty than the one the peg-leg sailor advocated.

▼▼▼▼▼▼▼▼▼▼▼▼

Six Negro Songs from the Colorado Valley

GATES THOMAS

When I was a boy on my father's plantation near Winchester I used to hear the Negroes singing at whatever they did— chopping cotton, topping corn, or scooping dirt with a team of mules to build a tank. After going to college and becoming a teacher I became interested in the study of Negro songs as a phase of folklore. I wrote down all of the old songs that I could remember and added new ones as I learned them. In this way I have built up a sizable collection, from which the following six songs have been selected. They are, or once were, current in the neighborhood of Winchester, including an area about thirty miles across with its edges touching Bastrop, Smithville, Flatonia, La Grange, and Giddings. The Colorado River runs through the middle. The first of these songs I heard in 1886 and the last in 1906; the others fall in between these dates.

THE OLD HEN CACKLE

>The old hen she cackle, she cackle in the corn;
>The next time she cackle, she cackle in the barn.

>*Chorus:*
>Well, the old hen she cackle, she sholy gwain to lay.

>The old hen she cackle, she cackle in the loft;
>The next time she cackle, she cackle further off.

>*Chorus:*
>Well, the old hen she cackle, she sholy must-a laid.

>The old hen she cackle, she cackle in the lot;
>Well, the next time she cackle, she'll cackle in the pot.

>*Chorus:*
>The old hen she cackle, well, she sholy ought to lay.

ONE MORNIN'

>Got up one mornin', grabbed my gun,
>Shot at my babe and started to run;

>Started to run down the Katy track;
>Mr. Loessin[1] got his Gatlin' for to bring me back;

>Made a good run, but I runned too slow,
>He landed me over in the Jericho;

>He put me in the jail-house, I fell on my knees;
>The first thing I noticed wuz a big pan o' peas;

>Well, the peas wuz hard and the bacon wuz fat,
>But you ought'r seen the Niggers wuz grabbin' at that.

HUNTSVILLE-BOUN'

>Last Saturday mornin' about the dawnin' of day,
>The sheriff done come and arrested me, poor boy,
>And 'livered me to the county jail.

[1]Former sheriff of Fayette County; pronounced Lucine.

Them jurymen foun' me guilty, the jedge he did say,
"This man's convicted to Huntsville, poor boy,
For ten long years to stay."

Black mammy said, "It's a pity"; my luluh[2] said, "It's a shame;
They're takin' my man to Huntsville, poor boy,
For ten long years to stay."

Upon the deppo platform we all stood waitin' roun',
Waitin' for the train for Huntsville, poor boy,
Jest waitin' for the train to come down.

The train run into the deppo, the sheriff he did say,
"Get on this train for Huntsville, poor boy,
For ten long years to stay."

Now if you see my luluh, please tell her for me,
I've done quit drinkin' and gamblin', poor boy,
And gettin' on my sprees.

MY LULUH

You go ride the big bay horse,
I'll go ride the roan;
If you get there before I do,
Just let my luluh 'lone, Nigger man,
Just let my luluh 'lone.

White man goes to college,
Nigger to the field;
White man learns to read and write;
Poor Nigger learns to steal, Honey Babe,
Poor Nigger learns to steal.

Peaches in the summer time, apples in the fall;
Thought I heard my luluh say she wouldn't take none at all,
        Nigger man,
She wouldn't take none at all.

Beauty is only skin-deep, ugly to the bone;
Beauty quickly fades away, but ugly holds his own;
Honey Babe, ole ugly holds his own.

If you don't quit monkeyin' with my luluh, tell you what I'll do:
I'll feel aroun' your heart with my razor, and I'll cut you
        half in two,
Nigger man, I'll cut you half in two.

[2]Luluh, sometimes a proper name, in the songs is generally a synonym for
"honey," "woman," etc.

Train runned into Palestine sixteen coaches long;
Took all the money I had to put my luluh on,
Nigger man, to put my luluh on.

Engineer blowed the whistle, fireman rung the bell,
Conductor hollered "All aboard." Well, it wuz, "Luluh,
     fare you well, Honey Babe."
It wuz, "Luluh, fare you well."

Luluh went to Kansas, I tole her not to go;
Well, now the ole thing is in Kansas a-hustlin' in the cole
     ice and snow, Honey Babe,
A-hustlin' in the cole ice and snow.

EAT WHEN YO'RE HONGRY

Chorus:
Eat when yo're hongry, drink when yo're dry,
An' ef a tree don't fall on you, you'll live tel you die.

The horses wuz mounted, the races wuz run;
Them ladies from Baltimo' came for the fun.

Oh, ladies, young ladies, don't think it unkin'
Ef I set down aside you and tell you my min'.

My min' is to marry a woman I knows,
Who will patch on my jumpers and make all my clo'es;

Who will wash 'em and ine 'em, and scrub up the flo',
An' keep the house tidy an' sweep 'roun' the do';

Who will cook up my vittuls and bake up my do',
And make down my pallet to lie on the flo'.

We'll eat when we're hongry and drink when we're dry,
And ef a tree don' fall on us, we'll live tel we die.

THE BOLL WEEVIL

Have you heard the lates', the lates' all yo' own,
It's all about them weevils gonna make yo' fa'm their home.
Gonna make it their home, Babe, gonna make it their home.

The boll weevil says to the sharp-shooter,[3] "Pardner, let us go,
And when we strike that cotton patch, we'll take it row by row;
For it's our home, Babe, for it's our home."

[3]A small insect like a midge, found along with the weevil and once thought
to be harmful.

The first time I seen him he wuz settin' on a square;
Well, the next time I seen him he wuz a-crawlin' everywhere,
Just a-huntin' him a home, Babe, just a-huntin' him a home.

The boll weevil sez to the farmer, "I ain't bothered a bit;
So when you plant that cotton, be sure you plant it thick;
For it's my home, Babe, for it's my home."

The sharp-shooter sez to the boll weevil, "You ain't treatin' me fair;
For since I seen you last time, you've scattered everywhere.
Done found you a home, Babe, done found you a home."

The farmer sez to his ole wife, "We are in a terrible fix:
Foolin' with the weevils gonna keep us in the sticks,
Without a home, Babe, without a home."

The ole wife sez to her husban', "I done my level bes'
Workin' with them weevils, and I ain't got but one dress.
It's full of holes, Babe, it's full of holes."

The farmer sez to his ole wife, "Well, what do you think of that?
I found a little boll weevil right in my Sunday hat;
Done found him a home, Babe, done found him a home."

The farmer said to the merchant, "It is the general talk;
The boll weevil's et all the cotton, and left us leaves and stalk.
We've got no home, Babe, we've got no home."

The merchant sez to the farmer, "What do you think of that?
Ef you ketch all them boll weevils, make you present of a Stetson hat.
You'll have a home then, you'll have a home."

The boll weevil sez to the sharp-shooter, "Pardner, what of that?
They say ef the farmer ketches us, gwain to give him a Stetson hat.
He'll have a time, Babe, he'll have a time."

So they took the little boll weevil and they put him on the ice.
He sez to the farmers, "I say, but ain't this nice!
But it ain't my home, though; no, it ain't my home."

Then they took the little boll weevil and buried him in hot sand.
He sez to the farmers, "Well, and I'll stand it like a man,
Though it ain't my home, Babe; no, it ain't my home."

The farmer said to the merchant, "I didn't make but one bale,
But befo' I'd bring that bale in, I'd fight you and go to jail;
For I've got to have a home, Babe, I've got to have a home!"

The boll weevil sez to the farmer, "What make yo' neck so red?"
"Tryin' to beat you devils; it's a wonder I ain't dead;
For you're takin' my home, Babe, just a-takin' my home!"

"Well ef you want to kill us, I'll sho-God tell yo' how:
Just bundle up yo' cotton sack and th'ow away yo' plow;
Then hunt yo' a home, Babe, then hunt yo' a home."

Some Texas Spirituals

MARY VIRGINIA BALES

Spirituals are perhaps the best known type of Negro folk song. They have been comparatively well collected and are as well preserved as any ever-changing folk music. It is no marvel that their value has been recognized, for the greater part are haunting in their naïve pathos. They make one feel that here is real emotion, that here the Negro has reached the peak of his musical and poetical expression.

Probably another reason why spirituals are so well preserved is that most of the Negroes refuse to sing any other kind of song to the collector. Mr. John Lomax told me of an incident that happened to him while he was collecting songs in the Brazos bottoms. He asked a Negro to sing him "The Boll Weevil," and the Negro said, "I'se sorry, Boss, but you gonna hab to ask dat wor'ly nigger ober yondah to sing you dat." I also found that the religious song is the only kind volunteered; and many times, before I could persuade a Negro to sing a spiritual, I had to furnish my whole religious history as a proof of my sincerity.

Spirituals travel from one community to another, carried by the "leaders," and as there are no set forms for the songs, the different groups sing them in their own manner. In this way variants arise. Spirituals not only spread throughout communities, but they slowly travel to different states. Naturally, this traveling brings about changes so marked that some versions resemble each other only in a line or two or in the chorus; furthermore, it makes discovery of the place of origin virtually impossible. The songs of this collection are Texas songs in that they are all sung in various parts of the state.

ALL I WANT IS DAT TRUE RELIGION

The Negro has draped all his moods from the gayest to the most tragic with the veil of religion; and through this veil some of the songs show a dramatic story. Take for example

167

the following song, which was given me by a pupil of the Fort Worth colored high school. If it were not for the refrains, the song might well be called a simple narrative ballad.

Come on, Death, why is you so slow?
   Hallelujah, hallelujah!
Jesus is waitin', an' I'm ready to go.
All I want is dat true religion,
   Hallelujah, hallelujah!

De doctah come in an' wus lookin' sad,
   Hallelujah, hallelujah!
"Dis is de hardes' case I eber had."
All I want is dat true religion,
   Hallelujah, hallelujah!

De doctah turn an' went out de do',
   Hallelujah, hallelujah!
"Doan think I eber come here no mo'."
All I want is dat true religion,
   Hallelujah, hallelujah!

Mudder an' fadder stan' 'roun' a-cryin',
   Hallelujah, hallelujah!
"O, Lord, my po' chile a-dyin'!"
All I want is dat true religion,
   Hallelujah, hallelujah!

Come on, sistah, an' give me a han',
   Hallelujah, hallelujah!
I'm goin' to rock study to dat promise lan'.
All I want is dat true religion,
   Hallelujah, hallelujah!

When I get to heaben I got nothin' to do,
   Hallelujah, hallelujah!
But to sit right down an' sing hallelu'.
All I want is dat true religion,
   Hallelujah, hallelujah!

I WANNA BE IN DAT NUMBAH

This song is a favorite with the Negro Baptist church at Hearne, Texas. The pastor claims that the song has been sung in the Baptist congregation since slavery days. The song has such a sweep of rhythm to it that one can hardly keep from swaying to the music and joining in with the lusty-voiced singers. It is probably of group origin, since the verses are made up of repetitions of one line.

> When de saints ob Gob shall lib,
> When de saints ob Gob shall lib,
> When de saints ob Gob shall lib,
> Good Lord, I wanna be in dat numbah!
>
> When dey march a-roun' de throne,
> When dey march a-roun' de throne,
> When dey march a-roun' de throne,
> Good Lord, I wanna be in dat numbah!
>
> When de saints go marchin' in,
> When de saints go marchin' in,
> When de saints go marchin' in,
> Good Lord, I wanna be in dat numbah!

JOB'S GOIN' TO HEABEN

The songs that show more complicated verse structure and more variation of theme are built upon the "call and response" plan. The "leader" calls out the leading verse, and the group answers with a refrain. The "leader," who goes from one community to another, has to be a man of some talent for singing and verse making, as well as a man who can rise to the demands of a hundred different occasions. He must have some sense of appropriateness and considerable ingenuity to aid his good memory. There are still a few of these men in Texas, but they are the product of community churches, not of dignified churches in towns and cities. M. B. Butler, of Hearne, is one Negro I am thinking of. He is known as "Blind Butler" by a third of the Negroes of the state. He is a preacher but is more famous as a song leader.

From every source, we learn that this "call and response" custom came from Africa, and therefore is not original with the American Negro. "A study of the spirituals leads to the belief that the earlier ones were built upon the form so common to African songs, leading lines and response. It would be safe to say that the bulk of spirituals are cast in this simple form."[4]

[4] J. W. Johnson, The Book of American Negro Spirituals (New York, 1926), p. 25.

So states James Weldon Johnson, an authority upon the spirituals of his race. The following song illustrates this oldest type of spiritual.

Emma Johnson, a Negro woman of Beaumont, told me that she learned "Job's Goin' to Heaben" from her parents, who came to Texas from Louisiana. The song is generally known in Southeast Texas. Since it is a direct paraphrase of Job 1: 13-17, with the addition of the refrain and chorus, there is no set number of verses or, in reality, set word order. Emma herself sang it differently each time, just as the spirit moved her. She could not even begin the song until I had read the Bible story to her for a while.

An' dere wus a day,
(Job's goin' to heaben!)
His sons an' his daughtahs
(Job's goin' to heaben!)
War eatin' an' a-drinkin'
(Job's goin' to heaben!)
Dere come a messengah,
(Job's goin' to heaben!)
An' said unto Job:

Chorus:
Job's goin' to heaben,
O Job!
Job's goin' to heaben,
Job! Job!

De oxen war a-plowin'
(Job's goin' to heaben!)
An' de asses war a-feedin',
(Job's goin' to heaben!)
An' de Sa-ba-e-ans
(Job's goin' to heaben!)
Fell upon dem
(Job's goin' to heaben!)
An' took dem away! Yea!
Chorus

Dey have slew de sarvants
(Job's goin' to heaben!)
Wid de edge ob de sword,
(Job's goin' to heaben!)

An' I alone
(Job's goin' to heaben!)
Am escaped
(Job's goin' to heaben!)
To tell to dee!
Chorus

Den say his wife
(Job's goin' to heaben!)
Unto him,
(Job's goin' to heaben!)
"Dost thou still
(Job's goin' to heaben!)
Detain thine interrity?
(Job's goin' to heaben!)
Curse God an' die!"
Chorus

He say to her:
(Job's goin' to heaben!)
"Thou speakest as a foolish 'oman.
(Job's goin' to heaben!)
Blessed be de name
(Job's goin' to heaben!)
Ob de Lord!
(Job's goin' to heaben!)
De Lord giveth,
(Job's goin' to heaben!)
An' de Lord taketh away!"
Chorus

JESUS RIDES A MILK-WHITE HOSS[5]

Biblical stories appeal to the Negro, not only because of the reverent awe he has for them, but also because of their simplicity and vividness. They omit enough detail to give the mind play and furnish an excellent opportunity for the Negro to use his graphic power of description.

Compare Revelations 6:2, "And I saw, and behold a white horse; and he that sat on him had a bow; and a crown was given unto him; and he went forth conquering, and to conquer," with the following spiritual:

Jesus rides a milk-white hoss,	*Chorus:*
No man can hindah!	Ride along, Jesus,
He rides him up an' down de cross,	No man can hindah!
No man can hindah!	Ride along, Jesus,
	No man can hindah!

I'M NEW BAWN[6]

For another example of the Negro's vivid and original treatment of Biblical subjects, note the manner in which Christ's birthplace, the statement Christ made to Nicodemus, and the Christian experience are all brought together in a stirring spiritual which my washerwoman, Nancy Washington, of Fort Worth, sang to me.

> Way ober yondah in de harvest fields
> Angels workin' on de chariot wheels!

[5] A variant of the second stanza of "Ride on, King Jesus" (*The Jubilee Singers,* by G. D. Pike [Boston, 1873], p. 208), one of the songs sung by the Jubilee Singers of Fisk University on their tour for funds during the seventies; and of "No Man Can Hinder Me," Allen's *Slave Songs of the United States,* No. 14. The music of both is different from that of this song. The line "He rides him up and down de cross" illustrates the hazards of oral transmission. In the earlier record it is "The River Jordan he did cross."

[6] All the verses here given and one more are in W. H. Thomas's *Some Current Folk-Songs of the Negro,* published, without music, in 1912 by the Texas Folklore Society. The additional verse is as follows:

> I'm so glad, I don't know what about,
> O good Lord!
> Sprinkling and pouring's done played out.

Chorus:
Tell all de membahs I'm new bawn,
New bawn, new bawn, new bawn baby,
Bawn in de mangah!
Tell all de membahs I'm new bawn,

New bawn, new bawn, new bawn baby,
Bawn in de mangah!
Tell all de membahs I'm new bawn!

Read de Scriptures, I am told,
Read 'bout de garment Achan stole!
Chorus

I went to de valley on a cloudy day,
My soul got so happy dat I couldn't get away!
Chorus

Away ober yondah got nothin' to do
But walk 'bout heaben an' shout halloo!
Chorus

JES' SUIT ME[7]

The song "Jes' Suit Me" was sung by a Negro of Elgin, Texas, in the south-central part of the state. Miss Eula Lee Carter, of Fort Worth, who contributed the song, said it was sung by her old Negro mammy and that the darkey wore out many a washboard to its swinging melody. The song has many more verses than Miss Carter could recall.

Dere ain't but one road to heaben,
An' it's right straight dar,
An' it's right straight back,
An' it jes' suit me,
An' it jes' suit me,
An' it jes' suit me.

John writ a letter,
An' he writ it in a haste,
An' he tole God's chillern
Dat dey better make haste!

An' it jes' suit me,
An' it jes' suit me,
An' it jes' suit me.

Ezekiel spied a train a-comin',
He step on boa'd,
An' it neber stop runnin',
An' it jes' suit me,
An' it jes' suit me,
An' it jes' suit me.

[7]"It Just Suit Me," in *The Negro and His Songs*, by Odum and Johnson (Chapel Hill, N. C., 1925), p. 121, contains the second and third verses.

MY LAWD'S A BATTLE AX

"My Lawd's a Battle Ax" is one of the most interesting songs that I have. Eva Miles, a Negro woman of Hearne, Texas, sang it to me. She said that it was composed by a man of Hillsboro, Texas. However, the song has all the earmarks of a true old spiritual, and a verse form which I would scarcely attribute to an individual's composition. I found one reference to "The World's Battle Axe" in Mr. R. E. Kennedy's *Mellows*, which would indicate that the idea of the song was much older than the contributor claimed, and that the song itself might possibly have come from Louisiana.

When I wus boun' in trouble,
An' didn't know what to do,
I open my mouf unto de Lawd,
Now de saints I mus' go through.

Chorus:
Oh! my Lawd's a battle ax,
A battle ax, a battle ax!
Oh! my Lawd's a battle ax,
A shelter in de time ob storm!

My Lawd did stan' befo' me
An' sweetly crossed His hands;
He said, "If ye love me,
Ye will keep my Comman'."
Chorus

I wus meditatin' wif my Lawd,
An' lifted mine eyes to Dee;
I said, "Thank God, now I'm saved!
Three times de light shine on me!"
Chorus

AN OFFERTORY

The queerest song I have discovered is a one-line song used for taking up the collection in a Negro church at Lufkin, Texas. Mrs. Werna Hargis, of Austin, who gave me the song, said that the Negroes sang it over and over as a dull, droning chant with slight variations of the melody.

All cum up an' numbah yo'self 'fo' de Lawd,
All cum up an' numbah yo'self 'fo' de Lawd, etc.

O HAN' ME DOWN DE SILBER TRUMPET, GABRIEL

It was late in the evening when my friend and I reached the colored part of Hearne. We went to see a woman who lived at a restaurant and who was reputed to have an excellent voice.

After much coaxing she appeared at the door of the old building and invited us in. Inside the shabby room the most noticeable piece of furniture was an old piano with all the ivories off.
A party must have been in progress, for there were several
young boys and girls present. When the woman was asked to
sing some very old songs to us, she evinced embarrassment
and said she did not know any. We insisted that she must
know one, and she finally began to sing "That Ole Time
Religion." Of course that was not what we wanted. She was so
disappointed in our reception of her performance that she
refused to sing again. Meanwhile one of the boys began to
bang out jazz on the piano, and we were soon forgotten in a
mad frenzy of wild dances and songs. An elderly woman
noticed our panic and called the party's attention to us. In their
chagrin, the woman got them to sing for us one religious song
which is well known in Texas at least. It was "Han' Me Down
de Silber Trumpet." The voices rang out with clearness and
gusto.

> If religion wus a thing dat money could buy,
> (O han' me down de silber trumpet, Gabriel!)
> De rich would lib an' de po' would die.
> (O han' me down de silber trumpet, Gabriel!)
>
> *Chorus:*
> O han' me down, O han' me down,
> O han' me down de silber trumpet, Gabriel!
> O han' me down, O han' me down,
> O han' me down de silber trumpet, Gabriel!

SERMONS

Sin-Killer's Sermon

JOHN R. CRADDOCK

The Reverend Sin-Killer Griffin, employed by the State as Chaplain to the Negro convicts of the Texas Penitentiary System, looked his part. His grizzly grey hair and mutton chop whiskers, his Prince Albert coat which almost touched his shoe tops, his dignified and courtly bearing, his deep and sonorous voice were most impressive. His ministerial manner was further heightened by a very slow walk, slow speech, and a long, long pause between questions as if he were consulting higher powers.

"Reverend," I said, "I hope you will preach your favorite sermon to the boys tonight. The Captain has agreed for me to record it, and I plan to deposit the records in the Folk Song Archive of the Library of Congress. A thousand years from now people can listen to the words you will preach."

"I'll preach my Calvary sermon," he assented. "Today is my Easter service."

The two long wings of the dormitory of the Darrington Farm, near Houston, where the convicts slept, were separated by a wide hall. My son Alan and I set up the recording machine here, running the microphone cable through the bars of one wing where the Reverend Sin-Killer had his pulpit and altar. He stood where his powerful voice could reach the three hundred convicts lounging on their beds in their pajamas or peering curiously through the bars at the strange doings. Some of the more devout worshipers—deacons and preachers out in the free world—were seated in a circle near the Reverend. At a sign from him the penitentiary song-leader led them in a swinging spiritual:

> Lord, I want to love my enemies in my heart,
> Lord, I want to be more humble in my heart....

When the song was finished the leader invited the "sinner friends" to come forward to the front seats. No one moved.

"Those that mourn shall be comforted," he said. "Let us mourn, brethren."

Something swept through that crowd, something powerful and poignant. No words were uttered, only waves of sound, impelling and pregnant, moans of unutterable woe. Then came silence which grew deeper and deeper.

"Thousands and thousands and multiplied thousands are cast off from the golden opportunities because they don't believe," the leader said. "Let us sing."

They sang a song, an impressive song, entitled, "Wasn't That a Mighty Storm That Blew the People Away," after which the leader led them in this prayer:

> This evening, our Father,
> We begin before death in early judgment,
> This evening, our Father,
> I come in the humblest manner I ever know'd,
> Or ever thought it,
> To bow.
>
> I'm thankin' Thee, O Lord,
> That my laying down last night
> Wasn't my cooling board,
> And my cover was not my winding sheet.
>
> O Lord, thanking Thee, this evening, my Father,
> That my dressing room this morning was not my grave.
>
> O Lord, thanking Thee, this evening, my Father,
> That my slumber last night was not for eternity.
>
> O Lord,
> Just bless the widows and orphans in this land,
> I pray Thee in Jesus' name;
> Take care of them, my Father,
> And guide them;

And, then, my Father,
When they all is standing in glory,
And Thou art satisfied at my staying here,
O meet me at the river, I ask in Thy name.
Amen.

After an impressive silence the leader, in a more casual tone, said: "You knows whether you are to eat the body and drink the blood of Christ. If you eat and drink the Lord's food unworthy, you eat and drink to your damnation." He distributed white crumbs of bread such as the men had eaten for supper and grapefruit juice from the prison commissary for the "wine." When all who dared had participated, Sin-Killer Griffin stepped forward, dignified and solemn, and took charge of the services.

"My dear brothers and sisters [the Captain's wife was the only woman present], sinner friends all," he began, and then, in poetic diction, impressively and hypnotically said:

The ears hears the voice
An' notify the eye where to look.
One day as I was walking along
I heard a little whisper but I saw no one;
Something was bringing about a disturbment—
That was the wind,
The water was jumpin' in the vessel.

The force of his voice, the intensity of his appeal, almost instantly brought from the audience exclamations:

Sho' nuff!
Sho'!
Amen!
Oh, yes!

Catching the spirit of his appeal, Sin-Killer took them into a song:

Dem little slippers dat my Lord give me
Goin' to outshine de sun [Repeat twice];
Dat little harp-h dat my Lord give me [etc.],
Dat little robe dat my Lord give me [etc.] . . .

From the enthusiasm aroused by this song Sin-Killer quickly plunged into his description of the Crucifixion:

Lightnin' played its limber gauze
When they nailed Jesus to the rugged cross,
The mounting began to tremble
When the holy body began to drop blood down upon it,
Each little silver star leaped out of its little orbit;
The sun went down on Calvary's blooded brow,
Lightnin' was playin' on the horse's bridle reins
As it leaped on the battlements of Glory,
When the morning star was breaking its light
On the grave.

All at once Sin-Killer broke away from his poetic chanting, and with a voice that pointed like his outstretched finger, shouted:

"You keep foolin' with the Master and He will shake the earth again."

From this brutal warning he went from one dramatic situation in the Old Testament to another, skipped lightly to the New Testament, and back again: Moses and the burning bush, Jacob's sacrificing Isaac, the breaking of the seven seals and other scenes from Revelations—all these came forth in dramatic intensity. When Sin-Killer had to catch his breath, he started them to singing a song while he mopped his face and kept up the growing excitement of the congregation by a shouted word which fitted perfectly into the tempo of the song. Then he went back to his sermon:

Roman soldiers come riding in full speed on their horses,
And splunged Him in the side,
We seen the blood and water come out.
Oh, God A'mighty placed it in the minds of the people
Why water is for baptism.
And the blood is for cleansin'.
I don't care how mean you've been,
God A'mighty's blood'll cleanse you from all sin.

I seen, my dear friends, the time moved on,
Great God looked down,
He began to look at the temple.
Jesus said to tear down the temple,
And in three days I'll rise up again in all sight.
They didn't know what He was talkin' about—
Jesus was talkin' about His temple body.

I seen while He was hangin', the mounting begin to tremble
On which Jesus was hangin' on;
The blood was dropping on the mounting,
Holy blood, dropping on the mounting, my dear friend,
Corrupting the mounting;
I seen about that time while the blood was dropping down,
One drop after another,
I seen the sun that Jesus made in creation;
The sun rose, my dear friends,
And it recognized Jesus hanging on the cross.

Just as soon as the sun recognized its Maker,
Why it closed itself and went down,
Went down in mournin'.
"Look at my Maker hanging on the cross."
And when the sun went down, we seen the moon;
He made the moon,
My dear friends, yes, both time and seasons—
We seen, my dear friends, when the moon recognized Jesus dying on the cross,
I seen the moon, yes,
Took with a judgment hemorrhage and bleed away.
Good God looked down.
Oh, the dyin' thief on the cross
Seen the moon goin' down in blood.
I seen, my dear friends, about that time they looked at that,
And when the moon went down, it done bled away.
I seen the little stars, great God, that was there
On the anvil of time,
And the little stars began to show their beautiful ray of light,
And the stars recognized their Maker dyin' on the cross.
Each little star leaped out of their silver orbit,
The torches of a unbenointed world . . .

It got so dark
Until the men who was puttin' Jesus to death
They said they could feel the darkness in their fingers.
Great God A'mighty, they was close to one another,
An' it was so dark they could feel one another and hear one another and talk,
But they couldn't see each other.
I heard one of the centurions say:
"Sholy, sholy, this must be the son of God."

'Bout that time we seen, my dear friends, the prophet Isaiah,
Said the dead in the graves would hear his voice and come forward.
They saw the dead gettin' up out of their graves on the east side of Jerusalem;
Gettin' out of their graves
Walkin' about, goin' down in town.
Oh! . . . 'way over on Nebo's mounting [shouted]
I seen the great lawgiver go up out of his grave and begin to walk about,

My dear friends, walking, because Jesus said,
"It is finished."
We notice, my dear friends, here about that time—
I shouldn't wonder, my dear friends,
The church will save you when you get in trouble.
I heard the church so many times singing;
When you get overwhelmed in trouble, the church said,
How can I die while Jesus lives? [Chanted]
How can I die while Jesus lives? [Chanted by Sin-Killer and entire congregation]

I seen the horses come stepping
On Calvary's bloody brow,
Pawing, my dear friends,
Seein' the next train was thunder;
An' the lightnin' was playing on the bridle reins Death had in his hands.
He come riding, he come riding,
An' the dying thief looked death in the face,
Caught sight on the opposite side of the horse;
He saw a new name written there;
He read the name;
And the name read like this:
"Death and Hell followeth him."
I heard the dying thief say,
"Lord, oh, Lord! Lord, oh Lord!
When Thou come to Thy Father's kingdom
I pray remember me.
Oh, motherless child, hangin' on the cross!
An' I want you to remember me."
Jesus, my dear friends,
The dying thief had so much confidence in Him,
Had so much faith in Him,
Jesus hung just like He was.

Jesus, Jesus, daggered in the side,
Blood drippin', great God.
Jesus caught a-hold of the horse, my dear friends,
Caught it by the bridle,
And the old horse begin to paw.
Oh . . . Elijah didn't catch a-hold of him when he was comin'.
Oh . . . Job didn't catch a-hold of him when he was comin'.
Oh . . . Great God A'mighty! Moses, the great lawgiver, didn't catch a-hold
    of him.
But over yonder, the incarnated Son of God [shouted]
Caught the horse by the bridle, and held him still [shouted].

Jesus begin to speak,
Says to the dying thief,
"Pay no 'tention to death."
Says to the dying thief,

Says, "This day your spirit will be with Me in Heaven."
Says, "Oh, yes, this day, will be with me."
I am not ashamed to own my Lord! [Chanted].
I am not ashamed to own my Lord! [Congregation intoned].
God meet the devil when He seen him comin',
He began to wonder where he was goin'.
You needn't wonder, but just keep still,
He's a comin' on down.
He'll let you know what he's comin' for.

And when he fastened the great dragon,
Great God, bound him for so many thousand years,
Seen him, my dear friends, when he got a-hold of death,
Twist the stinger away from death—
Death ain't got no dominion over a child of God.

I seen Jesus whisper from Hell to His Father,
Told him to send down angels of grace,
Let them roll back the stone;
Then stay there and "Let my mother know I am gone, as I said."
Great God A'mighty! [shouted].
We seen when God A'mighty with His own omnipotent power,
Good God, called Michael and Gabriel, both peaceful angels.

Praise God! Jesus then told the boys,
"Don't, don't, don't harm those peoples that is settin' at the grave;
Don't say nothin' to 'em;
I'll give power;
I'll cause the earth to quake ahead of you."
Good God! Those angels left God A'mighty's throne;
Yes, leaped over the battlements of glory,
I seen forty and four thousand in heaven,
Just in the moment, the twinklin' of an eye.
Great God! three and twenty elders
Each one left their seats
Cryin', "Holy, holy,"
And when the angels got near the earth, the earth began
To quake and tremble. The peoples began to say,
"What's the matter here?"
Good God A'mighty! First and second day, no harm, nothing happened,
But here on the third mornin', looky here!
The earth quaking!
Good God! The earth began to quake.

'Bout that time while they were watching the earth
The angels darted down and a-seated right by the side of 'em,
Rolled back the stone,
Took a seat by the side of 'em,
Never said a word to 'em,

But just set there.
And when the angels took their seats
Good God!

Jesus got up;
Yes, got up out of his grave,
Began pullin' off his grave clothes.
Great God! Taken the napkin from around his jaws,
Shook the girdles,
Then laid them in the grave.

We seen the angels watch old Mary and Marthy,
An' told 'em just about when the morning star would break,
Told the girls to go on down to the grave.

Every child of God, he had something to carry to Jesus.
Oh . . . how you abused me in this world!
An' how you caused me to shed briny tears!
How you caused me to stand with folded arms!

Sin-Killer closed with a mighty invitation for sinners to come forward but none did. Perhaps they had become hardened to his pleas. Alan had been able to catch only segments of the two-hour-long sermon. Every seven minutes a disc must be turned, every fourteen minutes a new one had to be inserted.

After Sin-Killer had bid farewell to the convicts he joined Alan and me. The loud speaker was turned so that the convicts could hear and three hundred of them leaned forward to listen —more intently than they had listened to the preacher. Sin-Killer was fascinated as his words came forth from the machine.

"Mr. Lomax," he said when the last word had passed out of the loud speaker, "for a long time I'se been hearing that I'se a good preacher—now I knows it."

GAMES AND GATHERINGS

The Cowboy Dance

JOHN R. CRADDOCK

Turning back to the West of pre-1910 days, before the automobiles and phonographs became numerous, before the country became too thickly populated, we find an honest, hospitable people who worked with a will and played with a zest. It was then truly the land of the open door, where the stranger was always welcome and a man's word was his bond. Here people lived a simple life of contentment, untroubled by driving ambition and free from all convention. Their "gatherings" were few, and at them the individuals felt themselves under no obligation to conform. Hence, the picnics, the "meetings," the "sociables," the dances, were all highly flavored with the individuality of the locality—but none more than the cowboy dance.

An old-time cowboy dance was not announced in any specified manner. The news was given out and scattered by means of the "grapevine telegraph." At the beginning, several weeks before the dance was to "come off," several men were deputized to "ride it up." These men made a tour of the country and invited every person they happened to meet, regardless of who it might be. The invitation usually contained the phrase, "Everybody invited and nobody slighted."

Following the invitation to the dance, there was always a noticeable bustle about the community. Even the steadiest working ranch-hands "knocked off" early, dressed in their "Sunday-go-to-meeting" clothes, and rode away in a mysterious manner. A cowboy often put himself to a great deal of trouble to take his girl to a dance. Buggies were always scarce in the ranching country, and sometimes it was necessary for the "puncher" who contemplated taking his "lady friend" to a dance to hire a buggy from a livery stable at the nearest town. A typical case of the trouble a cowboy will put himself to on an occasion like this is that of Bill ————, who had a girl living twelve miles from the ranch where he worked. To make arrangements with the girl, he rode twenty-four miles. To procure a buggy he rode sixteen miles to town and drove the same distance coming back, making thirty-two miles. Then he drove to the girl's home, covering the twelve miles, and thence to the dance, covering eight miles. After the dance Bill drove the eight miles back to the girl's house, the twelve miles to the ranch, and made the thirty-two mile round trip to return the buggy. In all, Bill covered a distance of one hundred and twenty-eight miles, in order to take his "best girl" to the dance.

Some time during the day on which the dance was to "come off," several of the neighbors "dropped in" to help prepare for it. The furniture was all moved into one room or into the yard. The home stock were fed early and turned into the "starve out," to make room for the visitors' horses in the corral. Pictures and ornaments were usually left in their places, these forming the only decorations for the rooms. The pictures for the most part were enlargements of the members of the family or near relations; the other ornaments, decorated cards upon which were printed such maxims as "Welcome," "God bless our home," "What is a home without a mother," and "God bless mother and father."

The people began to arrive about sundown. Each group was hailed with loud and merry greetings. Gossip occupied the time until the arrival of the fiddler, but when he put in his appearance, all concern and attention were bestowed upon him. The fiddler was usually a unique character. He was in most cases a lazy, shiftless individual who never was known to refuse a drink. He had an "improvised" vocabulary, he "opined" and "calculated" and considered his own judgment as final and infallible on all subjects. For a long time he would tune his fiddle before the admiring crowd. With startling skill he would fasten his knife to the bridge of it to intensify the sound. He had a rattlesnake rattler always on the inside of his fiddle as a charm against dampness. When the fiddler started playing, all signs of his habitual laziness vanished, and he became strangely animated. He "kept time" with his head and his foot simultaneously, moving and tilting his head to the variation of his music while he patted his foot. The fiddlers all learned to play without instruction; therefore each of them had a different interpretation for the tunes they knew.

When a sufficient crowd had gathered, the dancing began. The girls were lined up on one side of the room and given chairs. If there were not enough chairs to "go around," trunks and boxes were used. When a man wished to dance with a young lady, he went over to her and said, "Pardner for the next dance?" and if she had none, he added, "May I have the next?" If she gave her consent, the bargain was closed. If a man was refused a dance by a girl he was "stung" or "stood up" by her, and should he be "stung" twice in one night he was considered "slighted" by the lady, and he customarily would not ask her for another dance.

Each man who danced made a donation to the fiddler. The dance usually started with a waltz, which was very beautiful. The cowboy held the lady's right hand in his left and put his right arm about her. He was always considerate and held a large handkerchief in his right hand to keep from soiling the lady's dress.

After the dance had been "going on" for some time, those who came from a distance began to arrive. When these late comers got close enough that they could hear the music of the fiddle, they would "pour the quirt" to their horses and ride yelling up to the very door. The men often came as far as forty miles to attend a dance, and it always seemed that the farther they came the more popular they were with the girls.

When the square dance started, a "caller" was selected, who automatically became the center of all attraction. The caller was always some person who was forward and "loud-mouthed." He had a carefree way about him that was evident even in dress. His boots were apt to be of the fanciest pattern that could be had; he would likely wear his "lock-rowelled" spurs.

He would have a rattlesnake skin slipped over his belt, which he buckled on the side instead of in the center. His shirt was a fancy pattern and a flaming color; he wore a "stamped leather collar" with a gaudy tie, having a small section of cow's horn slipped over it to serve in place of a knot. A pair of new buckskin gloves hung from the pocket of his "peg-topped" trousers and a "Bull Durham" tag hung from a sack in his shirt pocket. He assumed an indifferent air and seemed utterly unaware of the importance attached to him. The caller sometimes led in the dance and called for it at the same time. Sometimes calling from memory, filling in forgotten parts with new words, and often inventing entirely new calls, he chanted the calls in a rhythmic monotone that fitted well with the music of the fiddle. The performance of the dancers varied with the calls of the caller.

The swinging formed the major part of the dance. One way of swinging was by grasping the hands as the couple passed; another was by the interlocking of the elbows as the dancers met, followed by a quick turn and a release. The dancers moved with a kind of shuffle that was timed to the music. The feet of the dancers as they pounded the floor in unison stirred up the dust from between the boards, and several times during the night the dance was halted until the dirt could be swept out into the yard. It was not an unusual thing for a girl to dance her shoe soles through in one night. The "punchers'" thick-soled boots of course lasted longer.

The "calls" of the cowboy dance were exceedingly picturesque. A few examples of these calls follow.

> Choose your partner, form a ring,
> Figure eight, and double L swing.

> First swing six, then swing eight,
> Swing 'em like swinging on a gate.

> Ducks in the river, going to the ford,
> Coffee in a little rag, sugar in a gourd.

> Swing 'em once and let 'em go,
> All hands left and do-ce-do.

> You swing me, and I'll swing you,
> And we'll all go to heaven, in the same old shoe.

Chase the 'possum, chase the coon,
Chase that pretty girl 'round the room.

How will you swap, and how'll you trade
This pretty girl for that old maid?

Wave the ocean, wave the sea,
Wave that pretty girl back to me.

Swing your partners, once in a while,
Swing them all in Indian style.

Rope the cow, and kill the calf,
Swing your partner, a round and a half.

Swing your partners before you trade,
Grab 'em back and promenade.

Grab your pardner and sail away,
Hurry up, it's breaking day.

Swing 'em round, and round an' round,
Pockets full of rocks to weigh 'em down.

There comes a girl I used to know,
Swing her once and let her go.

When you meet your pardner, pat her on the head,
If she don't like coffee, give her corn bread.

Three little sisters, all in a row,
Swing 'em once and let them go.

Old shoe sole is about wore out,
Grab a girl and walk about.

Swing 'em east and swing 'em west,
Swing the girl that you like best.

There was something about the cowboy dances that cast a spell over participants and onlookers alike. Those who were forbidden by the strict country church to dance came often to look upon the gaieties of their "sinner friends" with envy and hunger in their eyes. At first they might refuse stoutly the invitations to dance, but too often the tantalizing music of the fiddle and the high nasal twang of the caller's voice caused even the most religious to join in the dance. When a church member took part in a dance he was said to have "danced himself out of the church" and he had to be "saved" at the next revival. With some persons it was a habit to "dance out of the church" in the winter and to be "saved" at the "camp meeting" the following summer when dancing was not in vogue.

Black coffee was served to the guests in the kitchen, where the children were put to sleep on the floor. As for the men, there was always a little whiskey on hand somewhere; between dances some man would wink at another and motion with his head. Following this mysterious procedure, several of the men would leave the room, and the bottle would be passed around, each man taking a swallow. In some instances, the boys would forget and take too much and get on a "high lonesome." As long as the men behaved they were not molested, but when a man got "tanked up" and showed it, he was frequently "cooled off" by a series of blows on the head, and then carried away to the harness shed and locked up or guarded until he was sober or until the dance "broke up."

The dancers as they moved about the room presented a pleasing spectacle. Singling them out, one would be impressed by the great variety that the gathering afforded. Style was not followed so closely then as now, and the girls would be dressed in many ways. The dresses were long, reaching almost to the ankle. White dresses with light pink or blue ribbons were the most popular. Between dances the girls would "fix up" in the dressing room. In those days a girl would not powder her nose in public. The boys were dressed in various ways; some wore shoes and common suits, while others wore fancy handmade boots and all of the other regalia that make up a cowboy's "garb." The farmer boys would wear "hand-me-down" boots in their effort to copy the cowboy's dress.

The dance was often varied by amusing or exciting incidents. When a "new beginner" wanted to learn to dance he was given a little extra attention. All care was taken to get him "balled up." Some of the girls were unusually strong, and when they swung the "new beginner," they would sometimes send him reeling against the wall; the dance was prolonged beyond its usual length for his special benefit, that he might get "blowed" or "winded."

The dances usually lasted all night and into the next day. Some of the "punchers" who had ridden forty or fifty miles to

attend a dance might sometimes have to leave early in order
to begin work in the morning. When a man left he announced
his "farewell" dance, danced it, and departed. Sometimes,
though, after he had mounted his horse and started away, his
ears caught the strains of a favorite selection. When he heard
these, he could not resist the temptation to return for another
"farewell" dance. Then he danced in his "chaps" and his riding
clothes. His return often arose from his desire to "show off" his
new "chaps," quirt, or other trapping. As he reluctantly rode
away, he would sometimes give the cowboy's call. This call is
weird and melancholy; it is the call that the cowboy uses as he
rides around a herd at night to solace himself and to quiet the
restless cattle. This call is strange in that it cannot be imitated.
It comes from the depths of the cowboy's soul, mellowed by
loneliness and inspired by the spell of the prairies. It was a
fitting and impressive farewell from the lonely rider as he
started away on his long ride.

When the dance broke up, the people shouted to one another
as they "hooked up." After many farewells, they drove away,
shouting as they went. Each man "prided" himself on his "rig,"
and to show off he would try to "pass everything on the road."
The departing crowd would often leave the gates open expecting the last comer to close them, and the land owners habitually
rode their fences and shut their gates on the morning following
a dance. Some of the boys would ride over fences and leave
them down, or play such pranks as taking the gates off the
hinges and dragging them with their ropes. After the rattle of
the last buggy had died away, the "blowout" became a part of
the community history.

▼▼▼▼▼▼▼▼▼▼▼▼

The Snap Party in Mills County

MAE FEATHERSTONE

Among the games mentioned by Mr. William Owens as in-
sufficient for an evening's entertainment is the one called

Snap.[1] But the hill people of Mills County are not aware of this deficiency, for Snap has furnished them entertainment for many evenings stretching over a long period of years.

I do not know when or where Snap originated. It was brought to Mills County by the first settlers, who had played it in the older settlements along the Colorado River, Pecan Bayou, and Bennett Creek. To my knowledge, the game is still played in East Texas near Nacogdoches, in North Texas at Byers on the Red River, in West Texas at Imperial on the Pecos. But in none of these places is it played so much as in the hills of Central Texas.

The country dance and the play-party have existed in Mills County since settlement, but they have never been so popular as the Snap party, partly because many Mills County boys and girls have been brought up to believe that dancing is wrong. For this reason only the "rougher elements" of society attend the dances and play-parties. Then the town of Goldthwaite has never sponsored a public dancing place of any sort, and since the rural dances have always been the rendezvous of the county's bootleggers and the scene of its most sensational murders, it is easy to see why most Mills County boys and girls do not go to dances until they go to college.

The play-party has never been very popular in this locality, partly because of its similarity to dancing, but primarily because of the great popularity of Snap. For Snap is a game that everybody can play at the same time and that a group can keep on playing together for hours on end.

Most boys and girls do not begin going to Snap parties until they are thirteen or fourteen years old. But if there are older sisters in the family and no big brothers to take them to parties, the parents go and take the smaller children along. Since I was one of the smaller children in such a family, I started going to Snap parties many years before I was old enough to play, and I started playing the game years before I began going with an escort or "date" of my own. Thus I grew up going to a Snap party almost every Saturday night, often on Friday night, the year around, and every night during the Christmas holidays.

[1]William A. Owens, *Swing and Turn* (Dallas, 1936), p. xv.

On account of revival meetings during the summer months, parties were usually discontinued; but very often—during that period—our parties, like the old saloon which closed on election day and opened when the polls closed, would begin after church services were over and last far into the night. In winter time, parties began about eight o'clock and broke up towards midnight; the summer parties held on longer, those that began after church services lasting until three or four o'clock.

In setting and atmosphere the Snap party is similar to the country dance and the play-party. It is the game itself that is different. When a fairly large crowd has gathered, several Snap games, the number depending upon the size of the crowd, are played simultaneously. There is always one game in the "party" room, while other games proceed on the porch and in the yard.

It takes four people to play a game of Snap, the two who "hold up," the one who snaps, and the one who is snapped. During a game, the player passes through four stages: namely, being snapped, snapping someone, holding up with the person who has snapped him, and holding up with the person he has snapped.

The original way to choose a partner was to snap one's fingers at the desired person, and from that custom the game received its name. This method of snapping, however, has been discarded in Mills County. When one person snaps another at our parties, he usually says, "Will you come catch me?" or simply "Come catch me," but often such expressions as "Let's run a race," "Get started," and "Lady, take after me," are heard. Little variation from these forms of address is permitted. One night at a party, a visiting boy from Wichita Falls went over to one of the girls and, following the coaching he had received from some local joker, said, "Come catch me, chicken. I'm full of corn." The girl answered him with a brisk slap in the face, and the boy from Wichita Falls played no more Snap that night.

The game starts with a boy and girl "holding up"; that is, they stand facing each other holding hands. Let us call them John and Mary. Another boy, say Tom, snaps a girl, Jane. Tom then walks or runs around the couple standing, and Jane chases him. When she catches him, John leaves the game; Tom holds up with Mary; and Jane snaps another boy, Henry. When Henry catches Jane, Mary leaves the game, and Tom and Jane hold up. Henry now snaps a girl, and the game continues. Thus the game goes on in an endless procession of entering, holding up with two different people, and leaving the game.

The chief action of the game comes when the couple runs around the couple holding up. The movement differs according to individual players. Some couples walk calmly and sedately through a game, but in my home community we usually played very hilariously. I have often seen the players holding up almost thrown to the floor by a runner's "swinging around the corner."

Assuming that the young folk are playing outside the house, any girl who participates is definitely associated with four different boys in the cycle of one Snap game. Let us take a girl named Jane through a game. She walks out with Tom, the boy who snapped her. She catches him and returns to the house with John, the boy who is leaving the game. She then snaps Henry and returns to the game. After he catches her, Jane remains outside holding up with Tom while Henry and the girl leaving the game go into the house together. Henry returns with another girl, and after he is caught, Jane holds up with him while Tom goes into the house with the girl Henry snapped. This girl returns with a new boy, and after he catches her, Jane, who is leaving the game, walks into the house with the new boy. During the game, then, she has been associated with both Tom, who snapped her, and Henry, whom she snapped, two different times, and with two other boys once each.

Snap may sound like a dull and uninteresting game, but it is far from that. It keeps the crowd constantly changing and moving about, and after several hours of play, each boy has had ample opportunity to talk to every girl present. The game moves with such automatic regularity that one is scarcely conscious of anything except that life is moving about him and that he is a part of it. In my heyday of Snap parties, which extended from about 1928 to 1934, they were always gay and colorful, with much laughter, talking, and noise. Often the "party" room was so packed that one could hardly push through the milling throng, and the yard was usually crowded with games.

The games may progress fast or slow, according to the humor of the person who is snapping. Often an individual gets snapped in one or two other games and completely forgets the couple left standing in the corner of the yard by a lilac bush. Playing in two games at once is not at all uncommon, and sometimes one plays in three and even four at the same time. This causes long waits for some of the couples holding up, but very few of them really mind that.

Should a boy wish to be left alone with a certain girl for a while, the best way for him to manage is to snap his sister. For when brother snaps sister or sister snaps brother, it goes without saying that the snapper wishes to let the game rest. Unfortunate indeed are the boys and girls who have no brothers and sisters present at a Snap party.

Usually there were more boys than girls. At parties in my community we frequently had boys from places twenty-five and thirty miles away, while girls seldom went that far. Then the boys from town always came to our parties, but the girls never did unless some of us who lived in the country gave a party especially for our class in high school. These young men from Goldthwaite and Star and other more distant places were never popular with the home boys, and their presence often caused fights.

Among the girls at a party there were always a few whose parents forbade them to play Snap outside, and often the parents were there to enforce the rule. I have many times accompanied one of my girl friends out to the well ostensibly to get a drink but really to stand by the windmill and keep watch with a boy provided for that purpose while she played Snap. One of my best friends, however, dared not attempt this scheme, since her father, after forbidding her to play Snap in the yard, frequently did so himself. One night Jack, a boy whose father was very old and never accompanied him anywhere, snapped Sue, who, upon learning that the game was outside, replied, "My daddy won't let me play in the yard."

Later in the evening Sue snapped Jack.

"Where's the game?" he asked, and when she replied that it was in the dining room, he drawled, "No, my daddy won't let me play Snap in the house."

At a crowded party, games may be going on in all sorts of out of the way places. I have played Snap sitting on the corral fence, on the wash bench, and on the rim of a cement water-tank, and once, at a party on an old ranch, in the family grave-yard. But the oddest game of Snap in which I ever played was on donkeys. Once at a party, my cousin hitched his donkey, Jennie, to one gate post, and my brother hitched Napoleon Bonaparte, his Mexican burro, to the other. During the party some gay couple started a Snap game on the two animals. Instead of holding up by the gate, they got on the donkeys and took a ride while the person snapping and the person snapped waited for them. This game of taking a donkey ride instead of holding up continued until Jennie pitched the girl off in a grain field.

About 1932 a new type of Snap became common in Mills County. It was called "Swap-out," or "Car" Snap. It is played exactly like ordinary Snap except that the players sit in a car instead of standing up in the yard. And instead of running around the car and catching each other, the players merely get in or out of the car. The advent of this fad caused a great deal of indignation among the older people. Many mothers thought that "Swap-out" was improper and refused to permit it at their parties. But time cures all things. Today Swap-out is the most common form of outdoor Snap in Mills County. A few enemies of Car Snap still exist, however, and their daughters are not allowed to play that form of the game.

In recent years the rural dance has become more popular and the Snap party is beginning to disintegrate. Play-party games are played in the house, and Snap is played outside at the same time, and the combination works very nicely. But not so with dancing. The crowd either snaps or dances. The two simply will not mix.

Snap parties in Mills County are still gay and colorful, but they are not what they used to be. In appearance they are about the same. Dress among the boys ranges from blue overalls and cowboy chaps and boots to tailor-made suits and lettered football sweaters. A sprinkling of John Tarleton and A. and M. uniforms appears at them during the Christmas holidays. Girls always dress up for a party, and to the casual observer they at first all look alike. But the colors and cut of their clothes and their hair styles mark the difference between the stay-at-homes and those who are at home only for the holidays or vacation.

The old spontaneity and unbridled gaiety are gone. The Saturday night parties break up early so that the participants can go to the midnight show. There is less laughter and more drinking. The games move slowly, couples segregating themselves more. Yet among the boys and girls there exists the same hearty degree of friendship, for they are all children of the same soil.

"Hoping Out" in East Texas

GUY KIRTLEY

A drummer, caught one rainy night on the muddy roads of the piney woods in East Texas, stopped at a house and asked if he might stay till morning. "Why, shore," said the farmer. "Kin I hope tote yore grips?" The drummer did not understand the question until his host picked up his bags. "To hope" is "to help," but "to hope out" has more specific connotations. It is a term associated with a number of traditional customs whereby neighbors exchange work and enjoy each other's company. Surviving from pioneer days, these customs grew out of the settler's need for help in clearing his land, raising his log cabin, as well as meeting emergencies, such as sickness, accidents, and Indian attacks. They exist today in the farming communities of the piney woods, because misfortune can still strike down the strongest of men; grass can get ahead of the best hoe hand; and there is still many a task too big for one man and his family.

Log-rollings, house-raisings, sewing and husking bees were traditionally popular on the frontier. They were popular because they mixed work with a sociable time—a man got his new ground cleared of big timber or his cabin built from foundation to roof in a day for the price of a good dinner, a jug of whiskey, and a dance for the young folks.

Log-rollings are not so common now, but a number of customs in East Texas express the desire of the people to work and help each other. There are still raisings, and the swapping of work, and the getting together to perform community tasks, and other customs involving coöperation of each man and his next neighbor.

SYRUP MAKING

Economically and socially, the annual syrup-make is probably the most important of these practices. Coming as it does at the climax of the harvest season, it is often a festive occasion for both young and old.

Syrup is an important item of the farmer's diet, and he strives to have somewhere among his scattered patches of cotton and corn a quarter or half acre of ribbon cane upon which he depends for sweetening to go with cornbread and pork. A black billowing cloud of smoke rising high above the creek-bottom trees in late November indicates the site of a cane mill, where a roaring pine knot fire is cooking a run-off of syrup. It is an event eagerly awaited, for it is the custom of long standing that everybody who is not working at the mill is invited to come chew cane, drink cold juice, and eat "buckskin," or foam, while they visit each other.

Twenty years ago down on Bodan Creek in Angelina County, Uncle Barney Free staked his old three-roller cast-iron cane mill down for a run every year and made syrup for everybody around Pollok. He was the best syrup maker in that part of the country, where making was a fine art. All the farmers hauled their cane to him, taking their turn as he made up for all in one continuous run. The men helped each other, working in two shifts and taking syrup for payment or swapping work for help to make their own cane.

Uncle Barney would set up his mill just after the first frost and rush the season to beat the first hard freeze, which would sour the cane juice in the stalk. While the cane was being stripped and cut in the field for hauling, the long copper evaporating pan was fitted on a makeshift furnace of brick cemented with postoak mud. The cane mill was placed a short distance from the pan and set with heavy stakes driven deep in the ground about the wheels. When hauling from the field began, Uncle Barney lined the hands up at the mill: skimmers, juice boys, mill feeders, cane carriers, and, most important of all, a good fireman who knew how to handle pine knots.

Cane grinding began at daybreak on a frosty morning. A team was hooked to the long sweep and tied to a lead pole that drew the mules in a circular tread around the mill. The long-jointed stalks of cane, fed into the rollers three and four at a time by a nimble feeder, sent forth a steady flow of juice. Incidentally the cane was not ground at all, but was crushed between the closely-set rollers, coming out as "mill chewin's," or "bogus."

The furnace was not fired till there were two good barrels and a pan full of juice on hand. Unless a breakdown shut off the supply of juice, work went on night and day, and the pan was not cooled down till the cooking was finished. Uncle Barney presided over the pan and did not forget how important his job was. The dark rich liquid had to be watched closely from the time it ran into the evaporating pan until it thickened into syrup at the far end. Two skimmers were kept busy with their ladles, sieving off the green vegetable scum, or "skimmings," that rose to the top of the boiling juice.

The maker was always fascinating to watch as he worked with his ladle, dipping, stirring, and testing. He strained his keen eyes to read the lazy burst of a bubble, or he would let the cooking liquid drip from the edge of his ladle to test the break of its bead before he pulled the bung from the pan and let the finished syrup run into the pot. Syrup could be cooked too long, in which case it would soon turn to rock candy, or it could run too thin and there would be complaints because it took too many biscuits to hem it on a plate. Uncle Barney rarely made a bad run; given a good fireman and a steady supply of juice, he could run off a hundred gallons a day, from which he took a toll of one gallon in eight.

While the men folks worked with the cane, their wives were as busy as any two of them providing three hot meals a day and a midnight snack. This food had to be prepared in the kitchen and carried on foot or by wagon to the mill, where it was spread on the ground, picnic-fashion. The pick of the fall fryers were killed for the occasion. Cakes, potato custards, and lightbread were cooked in quantities, and the best of the year's canning was brought forth. Like the men, the wives took turns in helping each other out, and there was no end of lively competition among them to see who could feed their men the best.

The big time was at night when the mill was lighted with huge pine torches placed about on scaffolds. The crowd gathered then and there was always a great deal of laughing, hurrahing, and horseplay among the visitors and the men at work. The young folks came sparking and sat apart on a handy log, the young men peeling cane for their girls. The old folks, who had not seen each other for a relaxed moment since perhaps the summer revival, gossiped and sampled the syrup, comparing its flavor with last year's run from the same land. Those with "fitten" teeth chewed a stalk of cane; all would make repeated trips to the barrel for a cup of cold cane juice, the exotic taste of which cannot be compared with that of any other drink. The more adventurous whittled a paddle from a cane peeling and skimmed the leathery foam, or "buckskin," from the syrup-pot. Its candy-like flavor was delicious. The folks gathering at night were a part of the cane-grind, and customarily they were welcome. Sometimes they came from miles around, and there were few that did not engage several gallons of syrup to be delivered later for cash.

Uncle Barney is dead now, but his place at the pan has been taken by others, and the passing years have seen little change in the method he used in getting all to pitch in and help so that everybody would have a year's supply of sweetening.

The custom of taking payment in kind and swapping work is not confined to the making of syrup. "Two heads are better than one" and "Many hands can do wonders" are sayings frequently heard in the piney woods. If a man gets behind with his crop and "gets in the grass" because of too much rain or sickness, or because of the simple lack of help, it is customary for him to invite all his neighbors, men and women, over to give him a day's work to catch up. He sets a convenient time far enough ahead for all to be prepared to accept. Each will bring his hoe or plowtools. A good dinner will be laid for all. An ox in the ditch is the only excuse for a neighbor's not coming, for it is understood that the farmer in need will pay each back in kind with a day's work at lay-by, gathering time, or during the winter at wood-cutting or clearing land. This is a very practical form of barter where there is little cash money. And it is used to perform a multitude of lesser tasks such as splitting rails or making fence posts, where two men are required to drag a cross-cut saw and others to split and haul.

Hog-killing especially involves a great amount of extra help in the butchering, scraping off the hair after the shoat has been scalded thoroughly, and dressing and salting down hams and sides. Even during a blue norther the work must be done with dispatch. The lard has to be rendered and the chittlings cooked. The perishable parts, such as the liver and lights, the head, and the backbone, are distributed among the neighbors for immediate use. Needless to say, help is not lacking, for to help means a mess of fresh pork, which will be repaid when work is swapped with the coming of the next norther.

The custom of swapping work is employed by the women in the form of quiltings and cannings. The quick ripening of berries and plums creates an emergency that one woman cannot handle alone, and it is to the advantage of her neighbors that they bring their fruit jars and help her for a half of what each cans. Quiltings are still popular and the women spend many an afternoon together helping each other piece scraps for a quilt cover, or tacking a comfort on a quilting frame swung from the ceiling of the front room.

Families get the mayhaws for canning and their scaly-bark hickory nuts to be used in Christmas cakes by organizing all-day hunts into the river bottoms, carrying a dinner to be spread on the ground. At the end of the day the pickings are divided according to the size of the family of each picker. Similarly, when a man finds a bee tree, he calls his neighbors to help him cut it. The honey is divided, the bee colony going to the finder of the tree. Robbing a bee-gum also requires help, and to the one who doesn't mind a few bee-stings about his face goes a share of the rich spoils for the breakfast table.

RAISINGS

In pioneer days the lone settler could eventually fell enough trees, bark and notch them, and build his cabin by himself, but after getting his logs ready, he invited his neighbors to "hope him out." House raisings were popular because they gave a lonely people an opportunity to get together, visit, and eat a hearty meal. Raisings are still given in East Texas, when a crib, a cotton pen, a smokehouse, or a brush arbor for the summer revival is needed.

Anyone giving a raising in our community is expected to have all the materials on hand and ready, and to set a day convenient for all. When my father wanted to raise a mud-chimney on our house, we spent days in preparation. During the hot days of late July while we waited for cotton to open, we found a post-oak clay of good texture and gathered moss from the creek bottoms. We spent several days cutting and hewing timbers and crosspieces for the framework of the chimney. It was not until he had all the materials hauled and laid down at the house that we set a day and sent word around that we were giving a chimney raising and that there would be a good dinner for everyone who came. As it was a slack time of the year, most of the men of the neighborhood showed up with their families, as we expected.

With two hands for every job, the raising proceeded quickly.

A hole was cut in the house wall for the fireplace and a foundation laid for the chimney. Then four upright oak timbers, squared with adz and broad-ax, went up, and on these closely spaced crosspieces were nailed to complete the framework. The postoak clay was mixed with water and worked to a stiff consistency; then a double-hand portion of the mud was kneaded around a wisp of Spanish moss. The result was a pliable brick, or "mud-cat," about eight inches long and two inches in diameter. When completed, the mud-cats were thrown to a man on the chimney framework, who deftly wrapped them about a crosspiece, one after another until a tier had been completed. The waterboys, claymixers, catmen, and wrappers performed this chain of tasks. There was no interruption, because there was always a man standing around waiting to take over when another wanted to blow a while. There was no let-up either in the laughing, hurrahing, and bragging that went on, and the fun was redoubled when dinner was spread under the shade trees and the women joined the men for a rest during the heat of the day.

WAKES

Perhaps those practices of mutual aid that best preserve faith in human kindness are the traditional customs that have no selfish end in view, but are purely Samaritan in character. The sick and the afflicted, the widows and orphans are a community responsibility, and a man is bound to help as he can. "Setting up" with the sick is a deep-seated obligation assumed by the good neighbor, for the ill and the harassed family must be relieved by the neighbors, who take turns at the sickbed. When death occurs, they must "set up with the corpse," for it is a sin and a shame to leave a family alone with its dead.

The death wake is believed to have had its origin in primitive times when guard was kept over the body of the deceased to ward off evil spirits. The custom as it exists in East Texas today requires that friends come to comfort the bereaved, wash the body, and lay it out on a board in the front room, where it will remain all night lighted by an oil lamp and covered with a sheet until it is dressed and put in the coffin next morning. Some religious sects hold all-night ceremonies for the dead, but usually the death wake is quiet, arrangements for the funeral next day being made in low voices on the front porch or in the yard. Friends, close kin, and neighbors stay all night, going periodically to the kitchen for coffee, but always quietly. As soon as it is day, a group will assemble picks, shovels, and mattocks and set off for the cemetery to lay off the grave and dig it six feet deep. And no kin of the dead need touch a cold clod of clay.

The graves of the dead are not forgotten as the years pass. Graveyard-workings with dinner-on-the-ground are still held annually in many settlements. During August or September a day is set aside for the occasion and the whole community will turn out with full baskets, each person bringing a hoe, rake, or shovel. The cemetery is worked clean of grass, weeds, and bushes. Individual graves receive the careful attention of relatives of the deceased. New mounds are heaped up on those graves that have settled flat or caved in. Wild flowers and bits of colored glass are arranged on the newly spaded earth as a simple tribute to a mother, father or a son, dead all these years. Naturally the gathering is one of mixed emotions. There is the usual amount of laughing and talking, as among any hearty people, but there are also tears in the eyes.

Rope-Jumping Rhymes

VIOLET WEST SONE

When mesquite trees put out their leaves, and boys bring out their marbles and girls their skipping ropes—why, it's spring in Texas. In Rockport School, way down South on the Gulf, the skipping ropes are always much in evidence. Lithe young figures with nimble feet dance hot pepper, high water, rock the cradle, and double rope all over the sidewalks. But the most interesting part of the procedure is the chanting of rhymes in time to the regular swing of the rope. Some of these rhymes are adaptations of familiar verses, but most of them show evidence of recent composition and of the fertility of childish imagination.

One of the familiar ones used is:

"Mother, Mother, I am sick,
Call the doctor quick, quick, quick!"
"Doctor, Doctor, will I die?"
"Yes, my darling, bye and bye."
"How many hours will I live?"
One, two, three, four, five,...

And so on the counting goes until the nimble feet miss. This rhyme is also said with: "How many hearses will I have?" instead of "How many hours will I live?"

Another familiar one is:

One, two, three, four, five, six, seven,
All good children go to heaven.
All the rest go down below
To eat supper with Old Black Joe.
How many bad ones go below?
One, two, three, four, five,...

The old button-counting rhymes have been taken over by the rope jumpers:

What shall I be when I grow up?
Rich man, poor man, beggar man, thief,
Doctor, lawyer, merchant, chief,
Tinker, tailor, cowboy, sailor,
Butcher, baker, music maker,...

A machine-age supplement goes:

What shall I drive when I grow up?
Lincoln, Chrysler, Chevrolet, Ford,...

Of course, the name the jumper misses on answers the question. Usually the girl says, "Who shall I marry when I grow up?" instead of, "What shall I be?" Then when that important question is settled the jumper says:

What shall I wear on my wedding day?
Silk, satin, calico, rags, silk, satin, ...

A rhyme peculiarly suited to the Rockport region is:

> Down by the ocean,
> Down by the sea
> Johnny broke a bottle
> And he blamed it on me.
> I told Ma, Ma told Pa,
> Johnny got a lickin'
> And a Haw! Haw! Haw!
> How many lickin's did he get?
> One, two, three, four, five, . . .

A number of these counting rhymes are based on the love theme, as:

> Cinderella, dressed in yellow,
> Went upstairs to kiss her fellow.
> How many kisses did she get?
> One, two, three, four, five, . . .

Another version of the Cinderella rhyme is:

> Cinderella, dressed in yellow,
> Went down town to buy an umbrella.
> On the way she met her beau,
> Who took her to a ten cent show.
> How many kisses did she get?
> One, two, three, four, five, . . .

The same theme with a different setting is used in:

> Down in the meadow where the green grass grows
> There sat Rosemary sweet as a rose.
> Up jumped Johnny, and he kissed her on the cheek.
> How many kisses did she get right quick?
> One, two, three, four, . . .

Instead of using Johnny and Rosemary every time, the children supply the names of the jumper and her boy friend.
Another amusing rhyme is:

> My mother is a butcher,
> My father cuts the meat,
> I'm a little hot dog
> Running down the street.
> How many hot dogs do I sell?
> One, two, three, four, . . .

Not all of the rope-jumping rhymes are counting rhymes. Some use letters of the alphabet:

> Ice cream soda, Delaware Punch,
> Spell the initials of my honey-bunch.
> A, B, C, D, E, ...

And so on down the alphabet. The letter the jumper misses on is the initial of the best beloved. If she fails to miss the first round, she starts off with A again, increasing the speed of the rope. Sometimes the letters of the alphabet are said without the preliminary "Ice cream soda," etc.; then when the initial is determined by a miss, the jumper continues with "Yes, no, maybe so, certainly, yes, no, maybe so," etc., to determine whether he loves her.

All of the rhymes mentioned so far can be jumped with either a skipping rope or a long rope. The "rock the cradle" variety requires a long rope. The throwers swing the rope back and forth instead of over for this one:

> Grace, Grace, dressed in lace,
> Went upstairs to powder her face,
> How many boxes did she use?
> One, two, three, four, five, ...

A combination of "rock the cradle" and "over" is used for this one:

> Blue bells, cockle shells,
> E-ve, I-ve, over.
> I like coffee, I like tea,
> I like the boys, and the boys like me.
> Yes, no, maybe so, yes, no, maybe so, ...

The word *over* is the signal for the throwers to stop rocking the cradle and to throw the rope over.

Hot pepper is always a favorite with jumpers. A good way to get started off is to say

> Mable, Mable, set the table,
> Don't forget the RED HOT PEPPER!

It's no mean accomplishment to be able to jump "double rope." The throwers keep two long ropes going at once, throwing one with the left hand and the other with the right. The proficient jumper learns not only to keep her feet clear of both ropes, but to enter and run out at will, either "front door" or "back door," and to jump "high water," in which the rope is not allowed to touch the ground.

Most attractive of all are the action or gesture rhymes jumped with the long rope. The words suggest to the jumper what to do:

> Amos and Andy, sugar and candy,
> I pop in.
> Amos and Andy, sugar and candy,
> I pop down.
> Amos and Andy, sugar and candy,
> I pop up.
> Amos and Andy, sugar and candy,
> I pop out.
> Amos and Andy, sugar and candy,
> I pop through.

This is the most interesting action rhyme of them all:

> Shirley Temple went to France
> To teach the ladies how to dance.
> This is the dance she taught them first:
> Heel, toe, around we go,
> Heel, toe, around we go,
> Salute to the Captain, bow to the King,
> Make a dirty face at the ugly old Queen.

A similar action rhyme is:

> Last night and the night before
> Twenty-four robbers knocked at my door.
> I asked them what they wanted,
> And this is what they said:
> "Spanish dancer, do the split,
> Spanish dancer, show your shoe,
> Spanish dancer, that will do."

The first rhyme I ever saw jumped was "Teddy-Bear." There are several versions of this rhyme, one of which is:

> Teddy-Bear, Teddy-Bear,
> Turn around.
> Teddy-Bear, Teddy-Bear,
> Touch the ground.
> Teddy-Bear, Teddy-Bear,
> Show your shoe.
> Teddy-Bear, Teddy-Bear,
> Skit, skat, skiddoo!

And the jumper runs out. She may return with this version:

> Teddy-Bear, Teddy-Bear,
> Go upstairs.
> Teddy-Bear, Teddy-Bear,
> Say your prayers.
> Teddy-Bear, Teddy-Bear,
> Turn out the light.
> Teddy-Bear, Teddy-Bear,
> Say Goodnight.

Children's Games in Fredericksburg

JULIA ESTILL

While thumbing through a small volume of *Selected Verses* by Harry Lee Mariner, who for many years cheered thousands of readers with his lines in both the *Dallas* and *Galveston News*, I found a little poem entitled "I Spy!" that awakened memories of my own childhood days.

It took me back to the spreading canopy of a large mulberry tree near a school building of amber-colored stone atop a gently sloping knoll on the school grounds in the town of Fredericksburg, Texas.

The smaller children, both boys and girls, are about to choose sides for an exciting old German game their grandmothers used to play—"Voegel zu verkaufen!" ("Birds for Sale!").

The two most aggressive youngsters in the group become the self-appointed leaders, each of a side. Choosing then begins, the fleetest runners being prime favorites and first selected.

All on the seller's side are given names of birds, who flutter inside a ring drawn on the ground to represent the cage. Close at hand is a similar ring in which the buyers move about restlessly. When the chief buyer approaches the seller's domain, the birds are all a-flutter, especially if the visitor is a dapper lad who will pay a lot of coin for a bird of fine plumage. Greetings over, bargaining begins.

"What kinds of birds have you?" queries the customer.

"Sparrows, hawks, red birds, blue birds, yellow birds—'most any kind you want," replies the salesman proudly.

"I should like a blue bird," promptly answers the customer. And he looks longingly at a fluffy flaxen-haired little girl in a blue-checked pinafore with blue bows on her pigtails.

The shrewd salesman, seeing the trend of affairs, and sensing a rival for the fair birdie's favor, screws up the price. But even though twenty-five "bucks" is steep, the customer accepts the "challenge," and promptly and resoundingly slaps the out-stretched palm of the salesman twenty-five times, watching, out of the corner of his eye, the dainty bit of fluff about to take wing at the farther end of the aviary.

The last dollar paid with a deal of vehemence, the chase is on, the birdie stretching her winglets and limblets in flight before the sale is quite complete; for she doesn't want to be caught. (Or does she?)

The bargain-hunter is soon in hot pursuit, the chase usually ending in capture. And a breathless, bedraggled blue-bird comes trailing along, led by a jubilant captor.

If the bird that has been bought is a Texas roadrunner, how-ever, he usually outdistances his pursuer and returns to the cage from whence he came, vociferously welcomed by his fellow fowls who feel that he bears a charmed life, as all Texas roadrunners should do.

But children soon tire of a game; and presently, up against the trunk of the mulberry tree, a disgruntled owl, who doesn't give a hoot about the old game, will call: "Aw, let's play 'Blinde Kuh, ich fuehre dich'" ("Blind cow, I'll lead you").

Immediately there is a scramble to hold hands and form a ring where the blind cow is to be impounded, a keeper and a cow are chosen, and the former leads the blindfolded cow into the circle of children who now represent *spoons*.

"Blinde Kuh, ich fuehre dich" ("Blind cow, I'll lead you"), declares the keeper importantly.

"Wohin?" (Whither?") queries the blinded victim.

"In Keller" ("Into the cellar"), the keeper responds.

"Wass soll ich da?" ("What shall I do there?") anxiously queries the cow.

Then comes the provoking reply, followed by suppressed giggles from the encircling spoons: "Dickmilch fressen!" ("Lap up the clabber!")

Then the animal protestingly announces: "Ich hab' kein Loeffel!" ("I have no spoon!")

But, nothing daunted, the keeper commands briskly: "Such' dich ein!" ("Find you one!") and backs away hurriedly as the cow gropes blindly about with outstretched arms in the direction of muffled giggles, and the enlivened spoons squirm out of the way.

Sooner or later, however, a spoon is caught and forthwith transformed into a blind cow.

Thus the game continues until an authoritative voice calls: "Wollen Stimmchen spielen!" ("Let's play voicelet!"); and immediately all the players scamper about seeking fresh hands to clasp and reform the circle.

Usually the child suggesting the game will be *It*, the blind-folded interrogator who will occupy the center of the circle. With an important air, he takes his place and, after the players have spun around dizzily a time or two, he pokes about with his stick trying to locate a victim.

Having "spiked" one, he demands, "Stimmchen!" ("Little voice, please!")

Usually the response comes in a mousey squeak or a basso profundo, the center trying to identify the voice. If he is a good guesser, the victim takes his place in the center, and the game continues.

A game of the ring variety very popular in early days of the Fredericksburg colony, when Schoolmaster Heinrich Ochs ruled supreme in the schoolhouse on the public square, was, according to octogenarians like Miss Ida Hennersdorf, a resident of Fredericksburg today, "Esel, lass dich hoeren!" ("Donkey, air your voice" or "Bray, donkey, bray!")

The players, impersonating animals and fowls, sit in a circle with ultra-sober mien, while the ringmaster and the donkey, chosen by their fellows, occupy the center. Forthwith the ringmaster, in a voice like the crack of a whip, commands: "Esel, lass dich hoeren!"

Then the donkey brays loud and long, while the ringmaster watches closely for grins or even ghosts of smiles on the faces of those seated in the circle. If any of them smile, laugh, curl their lips, or show their teeth, they forfeit a prized possession. Besides, one sitter may be called to change places with the donkey.

Imagine the fun of redeeming forfeits later.

Another game handed down through several generations in rural communities in Gillespie County is nameless, as far as I can learn; but, I am told, it is very enjoyable.

While the children participating sit on a bench outdoors, a chosen player advances to one of them and laughingly repeats these lines while thumping him on the thorax:

> "Stumm, stumm wie Buttermilch.
> Lache nicht; weine nicht;
> Zeich deine, kleine Weisze Zaehne nicht."
> ("Dumb, dumb as buttermilk!
> Laugh not; weep not.
> Show not your little white teeth.")

Naturally the nearness of the laughing leader's face and his "thoraxal thump" will provoke a grin on the victim's countenance. As a result, he is hoisted upon the locked hands of two other players and swung lustily to and fro. More than likely, he topples from his perch; and the spectators laugh derisively.

The girls enjoy playing "Kluck mit Huenkel" ("Hen with Chickens"), a larger child impersonating the hen, who fends and keeps behind her a long line of "baby chicks" swinging to one another's waists, the first firmly clutching the mother hen.

Suddenly a "Raubvogel" (bird of prey) appears. The mother hen sounds the alarm, and the chicks, chirping excitedly, fly from left to right, still clutching one another tightly and trying to avoid the advances of the hawk, the hen doing her part valiantly but to no avail. The chicks are caught, one by one, and the game begins anew.

Another game of the 1870's was called "Heintzelmaenchen" ("Little Pixie"). It was staged, according to Miss Hennersdorf, on the long stone gallery of a one-story store on the corner of

Upper Main Street, where the neighborhood children often gathered late in the afternoon or early evening.

The first comers each choose a gallery post. After the posts have all been taken, the next one to appear is the Heintzel-maenchen. Then begins the chant by the children clasping the gallery posts:

> "Heintzelmaenchen hat kein Endchen;
> Kann kein Endchen finden."
> ("Little pixie has no corner;
> Cannot find a station.")

The pixie, meanwhile, as posts are being exchanged by excited children, attempts to secure a station of his own. If he is successful, another "Heintzelmaenchen" takes over.

Perhaps the most popular of all the games for young children was "Zieh durch," a German version of "London Bridge." It involves the repair of a broken bridge that is rebuilt and rebroken many times before the game ends.

Marching in single file, the players, each with his arms locked about the waist of the child preceding him, chain-fashion, pass under an archway formed by two youngsters who stand opposite each other with uplifted arms and clasped hands, both having previously selected a piece of jewelry to represent.

All the players chant these lines:

> Zieh durch, zieh durch,
> Durch die gold'ne Brucke.
> Sie ist entzwei; sie ist entzwei,
> Wir wollen sie wieder pfluecken.
> Mit was? Mit Glass.
> Mit einerlei, mit zweierlei,
> Der letzte soll gefangen sein.
>
> (March along, march along,
> Under the bridge of gold.
> She's cut in two, she's cut in two,
> We'll patch her up to hold.
> Alas! With glass?
> Just one or two old things will do.
> We'll catch and keep the last one through.)

The child who happens to be underneath the archway when the chant ceases is caught when the "portcullis" falls, and is questioned as to which article of jewelry he prefers—a gold watch or a gold bracelet, for example. Then, his selection made, he scurries to the side he has chosen and clasps the child before him about the waist.

Thus the game continues until the bridge is repaired. Then the tug-of-war begins; and eventually the "archway" is pulled apart only to be rebuilt in the space of a few minutes.

SAYINGS AND PROVERBS

Familiar Sayings of Old-Time Texans

MARY JOURDAN ATKINSON

When Austin's colonists came to settle on the Brazos, they brought with them the varied idioms of the older states, many of which were ancient in Europe before Columbus first sighted the Bahama Islands. But language always takes color from its environment, and many of the sayings of the old world when brought to the new were gradually translated into figures expressive of American life. In the South and Southwest the work of men and women on the plantations and small farms, the business of riding over great ranges, of hunting Indians and game, of just living next to the ground with the implements of the soil in hand naturally brought to mind such comparisons as "sticking closer than a cocklebur" and "being knee high to a grasshopper."

As another example of a saying produced by local conditions, consider "plotting against the whites." This phrase, so suggestive of the danger and distress endured on Indian frontiers, is now never used in actual seriousness; but wherever a group has withdrawn for momentary conference, some friendly voice is sure to inquire: "Well, are you plotting against the whites?"

The sayings and similes that follow have been gathered mostly from the speech of native Texans, though many of them are current in other regions.

I've seen wilder heifers than you milked in a gourd, ma'am.

Teach your grannie how to suck eggs!
Teach your grannie how to pick ducks!

213

Just as well go out and bay at the moon as ask that old skinflint for money.

He might as well be singing psalms over a dead horse as trying to make a doctor out of that boy of his (or attempt anything considered preposterous).

He might as well try to eat sugar (or soup) with a knitting needle.

They'll live at the top of the pot for a while, I reckon (live high).

He'll shoot a punkin and churn; that's what he'll do. (He'll "make a fizzle," "play Hob.")

He hasn't got as much sense as last year's bird nest with the bottom punched out.

He found a mare's nest; that's what he found.
He found what the little boy shot at. (Nothing.)

He does not amount to a hill of beans.

He's mighty small potatoes and few in the hill.

He amounts to about as much as a notch on a stick and the stick thrown away.

Anything he says cuts mighty little ice.

When he says "frog," she jumps.

He has about as much use for that as a hog has for a sidesaddle.

He couldn't sell ice water in hell.

He rattles around in his office like one pea in a pod.

He has brass enough to make a boiler and sap enough to fill it.

His feathers fell when I told him that.

He sits around like a notch on a stick.

He jumped on to that like a duck onto a June bug.

He played the wild (or the wilds) when he did that.
He just about played whaley.

He does not know A from Adam's off ox: does not know B from bull's foot.

He's so ugly that he has to slip up on a dipper to get a drink out of it.

He's ugly enough to turn sweet milk to clabber.

She's so cross-eyed that when she cries the tears run down her back.

The old codger's as slow as molasses in January; also, as slow as Christmas.

There's a nigger in the woodpile.
You'd better look out; there may be a bug under the chip.

Oh, butter wouldn't melt in his mouth now. He's in the middle of a bad fix, got the worst kind of cold feet, and wants me to help him out.

He's as polite as a basket of chips; sugar wouldn't melt in his mouth.

I would not believe him if he swore to it on a stack of Bibles a mile high.

He'd steal the nickels off a dead man's eyes.
He'd rob his grandmammy's grave.

You must have sewed that with a red hot needle and a burning thread, but it will never be seen on a galloping horse and him in a trot.

It made a noise like pourin' peas on a dried cowhide. (This might be a description of any kind of sound, even of music.)

I'll ride Shank's pony, or mare (walk).

He's goin' around with a chip on his shoulder.

He's a regular Strap Buckler (Buckner); i.e., drinks like a fish.

I'll knock him windin' and brick-stinin' if he fools with me.
That knocked him sky-westward and crooked eastward.

He's too lazy to scare the flies out of his mouth.
He's too lazy to shuck corn if you gave it to him.

They didn't even give him the cork to smell. (May be taken literally but often used to express a perfect job of fleecing.)

The house was seven ways for Sunday.
The house was every way for Christmas.

Then hell broke loose in Georgia.

She's one of the old blue hen's chickens; i.e., a "hell cat," a termagant.

They just literally limb-skinned and jay-hawked that tree.

She has on a brand splinterfire new dress.
She's flirting like a Spanish filly.

There are more ways to kill a dog than to choke him to death with butter.
There are more ways than one of breaking a dog from sucking eggs.

You could ride to mill on that knife without any blanket (it's so dull).
That knife would not cut hot butter in June.

He's in a regular jack-pot now.
He's up Salt Creek (in trouble).

As well argue with a wooden Indian (or wooden man).

I killed him too dead to skin. (The death is likely to be figurative, as in an argument. To understand the figure it must be remembered that an animal that has been dead a long time is too putrified to skin.)

Everything's frozen as stiff as stilliards.

His name is Mud.

I don't know him from Adam's off ox. (Corrupted to Adam's all fox.)
I don't know him from the side of sole leather.

That beats a hen a-scratchin'.
Don't that just beat a hen a-lopin'?

Just hold your horses till I get through. (Be patient.)
You hold your potato till mine gets cold.

He pulled his freight in a hurry.
He ran like the devil was after him.

He's steppin' eleben now (stepping high).

Wait till we see how the cat jumps.

Don't kick till you're spurred.

The chickens will come home to roost. (This means in a bad sense what "cast your bread upon the waters," etc., means in a good sense.)

A rich man for luck and a poor man for children.

Them as has must lose, 'cause them as hasn't can't.

He's too big for his breeches.

He'll get hanged as high as Haman.
That horse will throw him so high that the birds'll build nests in his ears before he hits the ground.

She gives me the hebe-jebes (also, the heaves).

The rain was a regular gully-washer and fence-lifter (also, a gully-washer and root-searcher).
It's raining bull frogs and heifer yearlings.

I wouldn't marry him if he was the last man on God's green earth.

That galoot's not worth the powder and lead it would take to blow him up.
That guinea's not worth his salt (also, not worth his found).

She's sashayin' (or galavantin') all over the country.

Lord, take care of the poor and us rich devils will look out after ourselves.

I've a crow to pick with you.
I've a row to hoe with you.

He's a regular wheelhorse when it comes to doing work.
He's a stem-winder and go-getter.

You can't hear your ears in this place.

Miss Emma has set her cap for that young man.

That's a grey mare of a different color.
The shoe is on the other foot now.

That was the last button on old Gabe's coat.

I took my foot in my hand and walked. (An expression of independence.)

That buck had a set of antlers on him that looked like a rocking chair.

When I told him that he had to fork up $500, he bellered like a bay steer.

This pony paces like a rocking chair.

Sweating like a nigger at election.

Not room enough to turn around in.

His eyes bugged out (or bulged out) till you could have roped them with a grapevine.

A voice on him like the bulls of Bashan.

Layovers to catch meddlers. (A curious answer made to inquisitive children. What is the origin?)

We'll put the big pot in the little one; also, put the big pot in the little one and fry the skillet. (Celebrate, have a regular *blow-out*— a word used long before the automobile was invented.)

It happened in two shakes of a sheep's tail.

The whole cavayard, outfit. (From *caballada*, Spanish for a herd or bunch of horses; a term in common use all over the ranch country of the Southwest.)

Grandma's Sayings

A. W. EDDINS

Grandmother was a pioneer Texan, who came to Blue Ridge, Collin County, in the early 1840's. Left a widow by the war, she was sustained in her hard struggle to raise her large family by many quaint sayings full of wisdom and knowledge of life. Here are some of them.

> If you make your bed hard, you can turn over oftener.
> You can never get all the possums up the same tree.
> There was never a persimmon except there was a possum to eat it.
> Leave her alone and she'll come home to her milk.
> Lick by lick the cow ate the grindstone.
> The higher they go, the lower they fall.
> She will soon wish she was back under her mammy's bed playing with the cats.
> Cut your peaches, gals; thunder ain't rain.
> Come light, go light.
> Nothing ever went over the devil's back that didn't come back under his belly.

Fox is the finder; the stench lies behind her.

The hit dog is always the one that howls.

Before my face, honey and sugar; behind my back, you old wooden-legged devil.

Short visits make long friends.

The polecat can't tell the buzzard that he stinks.

Big talker, little doer.

There are more ways to kill a dog than by choking him to death on hot butter.

The man who dances pays the fiddler.

Let sleeping dogs lie.

Don't dig up more snakes than you can kill.

Enough of a good thing is enough; too much is a dog's bait.

What can't be cured must be endured.

The morning rain is like an old woman's dance, soon over.

Talk is cheap, but it takes money to buy whiskey.

It's not what you want that makes you fat, but what you get.

More cotton will grow in a crooked row than in a straight one.

Lots of hands make light work, but many mouths make empty dishes.

Old-Time Negro Proverbs

J. MASON BREWER

For the most part the proverbs given here have been taken from the speech of ex-slaves and elderly Negroes living in central Texas, if not on farms then with a rural background. However, such proverbs are to be heard in the homes of the best educated Negroes of the country as well as in those of the lowliest.

While the pithiest and most savory proverbs seem to have come directly out of the Negro's own wisdom as well as environment, some of them are but transmutations of older expressions into the language and experience of the Negro. Thus, as the Bible has it, "Whatsoever a man soweth, that shall he also reap." As the old-time Negro has it, *Yuh kin sow in mah fiel' ef yuh wants to, but when hit comes, hit'll be in your'n an' yuh won't know how it got dere.*

As a slave, so far as his life was reflected in song and proverb, the Negro's primary interest seems to have been in God and religion. The much exploited "Work Songs" and the proverbs dealing with work probably developed during and after Reconstruction, at a time when the master no longer provided food, when the Negro had to rustle for himself and family and could not logically continue to pray God to take him "home" and free him from slavery.

Ol' Massa take keer o' himself, but de niggah got to go ter God conveys about the same idea as that in a saying once current among vigorous frontiersmen: "Lord, take care of the poor and us rich devils will look out after ourselves."

God and Freedom were with many slaves synonymous. *Yuh mought as well die wid de chills ez wid de fever* not only goes back to a common plantation malady but was interpreted for me as meaning, "You might as well get killed trying to escape as to remain a slave and die in slavery."

De quickah death, de quickah heaben, I heard an old woman say, and then she sang a song to enforce the idea of the proverb:

> Oh Freedom, Oh Freedom,
> Befoh Ah'd be uh slave
> Ah'd be buried en mah grave
> An' go home tuh mah Jesus an' be saved.

Much of the slave's time was spent in trying to find ways and means of escape. *Don' crow tel yuh git out o' de woods; dey mought be uh beah behin' de las' tree* meant, "Don't be careless about talking to people you see, until you get to the Underground Railway. You might get caught and returned to your owner."

Don' say no mo' wid yo' mouf dan yo' back kin stan' is an admonition to slaves to speak briefly and seldom, not only to the master but to other slaves. Frequently the slaves would discuss the possibilities of escape among themselves, and be overheard by the overseer, some tattling slave, or the master himself; then their backs paid for what their mouths had said.

Yuh got eyes to see and wisdom not to see was an injunction to the slaves not to tell on each other about the neglect of duty, some secret visit to a neighboring plantation, the theft of a chicken or a pig, or any other wrongdoing.

Evah bell yuh heah ain't uh dinnah bell carries with it the idea that there was also a "rising bell" in the morning which called the slaves up for the day's work.

Of my entire collection I assign the most originality to a proverb given me by Aunt Milly Hicks, of Austin: *De one dat drap de crutch de bes' gets de mos' biscuits.* "What do you mean," I asked, "by drappin' de crutch?" "Dat means," explained Aunt Milly, "de one dat curt'sy de bes'." "Oh," I said, "you mean the one that could bow the most polite?" "Yas, suh, yas, suh, dat's hit," answered Aunt Milly, "an' Ah allus got de biscuits." This proverb carries with it more than Aunt Milly could express. It expresses the idea that the most polite slave got the easiest job on the plantation.

Don't let no chickens die in yo han' implies the traditional connection of the Negro with chickens. The idea is that when the dead chicken is on the ground instead of in his hand evidence against the darkey who has killed it is less incriminating.

As inevitable as chickens is cotton. The obvious meaning of *Dirt show up de quickes' on de cleanes' cotton* is that a bad deed shows up more distinctly on a person of good character than on a person of already bad repute.

Distant stovewood am good stovewood meant that the biggest trees don't grow on the edge of the woods and that if a man wanted big back logs for his fireplace, he would have to go to extra trouble to get them.

Muddy roads call de milepost a liah belongs in the category of work proverbs.

Whut yuh don' hab in yo' haid yuh got ter hab in yo' feet. "Dat me'ns lak dis," said Uncle George McKay. "Lak ef yuh goes to de sto' fer some grub an' yuh fergits ter git it all, den yo' feet hab ter take yuh back anudder time fer whut yuh didn't git de fus' trip."

Dere's uh fambly coolness twixt de mule an' de singletree does not so much say that a mule sometimes kicks the singletree to which his traces are hooked as that two people bound together, as man and wife, do not always work in harmony.

Although the ex-slave was grateful to God for his freedom and "God's chillun" were not supposed to dance, among the first of the freedman's free acts was a surrender to the rhythmic nature inherited from his African ancestors. He had, as a slave, developed into an excellent clog and tap dancer but had not been free to cultivate the social dance. The "platform dance" and the "cakewalk" came with Emancipation and the freedman revelled as much in dance and song as he had formerly revelled in church worship. Certain proverbs seem to date from this era of dancing and the freer courtship that came with it.

Don't take no mo' tuh yo' heaht dan yuh kin kick offen yo' heels meant, "Don't worry so much about jilts in love that you can't go to a dance and dance your troubles away."

Evahbody say "goodnight" ain't gone home may have evolved as a result of this social freedom enjoyed by the freed slave, especially by courting couples.

The philosophy of Negro gossip is summed up in the proverb, *Two niggahs 'll draw fo' niggahs an' fo' niggahs draw eight.*

To the Negro religion is all-important. I began this account with slave proverbs on God and religion. I shall end with a proverb connected with religion and possibly with Reconstruction days: *Stah won' shoot fer de sinnah.* I have been told that when during Reconstruction Negroes attended a revival or a camp meeting and became converted, they would, if in doubt as to the authenticity of the conversion, ask, on the way home from the service, the Lord to "shoot" them a star. If then the convert saw a shooting star, it was a sign that he was really converted; but if he did not see a star shoot, there was still something lacking to his conversion—he had not yet been "born again"—and he was still a sinner. I recall hearing of only one instance in which a Negro who had asked for a shooting star failed to be convinced, when he saw it, that he had been born again and "washed in the blood of the Lamb."

A rousing revival was being conducted in Bell County, soon after the close of "the War," and finally Uncle Seth, who had not yet professed religion, was persuaded by his wife and chil-

dren, members of the church, to attend the meetings. Before
the services were over he had gone to the mourners' bench and
professed religion. But that night on the road home, his faith
began to weaken. Knowing well the star test, Uncle Seth
decided to try it out.

"Gawd," said Uncle Seth, "shoot me uh stah." In a few minutes he saw a star shoot across that part of the sky where he
had his gaze directed. Not satisfied with this, however, when
about halfway home, he repeated again, "Gawd, shoot me
anudder stah." In a few minutes he saw another star shoot.
This was not yet sufficient to get up Uncle Seth's faith; so when
he was almost home, he said, "Gawd, looks lak hit's kinda hard
fo' me to get up mah faith. Ah tells Yuh what Yuh do. Shoot
me de moon."

"The moon!" replied God. "I wouldn't shoot yuh de moon
fer all de niggers in Texas."

Dichos from Austin

SOLEDAD PÉREZ

Spanish-speaking people have a very rich heritage of proverbs
and sayings. Here is a selection from a large number that I
noted among the Mexican population of Austin during the
course of a year's time. These *dichos* are typical rather than
unique; they could no doubt be found almost anywhere else in
the Spanish Southwest. First I have given as literal a transla-
tion as possible and then a rendering into idiomatic English
or the equivalent English proverb or saying if one exists.

A boca cerrada no entra mosca.
 Flies do not enter a closed mouth. A closed mouth catches
 no flies.
A buen hambre no hay mal pan.
 To a good appetite no bread is bad. Hunger is the best sauce.
Ahora es cuando, yerbabuena, le has de dar sabor al caldo.

Now, mint, is when you must give the soup flavor. Strike while the iron is hot. Now's your chance.

Al haber gallinas hay gallos.

Where there are hens there are cocks. Sugar draws flies.

Al mal paso, darle prisa.

Hurry over a bad road. When the going is bad, hurry. The sooner, the better.

Al que le apriete el zapato, que se lo afloje.

He whose shoe pinches him should loosen it. The foot best knows where the shoe pinches.

Al que le duela la muela, que se la saque.

He whose molar hurts should have it taken out. This expression has the same meaning as the one above.

Al que no le guste el juste, que lo tire y monte en pelo.

He who does not like the saddle may throw it away and ride bareback. Take it or leave it. Here the word *juste* replaces the correct *fuste*.

Arrieros somos y por el camino andamos.

We are mule drivers and we are walking on the road. We are human beings and walk along the road of life together. We are all in the same boat.

Cada oveja con su pareja.

Every sheep with its partner. Birds of a feather flock together.

Cada pobrete lo que tiene mete.

Every poor man contributes what he has. To put in one's two cents' worth.

Cincuenta años en la marina y no conoce una ballena.

Fifty years in the navy and he doesn't know a whale.

Cuando ven el palo caído todos quieren hacer leña.

When people see a fallen tree, all want to make firewood. The tree is no sooner down but everyone runs for his hatchet. This expression is applied to people who begin to take advantage of someone who has suffered misfortune.

Da y ten, y harás bien.

Give and take and you will do good. Be liberal but prudent. Give and spend and God will send.

Dar atole con el dedo.

To give gruel with the finger. To deceive with words or acts, especially to deceive one's husband.

Dar gato por liebre.

To give a cat for a hare. To deceive, to cheat.

Díme con quien andas y te diré quien eres.

Tell me with whom you associate and I will tell you who you are. A man is known by the company he keeps.

Dios los creó y ellos se juntan.

God created them and they get (or flock) together.

El flojo y el mezquino dos veces andan el camino.

The lazy and the stingy walk the same road twice.

El hábito no hace al monje.

The habit does not make the monk. Clothes do not make the man.

El pan ajeno hace al hijo bueno.

The bread of another makes the son good. He who has to work for his bread appreciates what he had at his father's table.

El pecado se dice pero el pecador no.

The sin may be told but not the sinner's name.

El que boca tiene a Roma va.

He who has a mouth goes to Rome. He who speaks is heard.

El que la hace la paga.

He who does it will pay for it.

El que no quiere ruido que no críe cochinos.

He who doesn't want noise should not raise hogs. Don't make trouble if you don't want trouble.

El que no se arriesga no pasa la mar.

He who takes no risks will never cross the sea. Nothing venture, nothing gain.

El que para tonto nace hasta guaje no para.

He who is born (to be) a fool will not stop until he becomes an (empty) gourd. He who is born a fool is never cured. Once a fool, always a fool. The *guaje* is a dry empty gourd.

El que por su cuenta es buey hasta la coyunda lame.

He who allows himself to be made into an ox will even lick the (yoking) straps. He who allows himself to be made into a cuckold must wear the horns.

El que solo vive solo muere.

He who lives alone dies alone.

El que tiene buen voto se hinca a cualquier santo.

He who has a good votive offering may kneel to any saint.

En martes ni te cases ni te embarques.

Do not marry or board a ship on Tuesday. The superstitious beliefs Mexicans associate with Tuesday correspond to those Americans associate with Friday.

Entre la espada y la pared.

Between the sword and the wall. Between the devil and the deep blue sea.

Entre menos burros, más elotes.

The fewer donkeys, the more cobs. The fewer, the better (cheer). *Elotes* (corn cobs), dried as well as green, are given burros to eat.

Hasta que te cases, mira lo que haces.

Until you marry, watch what you do. Until you marry, watch your step.

Hay muchachos viejos y viejos muchachos.

There are young men who are old and old men who are young. Some young men are old, some old men are young.

Hay muertos que no hacen ruido y son sus penas mayores.

There are dead men who make no noise and their sorrows are greater. This saying is applied to secretive or hypocritical persons whose true character is discovered by accident.

Haz bien y no mires a quien.

Do good and don't see whom you do it to. Do good and shame the Devil.

Ir por lana y volver trasquilado.

To go for wool and come out shorn.

La limpieza no está reñida con la pobreza.

Cleanliness has not fallen out with poverty. Poverty is no excuse for uncleanliness.

La necesidad tiene cara de hereje.

Necesidad (poverty) has the face of a heretic. Beggars aren't welcome.

Las doce en punto y el buey arando.

It is twelve o'clock and the ox is (still) plowing. It is twelve o'clock and all is well.

Las doce han dado y el gato armado.

It is twelve o'clock and the cat (is) armed. This means that people have been engaged in a particular activity for hours but the end is not in sight.

Le dan en el codo y aprieta la mano.

They ask him for some money and he closes his hand.

Lo que se hereda no se hurta.

What is inherited is not stolen.

Los golpes hacen al jinete.

Hard knocks make the rider. Practice makes perfect.

Los muertos al pozo y los vivos al negocio.

The dead to the grave and the living to their business. Let the dead bury the dead.

Más vale andar solo que mal acompañado.

It is better to walk alone than in bad company.

Más vale malo por conocido que bueno por conocer.

Better a known evil than an unknown good.

Más vale pobre que solo.

It is better to be poor than to be alone.

Más vale sucio en casa y no limpio en el camposanto.

It is better to be dirty at home than clean in the cemetery. It is better not to overwork and live longer than to overwork and die quickly.

Más vale tuerto que ciego.

Better to be half blind than all blind.

Más vale maña que fuerza.

Craft is better than force.

Nadie sabe para quien trabaja.

No one knows for whom he works. This expression means that persons who leave money and goods never know who will enjoy what they leave behind.

Ni tanto que queme al santo, ni tanto que no le alumbre.

Not so much (candlelight) as will burn the saint, nor so little as will leave him in the dark. Be moderate.

No es tan bravo el león como lo pintan.

The lion is not as fierce as he is pictured to be. The Devil is not so black as he is painted.

No le busques tres patas al gato porque le encuentras cuatro.

Do not look for three of the cat's paws because you will find four. Do not look for trouble, because you will find it. Let sleeping dogs lie.

No hay mal que por bien no venga, ni enfermedad que dure cien años.

There is no evil that does not bring some good with it nor illness that lasts a hundred years. It's an ill wind that blows no good.

No hay más amigo que Dios ni más pariente que un peso.

There is no better friend than God nor better relative than a peso.

No tener ni saliva.

Not even to have saliva. Poor as a church mouse.

No todos los que chiflan son arrieros.

Not all who whistle are mule drivers. This saying means that appearances are deceiving.

Ojos que no ven, corazón que no siente.

Eyes that see not, heart that feels not. What the eye sees not, the heart rues not. Out of sight, out of mind.

Panza llena, corazón contento.

A full belly, a happy heart. When the belly is full, the bones are at rest.

Para eso son los bienes, para remediar los males.

Goods are for this, to remedy evils.

Parece que no quiebra un plato, y todos los tiene mochos.

It seems as if she wouldn't break a plate, but all her plates are chipped. It seems as if butter wouldn't melt in her mouth. This expression is used in speaking of a person who seems to be very innocent but is not.

Pobre del pobre que al cielo no va
Lo friegan aquí y lo friegan allá.

He is poor indeed who does not go to heaven; they beat him here and they will beat him there.

Quien todo lo quiere, todo lo pierde.

He who wants everything loses everything. He who covets all loses all. Want all, lose all.

Sacar dinero hasta de las piedras.

To get money even out of the rocks. To squeeze blood out of a turnip.

Tener suerte de gato boca arriba.

To have the luck of a cat (who lands) mouth right side up. To land on your feet.

Tonto y rudo pero pesudo.

Stupid and unpolished but rich.

Un garbanzo de a libra.

A chick pea that weighs one pound. This expression is used referring to a rare or unusual occurrence.

Un peso vale más que cien consejos.

A peso is worth more than a hundred counsels.

SUPERSTITIONS

▼▼▼

The Human Comedy in
Folk Superstitions

TRESSA TURNER

During several years of teaching prior to 1925, in Southwest Texas State Teachers College at San Marcos, R. C. Harrison canvassed students, representing scores of counties and varying cultures, for folk superstitions. Following his death, in 1927, Mrs. Harrison turned the extensive collection thus made over to the Texas Folklore Society. From it have been taken the majority of superstitions described in this account. It has been supplemented, however, by two other collections: one that I assembled from my home town, Kildare, in Cass County, Texas, and from Flatonia, in Fayette County, where I taught; the other made by J. Frank Dobie from students in the Agricultural and Mechanical College of Oklahoma, at Stillwater, where he taught during the years 1923-1925, plus a considerable number of superstitions from Texas sources.

Perhaps I have not arranged the superstitions as well as Mr. Harrison or Mr. Dobie might have done, but I hold the belief that I have more right to write of them than either of these gentlemen. It is mine by virtue of a superstitious gesture attending my advent on this earth. Arriving a month ahead of time, I caught my father at work away from home. He rushed thither as quickly as possible, but arrived only in time to see my black mammy, Aunt Mattie Faust, solemnly marching around the house with me—not yet bathed, but closely bundled in an old quilt—in her arms. Although he had fathered seven children before me, such proceedings were not familiar to him. When he asked Aunt Mattie what she meant, she, scorning his ignorance, replied: "Dis gonna keep de chile from having de measles and wetting de bed, whut wuks a woman to death." As to the efficacy of Aunt Mattie's gesture, I have no comment. My only point is that, coming as it did, it gives me a peculiar right to deal with superstitions.

MARRIAGE, LOVE, AND COURTSHIP

If you sleep with a piece of wedding cake under your pillow, you will dream of the one that you will marry.

Cut a boiled egg in equal parts, remove the yolk from one half, and put salt in its place. Then fit the halves back together and eat the whole egg just before retiring for the night. Whoever brings you water in your dreams will be the one you will marry. A kindred version of this superstition directs you to eat a thimbleful of salt just before going to bed. You will dream that someone brings you water, and that person will be your future husband or wife. If the latter version is carried out by two girls, silent all the while, it is called a "Dumb Supper"— a very old superstition.

Another form of "Dumb Supper" is for a group of girls to prepare food in unison, eat equal parts of it at the same time, and then all go to the corner of a dark room and stand. No word must be spoken during the supper or period of standing. After a while each of the girls who is to marry will see her husband's image appear on the dark wall in front of her. The girl who does not see an image will never marry.

Put a holly leaf with nine stickers on it under your pillow, and you will then dream of the one you will marry.

Sleep with mistletoe under your pillow and you will dream of your future husband or wife.

Sleep with a mirror under your pillow for three nights, letting the third night fall on Friday. On the third night you will dream of the person that you will marry. Another version has it that one will dream of the same person all three nights.

To dream of a death is a sign of a wedding, of a funeral, an invitation to a wedding.

To dream of a baby is a sign that one will be happily married; but to dream of being married means that one will never get married. Mrs. R. O. Crane of Cuero says that she has known the latter superstition to fail.

If a girl will hang a horseshoe over her door, she can marry the first unmarried man who walks under it.

Place three bowls of water on a table, one full of water, another full of milk, and the third one empty. Blindfold a girl and have her reach for the bowls. If she touches the one with water in it, she will be an old maid. If she touches the one with milk in it, she will marry. But if she touches the empty one, she will die soon. Imagine how a trusting girl must have felt upon touching an empty bowl!

On Hallowe'en night a girl should take a comb and a mirror and go to a vacant house to comb her hair. If she will look at her mirror as she combs, she will see the image of her future husband looking over her shoulder into the mirror. This superstition is a good one, as good as the one Keats used in "The Eve of Saint Agnes."

On New Year's Eve go from one room to another and throw a shoe over your shoulder; then look in a mirror, and you'll see the one that you are going to marry.

Count fifty white horses, and the first unmarried man that you shake hands with after counting the fiftieth will be the man you will marry.

When a quilt is finished at a quilting bee, all hands gather around for the shaking of the cat, which must be black. The cat is tossed upon the quilt and is generously shaken till he jumps off. If he runs off close to an unmarried woman—and of course, he will, being shaken in her direction—she will be the next one of the group to marry.

By looking at high noon on the first day of May into a well —an old-time dug well—that has no shed over it, a girl can find out whom she will marry, or whether she will marry. If she is to marry, her future husband's image will appear quite distinctly on the surface of the water. But if she is not to marry, a coffin will appear. I know several women who saw strangers in wells. Later they met and married men whom they recognized by images they had seen in wells. The same knowledge can be obtained by looking into an open well at midnight on Hallowe'en or on May the first.

To find out if your sweetheart loves you, strike a match and let it burn as long as it will. If it burns up without breaking into two pieces, your sweetheart loves you.

You have as many sweethearts as you have white spots on your finger nails.

A girl will marry soon if she stumbles near the top of a stairway, but if she stumbles near the bottom, many a day will pass before she marries.

Cut a strand of hair from a girl's head and another from a boy's. Place both strands over a door. If both the boy and girl walk under the hairs, they will marry each other.

Upon hearing the first coo of a dove in the spring, take off your left stocking and look in the heel of it. There you will find a hair the color of that of your future wife or husband.

If the sun shines while it is raining, turn over a rock and look carefully under it for a hair. If you find one, it will be the color of that of your future wife or husband.

Don't sweep under the feet of a girl; if you do, she cannot get married.

If a maiden completes a patchwork quilt alone, she will never marry.

If a girl peels all the bark off an elm or blackgum toothbrush, she will lose her beau. (A hackberry twig makes a good toothbrush, too.)

When your shoestring comes untied, your sweetheart is standing on his head to see you.

When a pin comes out perpendicularly to your dress, your beau is out driving with another girl.

If you stump your toe, kiss your thumb and you'll see your beau.

If it is raining when a couple marry, they will have a dreary life.

If a girl, when washing dishes or clothes, gets her dress wet over her stomach, she will marry a drunkard. If she sings at the table, she will marry a crazy man. If she has a little coffee in her cup and pours more into it, she will marry a widower.

If the left thumb is on top when a man clasps his hands together, he will rule the house; if the right is on top, his wife will rule. If a girl's second toe is longer than her big toe, she will rule the house.

Then after you have found someone to marry, you must listen to admonition and warnings in regard to the wedding itself. A bride should wear something old as well as something new, something borrowed, and something blue. It is unlucky to try on the wedding ring before it is put on the bride's finger at the altar. It is bad luck for a bride to look at herself in the mirror before she is dressed or to glance behind herself while on the way to church. It is lucky to marry at full noon or with the flowing tide, or to see a flight of birds while on the way to the church.

> Monday for health, Tuesday for wealth,
> Wednesday the best day of all;
> Thursday for losses, Friday for crosses,
> Saturday for no luck at all.

The next rhyme for the different months of the year runs:

> Married when the year is new,
> He'll be loving, kind, and true.

> When February birds do mate,
> You wed, nor dread your fate.

> If you wed when March winds blow,
> Joy and sorrow both you'll know.

> Marry in April when you can,
> Joy for maiden and for man.

> Marry in the month of May,
> And you'll surely rue the day.

> Marry when June roses grow,
> Over land and sea you'll go.

> Those who in July do wed,
> Must labor for their bread.

> Whoever wed in August be,
> Many a change is sure to see.

> Marry in September's shine,
> Your living will be rich and fine.

> If in October you do marry,
> Love will come, but riches tarry.

> If you wed in bleak November,
> Only joys will come, remember.

> When December's snows fall fast
> Marry, and true love will last.

Upon the color in which one marries, it is predicted that:

> Married in gray, you'll go far away.
> Married in black, you'll wish yourself back.

Married in brown, you'll live out of town.
Married in red, you'll wish yourself dead.
Married in pearl, you'll live in a whirl.
Married in green, ashamed to be seen.
Married in yellow, ashamed of your fellow.
Married in blue, he'll always be true.
Married in pink, your spirits will sink.
Married in white, you have chosen aright.

GOOD LUCK SIGNS

It is good luck to carry a buckeye in your pocket; to wear a dime in the bottom of your shoe; to dream of a basket of eggs or of climbing stairs; to find a spider in your room, provided you do not kill it; to spit on a horseshoe and then take ten steps backwards; to touch the hump on a hunchback; to wear around the neck a string with a piece of clover tied to it; for a chaparral cock to run across the road in front of you; and for daddy longlegs to walk over you.

You will have good luck all day if you put your left foot to the floor first as you get out of bed in the morning.

If a buzzard's shadow goes directly over your head, you will have good luck the next day.

See a pin and pick it up,
All the day you'll have good luck;
See a pin and leave it lie,
To good luck you'll say "Goodbye."

BAD LUCK SIGNS

It is bad luck to go into the house with a rake, a hoe, or an axe on the shoulder; to walk over a grave; to trim the fingernails on Friday; to kill a bat, an owl, a blue bird, or a cricket; to dream of fruit out of season; to sweep the floor after dark (if you sweep the floor after dark the witches will ride you); to sit on a trunk; to walk with one shoe on and one off; to put the right shoe on first; to turn over a chair; to rock an empty chair; to carry a broom while walking; to give away parsley; to walk under a ladder; to walk over an ant bed (if you walk over an ant bed and do not step back over it, the ants will build nests in your grave); to wear one's wedding dress after the wedding; to kick the left foot against something and pass on without going back over the object.

It is bad luck to raise an umbrella in the house. On this superstition a clerk in a dry goods store said, "I have seen many customers refuse to let the clerk open an umbrella that the customer was inspecting."

If a ball team, while on its way to play a game, passes dogs fighting, it will lose the game.

If you go somewhere on one road and return by another, you will have bad luck before you get home.

Never turn back when you have started somewhere, unless you make a cross in the road and spit on the cross.

If a black cat crosses your trail, turn back or go around him, or you will have bad luck. In Dallas two boys walked half the night trying to go around black cats which appeared at every turn they made. Finally they turned back and started home. Just as they reached home, the superstitious one of the two found a $10.00 bill!

It is bad luck for a family to move a black cat. In fact, it is bad luck to move a cat of any color. If a cat comes to a house and then leaves of its own accord, it is a sign of bad luck. But if a cat comes and stays, it is a sign of good luck. If a cat that comes and stays is black, it will bring prosperity. For every cat that one kills the killer will have seven years of bad luck.

For a rabbit to cross your trail going to the left is bad luck; to the right, good luck. Too, if a rabbit crosses your trail, calamity will come to the errand that you are on. By spitting and saying, "Damn that rabbit," you can ward off bad luck.

If a person doesn't knock on dead wood when he brags on himself, he will have bad luck. (Knocking on one's head won't suffice.)

If you spill salt and don't burn some of it, you will have bad luck. It is bad luck to borrow salt — and bad luck to thank anyone who lends you salt.

It is bad luck to pick up scissors that you yourself have dropped. If, however, some one else picks them up it is good luck.

Kiss your thumb to ward off bad luck when you stump your toe.

If a pupil drops his school books, he will have bad lessons the next day, unless he stamps his feet on the books.

Sleeping in the light of the moon will cause a person to go crazy.

A person will have bad luck if he looks at the new moon through trees or brush. If he looks at a new moon through a glass window, he will have bad luck all that moon.

If a person is sitting when he hears the first coo of a dove in a season, he will have bad luck, but if he is standing, he will have good luck.

If two persons walking on opposite sides of a post or some other such object will say simultaneously, "Yellow," they can ward off bad luck or a quarrel. Or, one may say, "Bread and butter," and the other, "Come to supper."

If a person is hit with a broom, he will have bad luck if he does not spit on the broom.

If a card player is having a run of bad luck, let him change his method of picking up the cards. For instance, if he has been picking up the cards as they are dealt, let him wait till the last one has been dealt before he touches his cards. So, too, if a man's betting is lucky, let him increase it by half. A person standing behind a player may "joner" (Jonah) him. It is bad luck at any time to carry a two-dollar bill, but poker players consider such a bill especially unlucky and will hardly receive one in a game.

To hear a screech owl's cry near a house is a sign of bad luck, perhaps loss of money, sickness, or death in the family. Bad luck can be avoided by turning over three times an old shoe or by a complete turning of all pockets present. I have been present at a good many turnings of the pockets.

If one's right eye itches, he is going to cry; the left, be pleased. The one whose right eye itches may "pass the buck" by saying to the person next to him, "My right eye itches." My schoolmates and I used to pass this sentence around till the teacher would ask what we were saying — which was exactly what we wanted her to ask us. Then we would tell her, thus passing the buck to her.

It is bad luck for a person to pull off his hat and toss it on a bed.

Never start anything on Friday that cannot be finished on Friday — or on Saturday, according to an Oklahoma version of the superstition.

A person will go blind if a devil's horse spits in his eye. Mexicans claim that if a cow swallows a devil's horse, which she may easily do while grazing, she will die. Like many another harmless creature, the mantis is supposed to be poisonous.

Burn up the hair that comes out when you comb your hair, or birds will build nests with it, which will cause you to go blind.

It is bad luck to step over a person who is lying down. If one steps over an adolescent who is lying down and does not step back over him in exactly the same way, the adolescent person will stop growing. If a child sits in or climbs out of a window, he will stop growing.

If children are allowed to play in the fire, they will develop the habit of wetting the bed.

If you dream of a snake, it means that you will have an enemy; of muddy water, that you will have trouble. Dreams told before breakfast come true.

It is bad luck to sing at the table. A more detailed version of this superstition has it that you will lose all of your teeth if you sing at the table.

It is bad luck for a dog to howl near the house of a sick person. Once a neighbor of ours was sick with a fever. His bird dog came and howled under his window about twelve o'clock one night. The women who were sitting up with him went home and sent their husbands back so that they would be there to help lay the man out. The next morning the man was dead. The women's faith had been rewarded.

If you kill a frog, your cow will either go dry or give bloody milk. I know of one instance of a frog's reproving a man's conscience for a debt he owed the local groceryman—mostly for chewing tobacco. This man's farm lay along Frazier Creek. Such heavy rains came in the spring that the creek went on a rampage, overflowed, and washed the farmer's crop away. Late one afternoon he rode his horse down to the fields along the creek. As he sat on his horse looking at where his crop had been, a big bullfrog over in the creek kept booming out, "You owe me; you owe me." Finally the man said to the frog, "What do I owe you for?" Thereupon about a thousand little rain frogs answered back in a rattling chorus, "Terbaccer, terbaccer, terbaccer, terbaccer."

To see one buzzard is a sign of sorrow. Sorrow can be avoided by watching the buzzard until he goes out of sight or flaps his wings, which a buzzard only occasionally does. I have seen many people exercising these precautions against sorrow. The turkey buzzard at Kildare forewarns of so many things that his powers defy a strict classification, but the following rhyme fairly well covers them:

> One for sorrow, two for joy,
> Three for a letter, four for a boy,
> Five for silver, six for gold,
> Seven for a secret that's never been told.

It is pretty commonly known that for a girl to whistle or a hen to crow is a sign of bad luck, and from the belief have come these rhymes:

> A whistling girl and a crowing hen
> Would drive the devil out of his den.

> A whistling gal and a crowing hen
> Always come to some bad end.

One of my earliest remembrances is of my grandmother's rhymed warning against the whistling girl. It bothered me until Uncle Jim Huggins told me that:

> A whistling gal and a flock of sheep
> Are two good things for a farmer to keep.

Thereafter I whistled peacefully, but the poor hen is still under the curse of bringing bad luck when she "outs" with her crowing.

If you dream of muddy water, a nude person, or of being married, someone in your family is going to die soon. If you dream of losing a front tooth, you will lose a relative in death soon; of a back tooth, a friend.

If you bathe between Christmas and New Year, someone in your family will die soon. This certainly belongs to the days before hot water and warm bath rooms.

If a man trims his fingernails on Friday, his wife will die before the next Friday.

If a rooster flaps his wings after dark or after he has gone to roost, someone in his owner's family will die soon. A crowing hen is thought by some to presage death.

If three people look in a mirror at the same time, the youngest of the three will die at once.

If two people comb a third person's hair, the older of the two will die soon.

Sweep under a sick person's bed, and he will never get up.

A shooting star is a sign of death.

If a person has a mole on his ear, it is a sign that he will drown.

If you pass a funeral procession, someone in your family will die soon. If you count the cars or wagons in a funeral procession, you will die soon. A rain upon a newly made grave means that someone in the deceased's family will die soon. Someone in the neighborhood will die soon if a grave is allowed to stand open. If a corpse is brought into a house feet first, someone living in the house will die before the year has passed.

Any kind of owl or bat in the house foretells death. At Kildare the horned owl, usually called the hoot owl, is particularly dreaded because of a belief that if he comes to sit on the foot of a bed and cry, the person to whom the bed belongs will die soon. Though the belief is widely held, my mother tells the only story that I know wherein an owl actually sat on a bed and prophesied death. This is her story. A Mr. Johnson was killed by a log train. At the very hour of his death, as it was later ascertained, an owl flew into the Johnson house, which was unscreened, and lit on Johnson's bed. It began its mournful sounds and refused to be removed. Yet when the report of the accident came, the owl left immediately. It would be hard to convince that family that the owl's visit was merely a coincidence.

Niles Graham, of Austin, woke up one night last summer to find an owl perched on the foot of his bed. No member of his family has died since, but one of his dogs had rabies and had to be shot.

Measure a baby's length, and you measure its coffin.

If a baby is allowed to look in a mirror before it is a year old, it will die before it is three.

If an old clock stops before it is run down or starts before it is wound up, someone will die soon. Glen Van Noy of the Agricultural and Mechanical College, Stillwater, Oklahoma, tells of two occasions when clocks stopped simultaneously with the death of people. One time he was sitting up with a person who was very ill. Just before the person died, Mr. Van Noy chanced to glance at a clock in the room, and it was running. Presently he looked at it again, and it had stopped, apparently at the exact moment that the sick person had died. Another time he was sitting up with his wife in a hospital in Miami, Florida, when a woman next door died. The nurse waiting on the woman told him that her watch stopped at the moment the patient died. "Grandfather's Clock," a song popular during the latter part of the nineteenth century, depended upon this motif. In January, 1935, the grandmother of a girl in Flatonia High School died, and the clock in her room stopped at the moment of her death. When I was told about this occasion, another girl present said that when her great-grandfather died, the clock in his room struck one hundred forty-seven times without pausing. This strikes me as the prize-winner.

A mirror that falls from the wall presages death. To break a mirror warns of a death. Death may be warded off by burying a piece of the broken mirror.

There will be a death in your family soon if someone sweeps toward you as you are entering the house.

A person who plants a cedar or a willow tree will die when

the tree grows to such size that its shade is large enough to cover his grave. This superstition is said to have come from the mountains of East Tennessee. It has probably excused lots of men from the work of planting shade trees.

If a person casts an evil eye upon an animal, the animal will die.

A horse or dog will die if his picture is taken.

LETTERS, NEWS, AND COMPANY

To see a red bird or to dream of a dead person is a sign that you will see someone unexpectedly. Also a buzzard's shadow going over foretells seeing someone unexpectedly.

If you pass a Japanese, kiss the back of your hand and you will see someone that you have long wanted to see.

If a rooster crows at the dead of night, ghosts are going to appear.

If a person takes two pieces of bread at one time, it is a sign that someone is coming hungry.

To drop a knife is a sign that a man is coming; a fork, a woman. The direction in which the knife or fork points is the direction from which the company will come.

If a straw falls from a broom that is being used, someone is coming.

A rooster's crowing means that company is coming—and from the direction that his tail points. If a rooster crows right in the door, it means hasty news. Sometimes, however, his crowing may have an entirely different meaning. Once an aunt of mine was spending the day with a neighbor. A rooster crowed so persistently that my aunt remarked that someone was coming, to which the other woman replied that it was a sign she was needed at home. As my aunt had not heard that version of the rooster's crowing, it riled her, and she went home in a huff.

If a housewife leaves a kettle uncovered, someone is coming.

If you drop a dishrag, someone nastier than you is coming.

You will hear hasty news if a "news bee" buzzes around

you; important news, if a glow is apparent after a candle has been snuffed.

If you find a pin, pick it up and you will get a letter. If a bird flies into the house, someone in the house will get a letter from across the ocean.

The number of grounds that float on your coffee cup denotes the number of letters that you will receive the next day. Also the number of gray horses that you see one day indicates the number of letters to be received the next day.

When the bottom of a person's left foot itches, he is going where he is not wanted; the right, he is going to walk on strange land.

When the hem of your dress turns up, spit on it and you will get a new dress. When a measuring worm crawls over a garment that you are wearing, he is measuring a new one for you.

When a butterfly lights on a girl's dress, she will get a new one the color of the butterfly. The following superstition makes a girl earn the dress prophesied. If she will bite off the head of a butterfly that lights on her dress and then throw the head over her right shoulder, she will get a new dress the color of the butterfly. To see a butterfly means that before the day is over you will see a friend wearing a dress the color of the butterfly.

If you spit on yourself—your hands, for instance—you will get a pair of new gloves soon.

You have a disappointment in store for you if you see one Catholic sister or nun; an agreeable surprise if you see two.

If two people bump heads, they are going to sleep together the following night.

If two people hoeing near each other strike their hoes together, it is a sign that they will have something good to eat for dinner and also that they will hoe together the next year.

WISHES

Make a wish and then open the Bible in three different

places. If you find "And it came to pass," your wish will come true.

If two people say things simultaneously, they should link their little fingers and make a wish. The one who finishes first should say, "Longfellow"; the other, "Shortfellow." Together they must say, "Hope this wish may never be broke." Or, they may finish by saying each other's names.

If you make a wish on seeing a falling star before it goes out of sight, your wish will come true.

Spit on a bridge, then go away, and the wish will come true.

If you make a wish while trying on another person's shoe, your wish will come true.

Place a person's ring on his finger, making a wish as you do so. Tell the person when he may pull off the ring, and if he does not remove the ring before the appointed time, your wish will come true.

Swallow whole a brown bean found among a bowl of white ones, making a wish as you do so. The wish will come true.

Kiss the hem of your dress when it turns up, making a wish as you do so.

At the sight of a white mule, a white horse—particularly two white horses—or a hay wagon—"send" a wish; but you must "stamp" it if you expect it to get to its destination and bring a return. To "stamp" it, place the tip of the right forefinger, or the ball of the thumb, to the end of the tongue as if licking a stamp, then press the finger-tip, or thumb, down on the palm of the left hand, as if adjusting a stamp to an envelope, giving the "stamp" a smart pat or slap so that it will stick. According to one version of the belief, the wish will come true only after one hundred horses have been seen and counted, the stamping act to be enacted for each horse. A white mule counts for twenty. Children, with whom this form of wishing is popular, usually lose count long before they reach the hundredth white horse.

If you drop a pair of scissors and they stick up in the floor, make a wish on them before picking them up.

MONEY

If you say "Money" three times before a shooting star goes out of sight, you will get some money.

If you do not put your tongue in the place from which a tooth is pulled, you will get some money, maybe a gold tooth.

A person who has money in his hand when he sees a new moon will make money the whole month. If you will shake your purse at a new moon and say, "Fill my purse full of money," you will get lots of money.

A person whose eyebrows grow together across his forehead will be rich some day; also the growth is a sign of jealousy.

Whoever can catch a hummingbird—or put salt on any bird's tail—will be rich some day.

If a man has a dime in his shoe when he marries, he will always have money enough.

If you dream of a diamond, you will be rich some day.

If your left hand itches in the palm, you are going to handle money; if the right palm itches, you should scratch it on wood, making at the same time a wish; you will get some money and your wish both.

Count the "miller" bugs on water. For every bug counted, you will get a dollar.

When you see a lizard, say to him, "Lizard, lizard, show your money." If he shows his money, you will get some money. A lizard shows his money by opening wide his mouth or flaring his jaws so that something red may be seen. The chameleon shows his money best. The sandsifter will drop his tail if sufficiently excited, but he will not show his money.

In order to have money the year round, bake a poppyseed cake at Christmas and have some of it left for New Year.

People who burn onion peels will have money.

REMEDIES AND CURES[1]

Rub a wart vigorously with a gold band ring and say, "Hocus, pocus, presto, warts, go away." Soon the wart will disappear.

[1]See the section entitled "Cures" in the present volume.

Rub spittle on a wart seven times a day for seven days to make it go away, or spit in one hand and rub the wart with the spittle for five minutes, saying as you rub, "Wart, wart, go away." The wart will disappear within five days.

Rub a wart with a bean and throw the bean in a well. When the bean decays, the wart will go away. Or steal a piece of bacon from a neighbor, rub the wart with it, and then bury the bacon. When it decays the wart will go away. A woman in Flatonia has a very learned brother-in-law who removed a wart in this way. If a remedy works for the learned, surely it must be effective for the less learned.

Rub a wart with the jawbone of a horse or mule; hide the bone from the one who has the wart; if he cannot find it, his wart will go away.

A raw Irish potato carried in a pocket or a nutmeg tied to a string and worn around the neck will prevent rheumatism.

A tea made from bear grass roots will cure rheumatism.

A sure cure for rheumatism is extract of poison oak. Boil the leaves and stems of poison oak till the juice is well extracted. Then take two drops of the juice in four ounces of water before each meal.

Equal parts of turpentine, sweet-gum, and beef tallow melted and mixed make a good compound for rheumatism. Rub the mixture on the rheumatic parts.

Boil snake root till all the juice is out. Mix the juice with water and whiskey and take every two hours for rheumatism, jaundice, and chills.

Tea made from the white lime of chicken droppings or from sheep balls is a cure for baby's colic.

A sure cure for four-month colic is asafoetida in whiskey.

To stop the colic in a baby, pull a hair from the mother's head and place it on the baby's head.

To prevent the nose from bleeding, drop a pair of scissors down the back steps, tie a piece of woolen string around the big toe, or wear a coin hung from a string around the neck.

Grease the bottom of a baby's feet with pure hog lard to cure a cold.

For a sore throat tie your old dirty sock around your neck at night.

A stye may be cured by rubbing it with a gold ring. Too, a person having a stye may get rid of it by going to the forks of a road and saying, "Stye, stye, leave my eye; catch the next one that passes by," or by saying to the first person who mentions the stye, "You're a lie."

Either butter and lime, or bear grass roots beaten to a pulp make a good poultice for boils, though nothing will draw a boil to a head so well as raw fat meat.

To cure hives in a baby, find a man who has never seen the child's father and have him blow his breath into the baby's mouth. Likewise have a seventh child to blow his breath into the baby's mouth. Catnip tea is good to break out the hives with.

A string of beads made of elderberries is good for a baby to teethe on. A string of beads made of different spices will cause a baby to teethe rapidly and painlessly.

Tickling a baby's feet will cause him to stammer.

An aged person can blow the fire out of sun-blisters.

Press your thumb hard against the roof of your mouth to stop a headache.

A sure cure for chills is to go to a dogwood tree before sunrise and stand beside it till the sun rises.

A successful cure for the itch is prickly ash salve. To make the salve, "Take prickly ash bark, scrape off the outside surface. Take about as much as you can hold between thumb and trigger finger, pieces to be about eight inches long. Put one cup of lard in a skillet, add the bark, and fry till brown. Now remove the bark and add one pound of sulphur. Stir till cold, then put in a close top can." This recipe was given to me by one whom I know to be proficient in the art of making prickly ash salve. Experience with this compound forces me to observe that the "close top" can is a measure of self-defense against the odors of prickly ash salve.

Tea made from the linings of a chicken gizzard settles the stomach; so does water in which writing paper has been soaked.

Mullein leaves boiled for several hours in a small quantity of water will leave a syrup that is a fine cough medicine.

Cut a green walnut and rub the fresh juicy part of the bark on a ringworm to kill it. Making a cross of soot on a kernel will cause it to disappear.

To cure a "bone-felon," run the affected finger around the neck of a bottle.

Asafoetida worn on a string around the neck will cure almost any kind of disease. In 1869 Uncle Jim Huggins was coming with his father and their families from Butler County, Alabama, to Caddo Parish, Louisiana. When they reached Rodney, Mississippi, they heard that the town was quarantined against smallpox. As Rodney was the most convenient place for them to cross the Mississippi River, they were anxious not to have to hunt another crossing. So Uncle Jim's father went on foot ahead of the wagons to see if he could arrange a rapid passage through Rodney. He consulted the town physician, who told him that if he would tie a bag of asafoetida around the neck of each person in the party, it would keep them from taking smallpox. This he did, and the whole wagon train passed safely through the smallpox-infested town.

A spider in a nutshell worn around the neck will ward off fever. In 1869 Uncle Jim Huggins and his folk arrived in Shreveport, Louisiana, where at that time there was an epidemic of yellow fever. Uncle Jim says that he saw men go out to the Red River docks and hang up eight or ten beef quarters to draw the yellow fever out of the town. He says that it worked, too, that the meat just turned yellow and fell from the bones.

Hot poultices of "dinner" tea leaves applied, one after the other, will cause the swelling to go out of a rattlesnake's bite.

The hoof-like substance from the inside of a horse's foreleg shaved finely and put in the hollow of a tooth will cure or prevent toothache.

To cure asthma go to a tree and measure your height on it, driving a nail into the tree to mark your height. When the bark grows over the nail, the asthma will go away.

Bluing water is mighty good for horses or dogs that have distemper.

K. Willard Brown, a Negro who lives at Kildare, recommends the following remedy as a cure for fits in a dog: "Resolve a fair size lump of bluestone in water. Den give it to him often and lots."

Give a foundered cow a lump of alum the size of a walnut and three raw eggs three times a day.

If a watchdog has ceased to do his duty, give him a piece of garlic on Christmas Eve and force him to eat it. He will then resume his duties.

WEATHER SIGNS

"When I want to believe that the weather is going to be good or bad, I make my own sign," says an Oklahoman. His remark probably explains the origin of many weather signs.

It will rain somewhere within sight every day in June if it rains June 1. The number of stars within a circle around the moon indicates the number of days that will pass before it rains.

It is going to rain soon when snakes fall from trees; when doodlebugs and angleworms come to the surface of the ground and crawl around; when ants fill their holes; when crickets congregate; and when the sun sets red for four consecutive days. If there is a red circle around the sun when it sets, it will rain three days later.

A snake hung up with his belly to the sun will bring rain. An old Cherokee Indian was by the Illinois River in the fall of 1923. He saw a stick come floating down the river with a snake on it; he went back the next day and saw another stick, much larger, with another snake on it. He predicted two floods, the second larger than the first. The floods came, all right.

When the wind blows from the east, rain will come; from the west, fair weather will come.

If a fog goes up, rain will come down; but if the fog falls, the weather will be clear. Heavy fogs for several mornings predict big rains forty days later.

Rain before seven,
Fair before eleven.

Evening red and morning gray
Will set the traveler on his way,
But evening gray and morning red
Will bring down rain upon his head.

If feathers get tangled in the mane of a horse you are riding, rain is coming.

If the sun shines while it is raining, it is a sign the devil is beating his wife around the stump, or that it will rain at the same time the next day.

If it thunders while it is raining, it is a sign that the Lord is scrubbing the floors of heaven. The thunder is the sound that his water barrels make as he rolls them over the floor.

If the sun sets clear, the next day will be fair.

A rainbow in the west means that a month of dry weather will follow.

"Dust devils" (whirlwinds) are an infallible sign of dry weather.

If it thunders shortly before or after Easter, there will be a dry summer.

A buzzard sailing high in the sky is a sign of dry weather. I have heard it said, too, that a buzzard's sailing high in the sky means that he was getting above rain clouds.

If birds hover in one place, or an old sow carries sticks and straw with which to build a bed, a cold snap is coming.

If it thunders in December before Christmas, there will be a bad cold spell of weather at the end of January or the first of February. If it thunders in February, it will frost in May and the following winter will be severe.

Wasps fly into the house when a cold spell approaches. So do flies, for that matter.

If a turtle bites a person, it will not turn loose till it hears thunder.

Stick a double-bitted axe up in the ground to split a norther.

Put feathers on the ground and stamp them to stop a rain.

Butcher hogs in the dark of the moon, and the meat will be firm and the lard will render abundantly; otherwise, the meat will be flabby and the lard skimpy.

Soap made in the light of the moon will be firm; in the dark of the moon, soft. The best time to make soap is between the last quarter and the full moon.

If you plant potatoes in the light of the moon, the new potatoes will grow large and be near the surface; but if you plant them in the dark of the moon, the potatoes will be small and grow deep in the soil. To prevent potatoes from rotting, borrow a potato from a neighbor and put it with your potatoes.

Melons and corn should be planted in the dark of the moon. The moon even affects the breeding of cattle, for a cow bred in the dark of the moon will have a male calf.

Cucumbers planted "on the twins" (during the zodiacal sign of Gemini) will bear a good crop.

Plant turnips on the twenty-fifth day of September.

The major part of a garden should be planted on Good Friday to insure a good yield.

Plant beans, peas, melons, all crops that yield fruit above the ground, before ten o'clock in the morning to keep the blooms from shedding before the fruit has formed.

MISCELLANEOUS SUPERSTITIONS

A dimple on the chin, the devil within.

For every gray hair pulled out of your head, two more will appear.

> Cold hands, warm heart; warm hands, cold heart.
> Cold hands, warm heart; cold feet, no sweetheart.

How to find lost articles: Throw a horseshoe over the right shoulder, and you will find the article in the direction to which the prongs of the shoe point; or spit in the palm of one hand and slap the forefinger of the other in the spit. Look for the lost article in the direction that the spit flies.

If a dog steps on a tooth that has been pulled, the child from whom it was pulled will grow a dog tooth.

If a person trims his fingernails on Sunday, he will do a wicked deed every day of the week.

A baby will grow up to be a thief if his fingernails are trimmed before he is a year old.

The following rhyme explains other complications that arise from the trimming of the fingernails:

> Cut your nails on Monday, cut them for news;
> Cut them on Tuesday, a pair of new shoes;
> Cut them on Wednesday, cut them for wealth;
> Cut them on Thursday to bring you good health;
> Cut them on Friday, cut them for woe;
> Cut them on Saturday, a journey to go.

Sneezing likewise has a variety of meanings that are determined by the day upon which one sneezes.

> Sneeze on Monday, sneeze for danger;
> Sneeze on Tuesday, kiss a stranger;
> Sneeze on Wednesday, sneeze for a letter;
> Sneeze on Thursday, something better;
> Sneeze on Friday, sneeze for sorrow;
> Sneeze on Saturday, your sweetheart tomorrow.
> Sneeze on Sunday, your safety seek,
> For the devil will chase you the rest of the week.

If you burn food while you are cooking, you are feeding the devil.

If a woman burns bread, it means that her husband will come home angry.

A simmering kettle foretells a fuss in the family.

If a woman pricks her finger with the needle when sewing, she will get a kiss for every prick.

If you wish to find the direction in which to look for water, find a doodlebug's hole, bend over it, and say, "Doodlebug, doodlebug, come get your bread and coffee." If the bug comes out and knocks up dirt, look for water in the direction that the dirt falls—which will be down.

A light left burning at night will keep danger away.

A person who can swallow the whole floater of a fish will learn to swim easily.

All left-handed people owe the devil a day's work.

Every time a star falls, someone is indulging in sin.

Go to a graveyard and jump over three graves, saying, "What are you doing in there?" The answer will be—nothing at all.

The following belief, said to be of Negro origin, tells how

to become a witch. Take a live black cat in a sack and put him in a pot of boiling water. Leave him there until the flesh has come off the bones. Then with a mirror before you, put the bones in your mouth, one at a time, till it becomes impossible to see yourself in the mirror. The bone that finally makes it impossible for you to see the mirror will be your witch bone. You can take it in your mouth and go anywhere without being seen.

A fisherman will have good luck if a frog jumps into the water and then swims directly to the bank.

A sailor does not want to serve on a ship the name of which ends in the letter *a*.

An ill person reported dead will live a long time.

A person has told as many lies as he has ulcers on his tongue.

A fever blister says, "I've kissed someone that I had no business kissing."

It takes a lazy man to be a singing-school teacher.

It takes industrious people to build quick fires and raise pepper. In order to make peppers hot, plant them while you are "mad."

Red pepper fed to hens will make them lay many eggs.

To keep weevils out of seed, keep the seed in closed cans with wood ashes.

A good way to get rid of chicken mites is to put freshly peeled pine poles in the chicken house for roosts. The mites will crawl off the chickens and onto the poles to eat the sap or resin, which will harden and hold them hard and fast. This is how we get rid of mites on the Turner Farm.

If you will cut off the hair at the end of a dog's tail and bury it under your front steps, the dog will stay with you and be your friend.

If the cows are lost, find a granddaddy longlegs and say to him, "Granddaddy, granddaddy, where are the cows?" He will lift one of his legs and point in the direction where the cows are.

The witches sweep the cobwebs (whippoorwills) from the sky on Hallowe'en night in preparation for a happy New Year.

CURES

Ranch Remedios

FROST WOODHULL

The question of a properly descriptive title for this account bothered me. Some people call remedios "Household Remedies"; some folks call them "Family Cures"; a few careful persons term them "Home Treatments"; but most of the folks in Southwest Texas call them "Remedios." A remedio is, I suppose, a Mexican remedy. "Remedy" unfortunately contains the hint of a warranty of efficacy, and, as Jimmy Slator said with regard to his remedios, "I give you these without warranty or guarantee on my part as to reliability or efficiency"; furthermore, the great majority of the treatments are Anglo-Saxon in their abrupt simplicity rather than Latin in their finesse. But usage covers a multitude of irregularities, especially in folklore, and after all a title doesn't mean much.

My original intention was to collect only ancient treatments for livestock, but cures commenced to come in covering ills ranging from drought, muddy water, and a lack of wind to teething children, gunshot wounds, and pigs with the stomach-ache. The party grew. I finally opened the doors and welcomed with growing enthusiasm everything that came; I found that treatments for labor pains and freckles were just as interesting as treatments for fistulas and dislocated stifle joints, and I hope that others may find them interesting too. I did exclude colored folks' treatments, however. It looked as if I had to draw the line somewhere, and I thought that someone else might like to give a party for them.

I wish to thank those who took the trouble to answer my various written appeals. I sent out 225 letters and got back 25 replies. Further, I wish to condemn certain of my associates who were "too busy" to make good on their promise to furnish remedios. Personal observation leads me to conclude that they were "too busy" hanging around drug stores and driving fast automobiles down roads their fathers drove buckboards over. For livestock treatments I am particularly indebted to Ab Blocker, Gallie Bogel, and George W. Saunders. I do not show the source of each remedio in the whole batch because that would take too much space. Remember, when you read "I" in this or that remedio, it does not refer to me but to whoever wrote it in.

Should some of the receipts sent in be taken with a grain of salt? Maybe, but not many. Mr. Ab Blocker stated that his were genuine, and he didn't smile when he made the statement. The average person would be kind of cautious in doubting Mr. Ab Blocker's word. In 1929 I sent out a mimeographed booklet of remedios to some of my friends and correspondents. One man said they were "meaty." He may have meant that they were "prime beef" or he may have meant that they were like javelina meat — too strong and easy to get enough of; but whatever reactions these remedios cause in others, I am satisfied with the reaction they had on the greatest of them all:

I have just finished the booklet on "Remedios" and outside of some of the Mexican superstitions I find it good; and of course the superstition part is not to be despised, as it lends a bit of color and humor to what otherwise might be a bit dry to some. I do know that certain people can remove warts without ever touching them, so perhaps some of the other remedios which are apparently charms may be perfectly OK and not altogether impossible.

Thanking you for the booklet and with kindest regards, I remain,

Very truly yours,

C. GOODNIGHT.

I. FOR ANIMALS

BELLYACHE (Horse) Set fire to a gunnysack, place in a bucket and hold under the horse's nose so that he breathes the smoke.

Bathe belly with strong red pepper tea, then make him drink half a pint of same. Patient will stampede, but lose cramps. See *Botts*.

BOTTS Hold a teaspoonful of turpentine under the horse's navel until the turpentine evaporates into the horse's stomach.

Don't feed horse or mule for 24 hours. Then give it one quart whiskey. Botts will all be intoxicated within one hour. Then give patient one pound epsom salts, in warm water. All botts will be exposed to daylight within two hours from taking salts. Next day give patient all ice water it wishes to drink and feed it all it wishes to eat.

Feed the animal green feed and drench with equal parts of water and molasses and give a dose of chloroform immediately after drenching. They turn loose to eat the molasses.

Make a strong tea out of tobacco and mix it with sorghum molasses. Be sure that it is sorghum molasses. Then drench the horse with the mixture, about a pint. Botts like sorghum molasses very much and they turn loose to eat the molasses and then they get sick on the tobacco tea.

Act quickly! Drench with sage tea and molasses. The bott worms turn loose to sup up the molasses and the sage tea stupefies them enough so that they pass on without further harm.

CHOLERA (Chickens) Use the inside of black-jack trees in their drinking water.

Feed dry clabber and soda, half and half.

CREEPS This is a form of disease which affects cattle during protracted droughts when there is no green feed for a long period of time. The animal walks with a rather stealthy gait as though it were trying to slip up on something. In the advanced stages the animal affected has a pacing or rocking gait. Treatment: (1) If the cow affected has horns, immediately saw the horns off as close as possible to the skull. Pull out the tongue as far as possible, then place a strip of bacon on the larynx of the animal, and hold the tongue until the animal has swallowed the bacon. Then take a sharp knife and cut off the end of the tail so that it will bleed freely. (2) Saw off the tips of the toes well up into the quick. (3) I personally have gotten better results by the use of three or four pounds per day of cottonseed meal in a feed trough together with a good filling of hay, for thirty or forty days. I will warrant this last treatment.

GLANDERS   Kill him before he gives it to other horses.

LAMENESS   From prickly pear thorns. A sure cure is to take a large beef bone and heat it in the fire, warm some tallow and spread it on the horse's leg and rub it in right good with the beef bone. This is the only thing that will melt the thorns inside the horse's leg and it is infallible.

Hot poultice of prickly pear leaves; applications of kerosene oil.

POISON WEED (Goats)   To cure a goat which has been stricken with poison weed, give the animal gum of camphor, a piece about the size of a pea. Don't try this unless you think the goat is going to die anyway.

PNEUMONIA (Goats)   Make a tea from the leaves of Jerusalem oak wood. Give the goat one-half teacup cold. Anything hot will kill the goat.

RABIES (Dogs)   When a dog has rabies, burn a cross on the dog's forehead with a branding iron. We had a shepherd puppy that was bitten by a hydrophobic wolf. We treated him this way and he lived to be an old, old dog.

RATTLESNAKE BITE   The remedy herein set out is one sponsored by the Mexicans in Southwest Texas, and I have seen it used on several occasions with good results. However, this treatment should be applied at once. Take a sharp knife and scarify the wound until it bleeds freely. Cut the tips from five or six blades of a Spanish dagger, stick them under the skin all around the wound, and leave them there for twenty-four hours. This perhaps does not sound so scientific, but you could try it sometime in an emergency.

Apply hog lard to the wound. Heat the lard and have

patient drink all possible. For animals drench them with warm lard out of bottle. A dog will eat the lard. Fat hogs are immune from snake bite.

Scarify flesh as deep as the fangs went, making at least two incisions where each tooth has hit. Apply fine salt. The animal will never swell or get lame. This applies to man as well. A good remedy for poisons, spider bites, centipede bites, even poison oak.

If the swelling is bad apply cold mud or clay as poultice. Change frequently in order to keep the poultice cool. Buffalo manure seems to be better than anything else; cow manure is good, but be sure to keep it cool. There is nothing better, however, than a large prickly pear leaf. Cut off the outside, pound up the pear, and apply as poultice, an inch thick if possible. Keep moist with water and change when it gets warm.

RUNNING FITS (Dogs)   Use four doses of gunpowder, or four small doses of chewing tobacco.

SADDLE SORES   Apply a decoction made from the roots of the Texas buckthorn.

Poultice with the mashed leaves of the creosote bush, or use an antiseptic lotion made by steeping the leaves and twigs of the creosote bush in boiling water.

Apply a salve or poultice made of jimson weed.

Spread strong bacon grease all over the sore; it will heal up and the hair will grow over it.

Apply old-time axle-grease.

Burn the *espinas* off a prickly pear leaf, split the leaf, and apply as poultice to the sore.

Wash the sore with cowboy urine. None of the remedies will do any good unless the horse is turned out. If the saddle is kept off him long enough the sore will heal up anyhow.

SCREW WORMS   I have two uncles that can cure screw worms in an animal without ever seeing the animal. I have seen 'em do it many times. All you have to do is describe the animal, where the cut is and how bad the screw worms are. My uncles never would tell how they did it but they sure can do it. They never see the animal at all. We had a wild mule that had screw worms in both hind feet so that the animal could not be doctored with ease or safety. I described the animal to one of my uncles who was four or five miles away, and he told me to go on back to the house, that the screw worms would drop out, and they did and the mule got well. — *Beal Jester*, Chief Deputy Game Commissioner.

SPRAINS (Horse)   Take a piece of cloth and make a pouch around the horse's ankle. Fill this with salt, tie it up and then wet the salt. I have used this remedy many times myself, and it takes the soreness out over night.

Apply tallow and rub with hot bone. A mutton bone is best. This is a good remedio.

Bathe sprained leaders with turpentine. Then light with match, let burn two minutes, and fan out blaze with your hat.

SWEENY   There are a lot of cures for sweeny. Loosen the skin and pull it up and then make a hole through it and sew a hair from the horse's tail through like you would sew a sack together. Another good one that I used lots of times was to rub turpentine on the sore with a corncob.

A silver dime under the skin on the shoulder is the only certain cure. Cut a slit in the skin on the withers, and insert the dime. It'll work around and make the horse absolutely well.

STRYCHNINE POISONING (Dogs)   Remedy I used when my hound dog got a poison bait intended for wolves was soap (washing) suds diluted with water forced into its throat through a bottle or powder horn, which immediately caused vomiting.

The Mexican remedy for this was branding a cross on the dog's forehead with a hot iron.

II. FOR HUMANS[1]

ANT BITE   Soda and vinegar mixed.
Mud or fresh cow dung.

[1]See also the section called "Remedies and Cures" in Tressa Turner's essay above.

Strong solution of salt.

ASTHMA Go down to the river and catch a frog. Pry open the frog's mouth and blow your breath into it. This must be done before daylight in the morning. The frog will die before sundown, but the asthma will go into the frog and will never bother the sufferer again.

Tea of the jimson weed.

Bee's honey mixed with sulphur; dose, a teaspoonful hourly until relieved.

Tea of the leaves of the evergreen sumac.

A drug made from the buttercup.

BED WETTING Feed patient the hind legs of a rat fried crisp. — *Marvin Hunter,* Bandera.

BIRTHMARKS Birthmarks on small babies will vanish if some one (in the case I heard about it was the grandmother of the baby), will get out of bed early and go to the baby's bed and lick the birthmark three times for nine successive mornings, without saying a word to anyone.

Rub the birthmark with a piece of raw meat, and then bury the meat. The scars will disappear.

BLADDER TROUBLE Make a tea from watermelon seeds. Drink a plenty.

BLOOD PURIFIER Dock roots are used extensively for purifying the blood.

Tea from cenizo plant; from joint fir; from sassafras.

BOILS Use poultice of prickly pear leaf. First bake and then split and apply to the boil while hot. This remedio has come to be so well known that even white rancheros use it on their kids.

To bring a boil to a head or draw out a splinter, tie a strip of fat bacon over the boil or the head of the splinter.

CATARACT Grind up egg shells into almost a powder and sprinkle them in the eye.

COLDS For colds and croup goat tallow is a good remedy.

The Indians used a decoction of the leaves of the horehound to cure colds.

Red chili peppers, swallowed whole like pills.

Drink tea made from broom weeds.

Wrap a wet cloth around neck, then a dry cloth over the wet cloth, before going to bed. Sure cure.

"Who in the hell would want a better remedy for colds than whiskey?" — *Governor O. M. Roberts.*

Colic   Take teaspoonful of soot in a cloth, pour over three tablespoonfuls of hot water, let steep a few minutes. Give baby teaspoonful every half hour.

Croup   Use flannel cloth saturated with lard, kerosene, and turpentine; apply to chest.

Boil or steam the leaves of horehound, draw off the water and make a syrup by adding sugar or farm-syrup, but preferably rock candy.

Mullein leaves are a very effective remedy for croup. Prepare by pouring hot water over the leaves, let steam for a few minutes, then draw off and sweeten a little.

Diabetes   Drink plentifully of a tea brewed from the branches and leaves of the *palo verde,* or *retama (Parkinsonia aculeata),* or the flowers, if in bloom. The elimination of sugar from the blood by the use of this tea has also made possible and successful many an operation that otherwise would have proven fatal. No special diet is used with this tea.

Fever   If a person has fever and is sick enough to be in bed, put some black feathers in a pan and burn them under the bed.

Plant sunflowers around the house as a preventive.

Borraja (borage) with lemon juice boiled and taken internally; dose, one cup at bed time, together with a foot bath in lukewarm water.

The bark of the roots of the dogwood is used to some extent as a substitute for quinine.

The mountain pink was one of the most dependable fever medicines known to the early settlers; it was collected under the name of quinine plant. The plants are collected while still in blossom, dried in the air, then soaked in good brandy, and a tablespoonful given the patient three times daily.

Fever Blister   When you think there is a fever blister

coming on your lip, rub behind your ear and rub on your lip. Do this three times in succession.

Put your little finger in your ear and get a little ear wax. Rub this on the blister.

FRECKLES   Wash the skin in buttermilk every day.

Slice raw cucumbers and rub on the face.

The very nicest old lady you ever saw admitted that my cures for freckles (buttermilk and cucumbers) were pretty good, but said that the very best cure was urine. It must have been effective because she certainly didn't look as if she had ever had a freckle.

HAIR TONIC   One of the best hair tonics is to boil, and wash the head with sotol (*Dasylirion texanum*). It will just make hair grow where there ain't no hair.

HEADACHE   Paste a leaf of cottonwood on each temple and leave it there until it falls off, taking the skin with it, and the patient will never be bothered again with this trouble.

Put mustard plaster on back of neck, and one under each foot; let them stay on five minutes and remove.

The Mexican *vaquero* often puts fresh mesquite leaves in his hat and wears it. Remedio is used by some white men. Mistletoe leaves chewed will also relieve headache.

HEADACHE AND SUNSTROKE   Hang a rattlesnake rattle in the crown of your sombrero.

LOCKJAW   I recently went to a place near Fredericksburg on an emergency call. The patient was a young man and I diagnosed the trouble as tetanus. The patient's mother came into the room as I concluded and asked me what I thought. I told her with some gravity that I was afraid it was lockjaw. To my great surprise, she replied in evident relief, "Oh, I'm so glad it is lockjaw; I thought it was fits." I thought that lockjaw was pretty bad and told her so, but she replied that she wasn't at all afraid of lockjaw, that she could cure that, but that she didn't know how to cure fits. I asked her how she did it and she said that the household remedy for lockjaw was cockroach tea. — *Prominent San Antonio Physician.*

LUNACY The buttercup plant was applied to the neck in the wane of the moon.

MALARIA Slice a lemon—rind, seeds, and all—and boil in a cup of water until there's about a cup of pulp left. Let it set all night and eat in the morning before breakfast. Repeat this for three days. My mother used this for ordinary colds as well as malaria.

PNEUMONIA Cook onions, thicken with cornmeal, and place over the lungs while warm.

Fry sliced onions with rye flour and make a poultice of it for the chest and lungs. My mother cured my brother of pneumonia with this remedy when the doctor had given him up.

RATTLESNAKE BITE Chickens are good if you can get them. Just kill a chicken and tear it open and put it over the bite, and in a few minutes the chicken will be all green. Some people cut the chicken open while still alive. It takes about a dozen chickens to get all the poison out.

In the absence of chickens bury the limb bitten in the ground and soak earth covering it with sweet milk.

Apply mixture of turpentine and gunpowder.

Use kerosene well applied to the wound immediately after the bite and open wound with knife.

The Texas milkweed (*Asclepias texana*) is said to be an Indian antidote for rattlesnake bites. Mr. Chris Herms, living near Boerne, Texas, relates the following incident: An Indian chief and five Indians were asking for food at one of the ranch homes. While eating, a member of the family rushed in to tell that one of the party had been snake-bitten, and was too ill to be moved. The chief, on learning the cause of the excitement, made a few motions to his men and they hurriedly scattered in every direction. In a short time, one of them returned with roots of the Texas milkweed. This they mashed and applied to the wound, while giving the patient half of it internally. The man became well in an unreasonably short time.

RHEUMATISM Carry an Irish potato in your pocket.

Teaspoonful common table soda three times a day taken in half a glass of water.

An ointment made from the poke-berry is used in the treatment of rheumatism.

If one is troubled with rheumatism, all that is necessary to get rid of it is to carry a buckeye about.

Nothing can beat rattlesnake oil.

Wear rattles of rattlesnake or carry them in pocket.

If you get some dirt out of the graveyard and walk over it for ten nights you will be cured of rheumatism.

There are certain kinds of rings that people wear for rheumatism. They resemble gold and have a silver-looking set in the middle. Mrs. Betty Miller, Pineland, wears these rings and she says if she pulls them off her finger her rheumatism becomes almost unbearable.

A neighbor of mine bought two rather costly rings of lead or some base metal. He said they helped his rheumatism.

Sleeping with a *pelón* (Chihuahua) dog is infallible.

TEARS To prevent tears while peeling onions, hold in mouth a darning needle that has been dipped in kerosene oil.

TEETHING BABIES If the baby is fretful when teething, string three large snake rattles on a red cord, put around child's neck, and do not remove until it is through teething.

The vertebrae of a salmon, strung upon a string and worn around the neck, will help a baby through the teething period.

A rattlesnake rattle in a tobacco-bag hung around the child's neck.

Let baby chew rattlesnake rattles, or if they are not handy, six-shooter cartridges.

The Curandero of Los Olmos

RUTH DODSON

AN AX IN THE HAND AND FAITH IN THE HEART

Prisciliano Martínez was born in the year 1858 and was reared in Brownsville, Texas. At the age of thirty he moved to another locality, one that happened to be nearer Don Pedrito Jaramillo at Los Olmos. He lived in that general area the rest of his life, following his work as a woodcutter. At the age of seventy-six he was still working. He told me that when he went into the woods that were dangerous on account of rattlesnakes, he would kneel down and supplicate God and the spirit of Don Pedrito, who protected him in his work; then he would go ahead with so much confidence that he would not even think of snakes.

The old man talked of cures that Don Pedrito had made in his family. He said one time his wife was very sick of a heart ailment. Finally they had consulted six doctors respecting his wife's sickness, and he had spent a great deal of money trying to have her cured. She had reached a very bad condition, and the doctor then treating her said that she couldn't live more than three days. They had thirteen children, and they all were crying, thinking that the hour of their mother's death had come.

At this point Don Prisciliano went to a friend and asked him as a favor to write a letter to Don Pedrito. The curandero replied very quickly. He prescribed that for five nights the señora drink a glass of water recently brought from the river, which was near at hand. She recovered and lived many years afterwards. The cost of the prescription was the ten cents that was enclosed in the letter for the reply; the cost of the doctors' treatments was a hundred dollars.

Another cure was that of Prisciliano's son, Pablo. When Pablo was only a few months old, he became sick. The remedy for him was that his mother put some cold water in a vessel and with a cake of soap between her hands soap the water well; and that in this same water she bathe the baby daily for eleven days. The mother disliked to put the sick baby into the cold water, but she had faith and did as directed. Pablo survived, and when he grew up he became a good vaquero.

Don Prisciliano told of being cured himself. Some heirs of a large ranch were dividing it, and they gave him employment as an overseer of the men who were hauling posts to build the fences. Some of these men resented him as their boss; they attacked him and beat him until he was unable to work. He set out to see Don Pedrito. As he traveled, he felt better. When he reached the presence of the curandero, Don Pedrito told him, without waiting for him to ask for a prescription, that there was nothing the matter with him, that he should return to his house and that he should then take a warm bath.

After doing this, the old man said, he got entirely well and continued his work — "with an ax in the hand and faith in the heart."

CURE OF A HORSEBREAKER

Silverio Ruiz became a horsebreaker when he was very young. From being hurt so many times in his work with wild horses, he was subject to hemorrhage of the lungs. At times, he said, when a horse would be bucking with him, he would have a hemorrhage that would bathe the horse's shoulder with blood.

Then one time when Silverio and his family were living in the home of his father-in-law, Don Pedrito arrived on his way through that part of the country. Silverio was not at home. Don Pedrito remained for a while and gave prescriptions to different members of the family who needed them.

When he was ready to leave, he bade them good-bye; when he reached the door, he turned and said to them, "All of you have thought only of yourselves, but of the one who is not here and who is more sick than any of you, not one of you has thought. But," he went on, "I am going to leave him a prescription. Tell him to buy a bottle of whiskey that sells for twenty-five cents, of the kind that is called 'mataburros,' and to drink it all at one time."

Silverio said that he complied with the direction and became very drunk. It is no wonder — mataburros means "it kills burros." Silverio fell off his horse and remained lying on the ground all night. By the next morning, he felt that

he was well; and from that time on he never again had
another hemorrhage.

THE CURE OF A HORSE

Mariano Ramírez did not own a horse. At a time when
most of the men in that part of Texas where he lived were
on horseback, he was afoot. He wanted to buy a horse but
he could never save enough money. One day, he said, he
went to a ranch where he had seen a horse that looked good
but that had been overheated at some time and was wind-
broken.

It occurred to Mariano that the manager of the ranch
might sell the horse very cheap because he couldn't be used
in the work on the ranch. Mariano's idea was to buy the
horse and then cure him.

First the manager asked sixteen dollars. Mariano had only
fourteen dollars, which he offered, saying he could pay no
more. The manager accepted, and Mariano took the horse
home.

The next day he wrote a letter to Don Pedrito, asking
for a remedy and sending a dime for the reply. Mounted
on the horse, he went very slowly six miles to the post office
to mail the letter. When he arrived, the horse was "rocking"
from the exercise. Mariano got off and tied his horse in the
shade of a tree, where he left him for some time to rest
before making the return trip.

In a few days, Mariano received the reply to his letter. Don
Pedrito told him to tie the horse where he could get neither
water nor anything to eat for three nights in succession, but
during the day to permit him to have all the water and feed
that he wanted.

Mariano did as instructed. The horse recovered and served
him well for a long time.

THE MARVELOUS CURE OF A SHEPHERD

Monico Hinguanza was a shepherd who had been sick for

All night Monico remained on his canvas bed,
rocked by the movement into a pleasant sleep.

some time. He took various home remedies, but they did him no good, and instead of getting better he grew worse.

His friends told him of the cures that Don Pedrito had made, and they advised him to go to the curandero. But as Monico lived sixty miles from Los Olmos, he thought it too difficult to make such a long trip.

Finally, when he found that he had to get help, he borrowed a horse and started out for Los Olmos Ranch and Don Pedrito. He reached there the second day at dark. It had rained and the creek was swollen; Don Pedrito's hut was near the bank.

When Monico asked him for a remedy, Don Pedrito got up and took a piece of heavy canvas and a pillow. Telling the shepherd to come with him, he took him to the edge of the creek, where the water made an eddy. He threw the canvas into the eddy, which caught it and extended it in the turn of the water; then he tossed the pillow onto the canvas. The curandero then picked up Monico and placed him also on the canvas, which instead of sinking supported him. All night Monico remained on this canvas bed, rocked by the movement into a pleasant sleep. In the morning Don Pedrito came and took him out of the water, sound and well.

Monico was so thankful that he made Don Pedrito, who had never married and had no family, a present of one of his boys, to live with him and serve him in all that he might command.

THE SPADE AND THE HOE

The wife of Tomás Treviño was reared at Rancho Davis, on the Rio Grande.

She said that at various times members of her family went from there to consult Don Pedrito, or they sent to get prescriptions. When she took sick of a stomach ailment, in which she felt suffocation, he prescribed that for nine nights she should put a glass of water at the head of her bed, and that the next morning she should drink it "In the name of God." With this treatment she recovered.

At another time, the wife of Tomás Treviño had a pain in

her side. The remedy for this was that for nine nights, at bed-time, she should wet the soles of her feet with water, and then she should soap them well and leave them that way all night. She did this and recovered from the pain.

Her mother had an eruption under one arm that lasted for a long time. She was unable to dress herself completely, because she couldn't endure a sleeve on that arm. When she consulted the curandero about this ailment, he told her to do nothing for a term of nine months. And at the end of that time, if she was still alive, she was to take a bath daily for nine days and to apply, with a feather, a certain ointment which was very diffi-cult to secure. Finally, Señora Treviño said, they were able to secure the ointment (its name she didn't remember), and at the end of the nine months her mother used it, as Don Pedrito had ordered, and was cured completely.

Once, on the way to Los Olmos, Señora Treviño's family stopped to spend the night with a relative. This relative had a daughter who was in poor health. She joined them to visit Don Pedrito too. When he saw the girl, he shook his head and mur-mured, "The spade and the hoe. But," he added, "so that the mother will have some consolation, I'll send her a remedy." He prescribed some baths for the girl.

In a short time the daughter died, as Don Pedrito had implied she would.

▼▼▼▼▼▼▼▼▼▼▼▼

Susto

SOLEDAD PÉREZ

Among Mexicans *susto* is a condition brought about by shock or fright. It may not be very serious or it may be fatal. It has many causes, such as the announcement of good or bad news, accidents, or any startling occurrence. The cures vary, but the most popular ones seem to be these:

1. Teas brewed from different leaves are given the patient. Some-

times a gold ring, a piece of red ribbon, or a clod of clay from the chimney is added to the tea.

2. Water sweetened with sugar or water with a little vinegar and salt is given to the patient.

3. The patient is swept from head to foot while a certain number of credos are repeated.

Let me tell the story of the curing of a case of *susto* that I witnessed in Austin. Mrs. Cecilia G. Vda. de Henríquez administered the cure to her own daughter, Rosa Henríquez. The treatment began on Friday afternoon and extended over three days, ending on Sunday.

First Mrs. Henríquez went out to the kitchen and placed a small *comal* (a flat iron grill for cooking tortillas) on the stove. Then she placed a lump of alum on the *comal* and came back into the bedroom. She made Rosa undress and lie face down on the bed with her arms outstretched in the form of a cross. Then covering Rosa with a sheet and taking a small broom made of green twigs and shaped in the form of a cross, Mrs. Henríquez proceeded to sweep Rosa from head to foot. As she swept, Mrs. Henríquez recited three credos. After this she took me out to the kitchen, where we looked at the alum. Something resembling foam had risen to the surface and Mrs. Henríquez gazed intently and then asked me to look at it.

"Don't you see the forms of two men fighting?" she asked.

"Well, yes," I hesitated, "but it's not very clear. Won't you show me exactly where it is that you see those two forms?"

She peered down and patiently outlined what appeared to be two forms of men with outstretched arms and doubled fists.

"I thought that was what had shocked Rosa and now I am sure," she said. "She never told me, but I found out that a man tried to assault her and her boy friend. Her boy friend had to fight with this other man, and it frightened Rosa very much."

Mrs. Henríquez then gave Rosa a tea that she had brewed, and I left after obtaining permission to come back to witness the rest of the cure.

On Saturday afternoon I returned. Mrs. Henríquez again placed the alum on the stove, swept Rosa just as she had done on the previous day, and gave her some more tea. Then Mrs. Henríquez and I went to look at the alum. She was very pleased.

"The cure is going to be very effective," she said. "Today, the figures of the men are barely visible."

When she asked me about it, I affirmed her statement.

On Sunday afternoon the cure was completed. As she had done previously, Mrs. Henríquez placed the alum on the stove and swept Rosa from head to foot, but she did not give her any tea. After this she said that she would be gone for a short time. I noticed a small bundle under her arm, but I did not ask what it contained. About forty-five minutes later she reappeared and told what she had done.

"I had to take the lingerie that Rosa was wearing on the day when she was frightened to the exact location where the attempted assault took place," she explained. "I have dragged the lingerie across the exact spot three times in one direction and three times in another so as to form the sign of the cross. Now I shall put the lingerie on her, and we shall know whether the cure is complete or not."

She then dressed Rosa in the lingerie, and we sat and chatted amiably for about half an hour. She asked Rosa how she felt, and she replied that she was sweating profusely. Mrs. Henríquez covered her with a blanket, and immediately afterwards we went into the kitchen to look at the alum. Nothing could be seen.

"I am very happy," said Mrs. Henríquez. "The two men who were visible on the first and second day have disappeared, and that means that the cure is successful."

When I left, Rosa was asleep, but she was still sweating profusely. Now Rosa is well and has returned to her work.

PLANTS

⌄⌄⌄

Folklore of Texas Plants

SADIE HATFIELD

A conversation which took place during my childhood stamped itself upon my memory very clearly because therein was offered a pleasant substitute for quinine. I shall report the conversation as nearly as I can remember.

"You should have been able to cure Ed's chills and fever with quinine," said one neighbor to another at a picnic as the women sat around talking.

"That's exactly what both the doctors said, but it did the poor child no more good than water. Besides it's awful hard to get him to take it. He is so little and puny, too, I hate to make him take it."

"Did you try chill tonic?"

"Yes, but as I was saying, I remembered an old remedy my grandmother used to talk about. She really believed in it. I do too now, but I don't want any of you to think that I am superstitious."

By this time everyone wanted to hear what the remedy was and urged her to go ahead.

"You-all will laugh and say I'm superstitious but it worked and it might help some of you if you'd try it.

"I thought about Grandmother's remedy a good deal and so one day before time for Ed's chill I took him to the creek and showed him different trees on the way and had him learn the names of some he didn't know. I was afraid he'd get mixed up. Then I showed him button willow and told him to get a branch of it first and to get eight other kinds of tree limbs and tie them together in the fork of the biggest tree he could find and not to let anybody see him do it. I told him if anybody rode by just to call me and when they had gone he could start over. Then I told him as soon as he had tied the limbs to the tree to back away nine steps, then turn around but not look back, not to return to that place or to talk to anybody about it.

"Then I walked away and didn't look back at him. I just crept along and after a good while he came to where we had agreed to meet in the shade of a live oak. He missed his chill, and from that day to this he's not had another one."

Recently I heard the following dialogue:

"Isn't that too funny about Mrs. B. putting that string of beads made from elderberry stems on her baby to keep it from teething hard?" said a daughter.

Her mother replied: "You shouldn't think it funny, you wore one when you were a baby. Grandma K. made you some and you wore them a long time."

"Not really?"

"We knew they'd not hurt you any, and we certainly weren't going to hurt her feelings by leaving them off of you."

One day an elderly woman came into my father's general store at Medina. In searching for change to pay her bill she had to unload the large pocket of her apron. Among the things laid on the counter was a small Irish potato.

"That," she said, "is to cure my rheumatism. See, it's getting hard. That shows that the rheumatism is going into it. If the potato gets soft, it won't do you any good."

I'd known folks who carried buckeye seed for curing rheumatism, but the potato was new.

In the early spring when the weather becomes inviting, the women of the hill country love to escape the dull routine of house work in order to tramp in the woods. Trailing turkey hens to their nests occupies much time in the spring. Not everybody has turkeys but everybody should have several "messes" of poke greens as early as possible. Often a party of women and children search for poke in the valleys of the two Medina rivers and in the narrow valleys of their many tributaries.

Poke is said to be poisonous unless it is gathered when very young and cooked right. It should be parboiled and drained three times, then fried in bacon grease. It tastes like spinach but is much better. Our latest dietetic information confirms the value of this poke-greens tradition.

The mullein which grows so abundantly about sheep and goat pens, in the river valleys and even in thin rocky hillside soil, is particularly valued because it makes measles break out, and because it helps cure colds and many other ills. Since the time of Pliny, according to Ellen Schultz, it has had many uses as a medicine.

Cenizo leaf tea is used for asthma. There are several remedies for dysentery. One may chew live oak buds or the white inside bark of mesquite, or drink tea made from them. Tea may also be made of the mesquite wax which forms when a tree is injured and the sap oozes out. Juice or sap of ragweed is also a remedy. Pound the ragweed until soft, put in a cloth bag and squeeze into a teaspoon.

For sore eyes, a poultice is made of madeira vine leaves.

Prickly pear leaves make good poultices for relieving a child's foot pierced by a prickly pear spine or a mesquite thorn. Choose smooth, thick, healthy leaves; peel carefully to remove thorns; scrape the fleshy inside and add salt; put on a closely woven cloth; heat in pan over hot water until hot through; tie on to the foot. This poultice draws and shrinks the flesh so that the thorn may be removed. It also lessens the pain and "takes out the fever." A hot prickly pear poultice also relieves swollen bruises and toothache.

It seems to me that children used to get many more "specks" in their eyes than now. A moistened sweet basil seed placed in the eye helps remove dust and small particles. The seed when wet forms a coat of white jelly-like substance which softens the "speck."

In the old days, when it was inconvenient if not impossible to buy cosmetics, and at a time when they were generally distrusted, powder to discourage a shiny nose was made from corn that had ceased to be roasting ears and was becoming horse feed. The grains were crushed and tied into thin cotton bags. These were dried. The bag was patted gently on the face to sift out the cornstarch.

Spice bush was one of the plants admired by a group of home demonstration club people while on a shrub hunt in Kerr County.

"This is a beauty bush," said one.

"Why do you call it that?"

"Oh, it's used to make you pretty," she said, patting her cheek.

For clearing a rough or muddy complexion caused by "the blood being too thick," the rich weed was often used. Whiskey mixed with the root tea kept it from souring. This is also called rosin weed because a resinous substance collects on the side of the vessel in which the roots are boiled. Perhaps you know it as ice weed, because the sap forms large curls or globular snowballs during heavy freezes.

Several kinds of wonderful smelling pennyroyals are plentiful, and on a few occasions I have known of their being used for perfume.

Many strings of beads can be had for the making. The black seeds of the wild china were—and are—the easiest to use for beads, and the most popular. I still have a string, a gift of two little girls who have long since grown up. The seeds of Eve's necklace make smaller beads but are just as attractive. A crimson necklace can be made from mescal beans. It takes longer, however, to collect and match them than the others.

Now that it is popular to use everyday things as jewelry, I expect most any day to see a cocklebur brooch. In this respect we are outdoing our resourceful pioneers.

Our early settlers had many dye plants to choose from, but the colors which might be produced were fewer than the plants.

For yellows, orange, and browns, there were cottonwood bark, pecan bark and hulls, walnut bark and hulls, Spanish oak bark and sap, smoke tree roots, twigs, or leaves, and ripe berries of sumac, Indian cherry, cotton, madroña bark and roots, goldenrod, cedar bark, berries, and twigs. Reds came from pokeberries, willow bark, roots of rough-leaf dogwood, and bloodweed sap; yellow-green and green from ash bark; blues and purple from baptisia or false indigo. Sumac dyes leather black. I've often wondered if that weren't the reason it is called "shoe-make" by everybody except botanists.

Old-timers tell of many wonderful plants that used to be found in the valleys and on the hills before they were over-grazed. These have become so rare as to be almost unknown now. For instance, it is said that a low-growing rose covered large portions of the country with fragrant pink blossoms in the early spring. It took me nearly a year to locate a few plants.

I blame the goats for this. They are so agile that few places are inaccessible to them. They have added much to the economic welfare of the hills, but they have eradicated many plants.

Data left by early botanists confirm this rose story.

"Did you know that the Indians used kinnikinnik for tobacco?" I have been asked on several occasions. It is said that early settlers also used it, mixed with tobacco, to make their smokes last longer.

Rhus virens is known not only as kinnikinnik, but shinikinnik, Indian tobacco, evergreen sumac. It is a honey-producing plant and is valued by stockmen, for it is an excellent browse plant.

It is rumored that Indians crushed or ground mountain laurel beans and put the mash in liquor so that it would make them wild as well as drunk. It is so potent that one-half a bean will do the trick. It is called mescal bean, big drunk bean, goat bean and *frijollito*. The Texas law against marijuana includes the mountain laurel.

The cypress tree, always a wonder to strangers, figures in many local stories. It grows bountifully on the north prong of the Medina River and its tributaries, but is not found on the west prong of the river. H. B. Parks once told me that it was one of the plants that have come down to us from the glacial age.

"Folks used to saw down a big cypress and give a dance on the stump," old people used to tell my brothers and me. We wished we could see just one such tree.

At the edge of our swimming hole in the Medina River, there was a large stump partly decayed. It was the biggest tree stump we had ever seen. We sized it up many times and discussed the possibility of its having served as a dance floor. I was still dubious, but when I saw the giant cypresses about the palace of Chapultepec in Mexico, I knew that the story was entirely probable.

ANIMALS

Texas Reptiles in Popular Belief

JOHN K. STRECKER

THE KING OF THE SWAMP

In many lowland localities, the Negro story of the "king of the swamp" is still current. According to this story, the "king" is a large moccasin, not the ordinary stumptail but a much larger creature. He attains a length of from ten to twelve feet and his body is as large around as a man's thigh. His home is usually the heart of a large, hollow cypress stump and here he holds forth for generations. He not only preys on large fish and an occasional water-fowl, but is very fond of eating other snakes, even other moccasins. Whenever there is a scarcity of other snakes, the Negro fishermen attribute this to the depredations of the "king," who is supposed to be jealous lest some other serpent may increase to such proportions as to be able to contest for his domain. A Negro once attributed the swollen condition of the corpse of a young boy who had drowned in a cypress swamp to his having "fust been bitten by de king moccasin."

THE COACHWHIP

After a coachwhip "flagellates" you (his technical name is *flagellum!*) into an unconscious state, he will run his tongue up your nostrils in order to find out whether you are still alive. If you are, he will continue the whipping process until life becomes extinct. In some localities the whipping produces only unconsciousness, never death. In others, the poisonous element enters into the story, and the snake poisons his victim with each blow of his quirt-like tail.

THE GREAT WATER DOG OF THE PLAINS

In the plains region of Western Texas, the large tiger salamander is a common animal. During the dry season it lives below the surface of the ground in deserted prairie dog and ground squirrel burrows. After the first heavy rain of the year, it comes forth to breed in the shallow lakes that dot the surface of the plains. The adult animal has a broad, flat head, four well-developed limbs, a long tail, and a smooth, moist skin; and large specimens attain a maximum length of ten inches. Small specimens are sometimes called "lizards" by the natives, while large ones are called "alligators." This animal, in common with all salamanders, goes through a larval, or axolotl, stage of existence before finally attaining the adult form. These larvae have large, plump, light-colored bodies, external gills, finned tails, and large broad heads, and in general appearance look not unlike small catfish. In this stage, the animal has a voracious appetite and feeds upon young spadefoot toads, toad tadpoles, grasshoppers, and other small creatures that either inhabit or accidentally fall into the lakes. The axolotl form is so different in appearance from the adult animal that it is usually given another name, that of "water-dog." According to some Texas cow-punchers, who somehow understand that the two forms are the same animal but do not understand the significance of the transformation, the tiger salamander is "one of the devil's brood; he can change from fish to lizard and then change back again!" He is considered a poisonous animal and classed with rattlesnakes, centipedes, tarantulas, and "vinagarones" (vinegarroons).

Along the New Mexican border is related a story of an enormous and extremely ferocious animal that formerly inhabited one of the salt lakes in Andrews County, Texas. It was an amphibious animal "resembling a great water-dog" and was said to feed almost exclusively on ducks and other waterfowl. It was said to make a terrific noise as it plowed its way through the water in the early morning, causing the ducks to arise in great flocks from the surface of the lake. It even put to hurried flight parties of gunners who became frightened at its ferocious appearance. A description of the animal given in a copy of a small plains newspaper of twenty-five years ago (unfortunately since lost) reminded one of the great prehistoric animals. "The 'great water-dog' has not been reported in recent years."

HORNED TOADS

If the strange and interesting horned lizard, or "toad," as it is called in the vernacular, were an inhabitant of the bayou counties of Louisiana and Eastern Texas, instead of the drier regions to the westward, where Negroes are less imaginative, folklorists would have much more material to place on record. In the Brazos Valley, you are told that "when a horned toad spits blood from its eyes and then bites you, it is sure death." When a horned toad attacks a red ant bed in the spring, the "king of ants" sends out a scout to discover whether the invader is thin (just through hibernating). If he is, the "king" sends out his soldiers and they sting the toad to death. There may be a basis of truth to the story of the ants' getting the better of their gigantic enemy, for in early spring I have found horned toad bodies in proximity to ant beds, emaciated and partly eaten. The animals may have been too weak to withstand repeated onslaughts of multitudes of attackers.

SNAKES SWALLOW THEIR YOUNG

All snakes swallow their young. This has been known for centuries but naturalists still refuse to give credence to the story. Ask any old Negro who lives in the woods and he will tell you of some instance. If he didn't see the act himself, one of his uncles or his grandfather did. It generally happens in this way. While in the woods, you suddenly come upon a female snake and her brood sunning themselves. At the first sound you make, the mother snake opens her mouth and the young snakes immediately seek refuge in the body of their parent. If you don't believe this story, kill the snake and you will find the young ones inside her throat. The brood may number a hundred or more, even if naturalists do claim that a female snake seldom gives birth to more than thirty-five young ones at one time.

WHEN SNAKES GO BLIND

Of course, snakes do shed their skins, and while the slough is hardening and becoming dry and loose, snakes are not in good physical condition and are inclined to strike aimlessly. This fact has led to the popular belief that in late summer snakes go blind. Many folk will tell you that during the "dog days" the rattlesnake is blind. "Look out for er blin' snake," say the Negroes. "He sho hev mo piz'n en when he kin see."

THE HAPPY FAMILY OF THE PLAINS

Out on the western plains, in the land of little rain and on its borders, lives, according to a fading popular belief, the most curiously assorted happy family in the world. There the prairie dog, the "prairie dog owl," and the rattlesnake all find home and companionship in the same burrow. Old-time cowpunchers knew this to be a fact, but the prairie dogs and the scientists have always disagreed.

A PROTECTION AGAINST RATTLESNAKES

When you are camping in rattlesnake country, coil a horse-hair rope around your bed and no rattlesnake will cross it. But a rattlesnake has been known to squirt his poison at his victim beyond the rope.

The Folklore of Texas Birds

JOHN K. STRECKER

BLACKBIRDS   When a blackbird sings near you, bad luck will come. This is clearly a distorted importation. American black-birds are starlings and their notes are harsh and unmusical. The European blackbird is the black thrush, one of the best songsters of the British Isles and temperate parts of the Continent. Ravens and rooks are black birds (in plumage) and it would be unusual to hear one of them singing. Probably some one got his black birds mixed. To kill a blackbird is to invite bad luck. This superstition is also an importation, but I have heard it in Texas. In England it is considered bad luck to kill a blackbird (black thrush) on account of its singing qualities.

BLUE JAYS   According to the old Negro belief, the blue jay, who, like other members of his family, is a familiar of evil spirits, is never seen on Friday, for he is then carrying sticks for fuel to the devil in hell. One theory, however, is that the infernal fires are fed by sand; therefore, some Negroes, and even some whites, hold that the jay takes sand rather than sticks to hell. I have heard of Negroes and whites who would quit working at a place near which jays had set up a chatter in order to get out of hearing of the sinister birds. Hunters frequently call jays "devil birds," because their cries arouse the game being hunted. Members of one of the Canadian tribes of Indians always attempted to kill the gray Canada jay, because they thought it warned enemies of their approach.

BULLBATS   Two species of nighthawks, one of which is divided by extremely technical ornithologists into several geographical races inhabiting different sections of the state, occur in Texas. Nighthawks fly earlier in the evening than do the more strictly nocturnal whippoorwills and chuck-will's-widows. They are usually called "bullbats" on account of the peculiar noise they make when they descend on the wing from a great altitude, the sound being produced by the passage of air through the stiff bristles that border their capacious mouths.

Old-time Negroes, who were often confused in their zoölogical classification, believed these birds to be bats of unusual size. However, in more recent years, the bat classification has been revised by these people and we now have "leather-winged" bats and "bullbats," or "feather-winged" bats. All nighthawks are supposed to be uncanny.

BUZZARDS A solitary turkey buzzard seen flying at a great altitude indicates rain. A buzzard sitting on a fence or tree and raising his wings — "airing his body" — also indicates rain. Several turkey buzzards circling at a great height predict the coming of a norther.

CHACHALACAS When the chachalaca cries in the night, it is a sign of rain. The chachalaca is a pheasant-like bird which inhabits the scrub in the Brownsville country, and this prophecy is strictly of Mexican origin.

COWBIRDS The cowbird, or cow blackbird, was, on account of its habit of picking the ticks from bison and cattle, called "buffalo bird" by the early pioneers of the West. The fact that these birds who derived so much of their food from the buffalo have a habit of assembling in noisy flocks and wheeling in flight caused both Indians and pioneers to suspect that they were warning the buffalo herds of the approach of men.

FLYCATCHERS The crested flycatcher, a small woodland bird that lays buff eggs curiously streaked with purple and reddish-brown and that generally uses in the construction of its nest the cast-off skin of a small serpent, is supposed to use the skin as a means of scaring intruders from the vicinity of its nest. I have been told this by both whites and Negroes in Kansas, Missouri, and Texas. There is nothing in the belief; several other species of birds occasionally use snake skin as nesting material.

KILDEES The "kildee," or kildeer, is a small plover widely distributed in Texas. It inhabits bottom lands and deposits its eggs on the bare soil, usually at the end of a corn row. Despoil a kildeer's nest and you will break a leg or an arm! The nests are very hard to find and many an egg-collector would be almost willing to suffer a fracture of one of his limbs if he could but discover one.

MOURNING DOVES Many years ago, nearly forty I should say, I read a short note on the diminutive ground dove by Mr. Troup D. Perry, of Savannah, Georgia. Mr. Perry stated that this bird was in that section of the South known as the "moaning" dove, and that Negroes believed that when it "moaned" frequently, some sick person in the neighborhood would soon be at death's door. The Carolina, or common, dove of Texas is even by the whites called "mourning dove" on account of its melancholy notes. According to bottom Negroes, this bird is also a "moaning" dove, and a prophet of approaching dissolution. Both the ground and common doves are found in southeastern Texas, and numerous are the Negro folk tales related of their uncanny power to predict death. There are hundreds of black people in East Texas who originally came from the old southern states, and they brought their mythology with them. Just as you must get your first glance of the new moon over your left shoulder, if you wish good luck, so "if you hear the first mourning dove note from above (in a tree or up the hill), you will prosper; if from below you, your course will thereafter be downhill."

NUTHATCHES Nuthatches are small insectivorous birds that inhabit the wooded regions of northern and eastern Texas. They have a habit of hanging with their heads down while they are searching for insects and are even said to roost frequently in the same manner. They are known as "devil-downheads" on this account, and many Negroes call them "devil-birds" because, as octogenarians say, "Dey is allays lookin' down towa'd deir master, de debbil." Two species, the white-breasted and the brown-headed nuthatches, are found in eastern Texas, the latter bird being principally confined to pine regions.

OWLS Very few members of the owl family have escaped figuring in folk tales. According to frontier belief, the burrowing, or "prairie-dog," owl shares subterranean burrows with rattlesnakes and prairie dogs, the curiously assorted company dwelling together in perfect unity! The barn, or "monkey-faced," owl is distributed in several color phases over most of the habitable globe. It is especially common in Texas and its presence and cries are believed to foretell changes of weather, good or bad luck, even approaching sickness or death. "Never disturb a barn owl that sits between you and the moon — it will bring bad luck," is an old English superstition that early migrated into Texas. A curious superstition concerning the screech owl comes from the Brazos Valley. I was told that when a small owl screeched incessantly in the neighborhood of a house, if one of the occupants were to turn over an old shoe, the bird's cries would immediately cease and it would betake itself to some other locality. When a screech owl screeches from the roof of a house which shelters a sick person, that person is doomed to die. An owl screeches or hoots often before an approaching gale. This is a weather sign still believed in many parts of Texas, but it was recorded by Virgil!

PAISANOS (See Roadrunners).

RAIN CROWS Every land in every clime has a "rain bird." In many countries the rain bird is some species of the cuckoo family. Throughout the greater part of the United States, the yellow-billed cuckoo is the "rain crow," this being the title applied to it by thousands of persons who know nothing about its family affinities or specific name. It is a very common bird in Texas and by both whites and blacks its melancholy notes are supposed to be uttered only before falling weather.

ROADRUNNERS OR PAISANOS Another member of the cuckoo tribe, the eccentric roadrunner or chaparral cock (the *paisano* of the Mexicans), is supposed to kill snakes by hedging them in by a surrounding wall of cactus branches. However, as the roadrunner dispatches serpents in another way (by repeated blows of its sharp beak) and as snakes can crawl over cactus spines with perfect impunity, the story probably started in the bizarre imagination of some South Texas Mexican.

SNAKE BIRDS The grotesque anhinga, or water turkey, inhabits swamps and the borders of lagoons in southeastern Texas. On account of its long, slender neck and reptile-like head, it is often called "snake bird." Southern Negroes assume that it is not only a familiar of poisonous moccasin snakes but that it protects these reptiles from their enemies.

SWALLOWS The migration of birds is a subject little understood by the generality of people, and it is not an unusual thing, even in this twentieth century and in the enlightened state of Texas, to find some person in the rural districts who still clings to the old European belief that, instead of migrating southward, swallows bury themselves in the mud of ponds and watercourses and there spend the winter. For do not these birds assemble in large numbers in September, suddenly disappear some evening, and keep out of sight until the following spring?

WHIPPOORWILLS The whippoorwill of the eastern United States occurs in Texas principally as a bird of passage, but a few no doubt breed in the extreme northeastern corner of the state. The bird usually called whippoorwill in central Texas is the larger chuck-will's-widow, which has quite a different cry. The following superstitions concerning the whippoorwill are not only believed by Negroes in all of the old southern states but are, as I have found them, current in Texas east of the Trinity River.

In case the cry of one of these birds (either whippoorwill or chuck-will's-widow) is heard near a house in which lies a sick person, it foretells death. The cry of a whippoorwill heard once in the night is a death sign, but if the bird cries out repeatedly, the hearer will live a long time. If a chuck-will's-widow is heard near a Negro's hut, it means misfortune to the occupant. It is unlucky for one to disturb a chuck-will's-widow in the woods, even in the daytime. Disaster will come to any person who destroys a whippoorwill's nest. While many modern Negroes are getting away from the superstitious fears of their ancestors, old patriarchs still shudder when they hear the cries of these nightbirds.

The poorwill, a rather uncommon cousin of the whippoorwill, is found in middle and southwestern Texas, far from districts inhabited by Negroes. Mexican sheep-herders, so I have been told by ranchmen, will not destroy the nest of this bird for fear that some misfortune will follow the act. A true whippoorwill is found in the mountains west of the Pecos River, but the bird is so rare as not to be generally known even where it exists.

WOODPECKERS The ivory-billed woodpecker (*Campephilus principalis*), the largest and most magnificent North American

representative of its family, was at one time an inhabitant of
the timber lands of East Texas but is now almost, or quite, extinct. It was a bird absolutely untamable, and its spirit was so
much admired by the southern Indians that its dried head and
neck were frequently worn by them as amulets in order that
the wearers might be infused with great courage. Remaining
representatives of a small band of Alabama Indians who a few
years ago were living in San Jacinto County, Texas, not far
from Shepherd, are responsible for this information, which
shows conclusively that the ivory-bill, wherever it occurred,
was respected by the aboriginal inhabitants of the South.

The slightly smaller pileated woodpecker, another magnificent species now becoming scarce, is known in East Texas as
the "logcock" and is supposed to be "King of the Woodpeckers."
I have frequently been told by old Negroes that a small woodpecker would never alight on a tree occupied by a nest of this
species or on a dead tree on which the big fellow was at work.
My personal observations, however, do not confirm these beliefs. The redheaded woodpecker and the zebra bird, or red-
bellied woodpecker, are two common species whose conspicuous appearance and eccentricities have caused them to be popular in Negro folk tales of the bedtime variety. When the
former species goes through its mating maneuvers, it is supposed by some black people to be displaying restlessness because of an approaching storm.

If a redheaded woodpecker taps on the roof of a house, there
will be a death in the family. Most American woodpeckers have
red on their heads, so that the subject of this superstition is
not a single species but an aggregation of species.

Thousands of perfectly respectable members of the woodpecker family, which minister to trees by relieving them of
borers and other destructive insects, have been killed because
they were suspected of being "sapsuckers." The real culprits
are three small woodpeckers of a single genus (*Sphyrapicus*)
that really do damage trees by boring into them for sap. Only
one of the three occurs in Texas, and this species is a winter
resident only.

WRENS   In East Texas, as well as in other sections of the

United States, children are warned not to blow their breath on a wren's egg for fear that it will not hatch. They are also told not to look inside this bird's nest, for if they do, it will be deserted by the owners. Those observers of the wrens' home life who have watched each day and have seen the first egg in the nest augmented by the addition of others until the full clutch of eight or nine were deposited, will hardly agree with this belief. In some Texas localities, it is considered unlucky to kill a wren.

The Paisano's Cactus Corral

J. FRANK DOBIE

Any animal is interesting to man not only for the facts about him but for what human beings associated with the animal have taken to be the facts. "No man," Mary Austin says, "has ever really entered into the heart of any country until he has adopted or made up myths about its familiar objects." Hardly any established fact about the paisano is as familiar to the public as some form of the story about the bird's corralling a rattlesnake with cactus joints and then either killing it or making it kill itself. The bird is certainly more interesting for this commonly believed and more commonly told story.

Nor am I prepared to deny that paisanos ever corral rattlesnakes. Perhaps they could. The act would be no more of a strain on nature than the building of a web by a spider to entrap a fly. It is claimed that snakes hear through the ground and that a sleeping rattlesnake could not be corralled without his becoming aroused. I do not know. The roadrunner runs lightly. But I make no argument, no denial. The stories are interesting. They are part of the history of the most interesting bird of the Southwest. Some of the narratives are very circumstantial — as all good narratives must be.

In May, 1933, I was introduced to E. V. Anaya, a practicer in international law, of Mexico City. He was reared on a haci-

The bird would carry a joint in its long
beak without getting pricked.

enda in Sonora, where he was associated with Opata Indians. He is as swart as a desert Indian himself and as decisive as Mussolini. The Indians and Mexicans of Sonora call the paisano *churella,* he said.

"Have you ever seen one kill a rattlesnake?" he asked. "No? Well, I have — once."

"I was out gathering pitahayas," he went on. The pitahaya, or pitalla, is a cactus fruit. "It was in the month of May — the month of pitahayas. I was just a boy, about 1908. I was with an Opata Indian.

"Just as we got to the top of a mesa, the Indian very cautiously beckoned me to come nearer. Then when I was close to him, he whispered, 'See the churella.'

" 'Churella,' I replied. 'What of it?' The bird is so common in that country that little attention is usually paid to it.

" 'This one is killing a rattlesnake,' the Indian spoke softly. 'Let us watch.'

"We crept up silently, until we were within twelve or fifteen yards of the churella. A rattlesnake lay coiled on the ground, out in a little open space, apparently asleep. The churella had already gathered a great many joints of the cholla cactus and had outlined a corral around the snake. The corral was maybe three feet in diameter.

"The churella was working swiftly. Cholla was growing all around us and the joints were lying everywhere on the ground. The bird would carry a joint in its long beak without getting pricked. He built the little corral up, laying one joint on top of another, until it was maybe four inches high. Then he dropped a joint right on top of the sleeping snake. The snake moved, and when he did, the spines found the openings under his scales. The snake became frantic and went to slashing against the corral. That made it more frantic. Then the churella attacked it on the head and had little trouble in killing it. The spines made it practically defenseless."

If a roadrunner were going to use any kind of cactus to corral or torment a rattlesnake with, cholla joints would surely be best suited to the purpose. Each joint is so spined that if one single thorn takes hold of an object and the object moves the least bit, another and then several other thorns will dig in. Instead of throwing off the cholla joint, movement causes the one thorn in the flesh to act as a lever for giving more thorns entrance. In the bad cholla country of Sonora I have ridden a native horse, wary of the thorns, that, nevertheless, caught several in his pastern. Then the only thing to do was to dismount, get a stick, and with it jerk the cholla joint directly out. I have seen a cave in that same country with enough cholla joints heaped in it to fill a freight car. They had been placed there by rats. The Papago Indians used to dispose of their dead by laying the body on open ground and then heaping cholla over it — a thorough protection against all beasts of prey.

Snakes, rattlesnakes included, eat rats. All kinds of rats in all parts of the Southwest build about their nests a defense of thorns against snakes and other enemies. The rattlesnake may not, as folk theory once held, be sensitive to the tickling of a hair rope; but he can't go like a shadow through an armor of thorns.

Not long after Lawyer Anaya of Mexico City told me his story of the churella, the cholla, and the rattlesnake, I went to see General Roberto Morelos Zaragoza in the city of San Luís Potosí. An ardent hunter and outdoors man, he was issuing monthly a small magazine called *Aire Libre* (Open Air), made up of hunting and fishing chronicles. The general's primary interest in wild life was that of a killer, but he was naturally alert and had made many observations on the habits of animals.

He called the paisano a *faisán* (pheasant) — the name the bird goes by around San Luís Potosí. "Yes," he said, "with my own eyes I have seen a *faisán* kill a very large rattlesnake. The *faisán* took a tuna (the Indian fig, or apple) from a *cardón* cactus, dropped it on the neck of the snake, and while the snake was maddened by the thorns pecked it to death on top of the head."

An old German mining engineer named Engelbert Brokhurst, widely traveled, learned, observant, and cranky, whom I met in Mazatlán, told me that Indians of the West Coast of Mexico regard the paisano as a sacred bird and will not kill it. They all

say that the bird corrals sleeping rattlesnakes and then torments
them to death with thorns.

The evidence, however, is by no means all from Indians and
Mexicans. *Black Range Tales* (New York, 1936) is a book of
reminiscences by an old-time prospector and miner named
James A. McKenna, of New Mexico. "One spring in Lake Valley," he relates, "my partner and I watched a pair of roadrunners. Morning after morning we met them outside the
tunnel where we worked. Not far from the mouth of the tunnel
a rattlesnake used to climb on a rock to take a sleep in the early
morning sun. [They were out-of-the-ordinary outdoors men
not to kill it.] It soon became plain to us that the roadrunners
had spotted the rattlesnake. One morning we saw them making
a corral of cholla joints and thorns around the snake. How
quietly they worked until the crude circle was nearly three
inches high! Then both birds ran with a strange cry towards
the cholla corral, waking up the rattlesnake, which struck instantly. Hundreds of fine sharp thorns were buried in the ten-
der underside of the snake's throat. The more he twisted and
turned, the deeper the spines of the cholla worked into his neck.
After a half-hour of writhing he lay still. The roadrunners hung
around long enough to make sure he was dead; then they
hacked him to pieces, which they carried off to feed their
young. Prospectors always keep on the lookout for rattlesnakes if they take note of a pair of roadrunners in the vicinity
of the camp."

Yet some critic has spoiled this story by claiming that a paisano does not have enough force in his beak to tear the flesh
from a rattlesnake carcass.

Something of a variation in the use of cactus thorns comes in
an account written by Hampton McNeill of the Texas Panhandle. Hunting quail one day, McNeill heard "some kind of
unfamiliar chuckling" going on just over a small mound. He
stepped up on top of the mound, and there a "chaparral
and a rattlesnake were fighting for life and death. The snake
was completely encircled by cactus leaves. Its head had been
pierced so many times by the cactus thorns that a match-head
could hardly have been placed anywhere on it without cover-

ing a thorn hole." The narrator probably had no magnifying glass to look at the holes. Remember, however, that the prickly pear in the Panhandle grows low and scrawny; the leaves (known to botany as pads) are not strongly jointed.

"The chaparral would run up to a cactus bush, take a good hold on a leaf with its bill, shake the leaf loose, and then return to the scene of battle. Using this thorny leaf as a shield, the chaparral would rile the rattler into striking at him. After the snake had struck several times, the bird would lay the leaf down near the snake.

"The chaparral repeated this action several times. In the course of time, the rattler seemed to become completely exhausted, for he would no longer offer resistance when the chaparral returned with more cactus leaves. Having brought up two or three leaves without arousing the snake to action, he then disappeared in the sage brush. The snake was not dead, but I put him out of his misery."

Philip Ashton Rollins, in his generally excellent treatise, *The Cowboy*, describes still another mode of attack whereby the bird uses thorns but does not bother with a pen. "The chaparral-cock," he says, "might stop its hunt for bugs, seize in its bill a group of cactus thorns, spread its wings wide and low, and, running more speedily than could any race horse, dodging as elusively as does heat-lightning, drive those thorns squarely into the snake's open mouth, peck out both the beady eyes, and then resume the hunt for bugs." According to the *gente*, a paisano upon finding a rattlesnake charming a rabbit, slips up and jabs a cactus joint into the waiting jaws of the would-be killer.

The more usual end, perhaps, of the story of the rattler corralled by cactus spines is that narrated by the Old Cattleman in Alfred Henry Lewis' *Wolfville*. "At last comes the finish, and matters get dealt down to the turn. The rattlesnake suddenly crooks his neck, he's so plumb locoed with rage an' fear, an' socks his fangs into himself. That's the fact; bites himse'f, an' never lets up till he's dead."

I am not sure of final findings but I have been informed by scientific men that rattlesnake venom injected into the blood system of the very creature carrying the venom will be as deadly as in the blood system of any other animal. Such an end is not impossible. According to the tales, then, there are three possible ways for the rattler to die after paisanos have corralled him. (1) He may bite himself to death; (2) he may have his brain punctured by the bird's beak just as it is sometimes punctured without benefit of the corral; (3) he may be brained by thorns themselves.

What would happen if a rattlesnake bit the paisano in a vital spot may be deduced from an account in a book first published in Cincinnati in 1847, by C. Donavan, *Adventures in Mexico.* During his captivity in the Mexican War, Donavan visited an extensive botanical garden near San Luís Potosí, and there became acquainted with *huaco* — the most celebrated herbal cure for snakebite in Mexico and the southern tip of Texas. The discovery of the medicinal qualities of *huaco*, Donavan learned from the natives, was attributed to a bird that "feeds upon snakes and reptiles." Indians in the far past noticed that after a combat with a snake the bird would "search for the herb and eat it." Thus they learned from the bird, which Donavan calls the guayaquil but which is patently the paisano, the "sure remedy" for snakebite.

From the paisano, too — perhaps — certain Indians of the Southwest took the idea of putting long fringes on their moccasins and leggins as a protection against snakebite, the fringes suggesting feathers to the snake. Indeed, the wands used to calm rattlesnakes in the Hopi snake dance are of feathers, though they are of the eagle, which preys on snakes.

Folklore in Natural History

ROY BEDICHEK

When a Texas sunflower gets good awake of a morning, it stretches itself a bit and forthwith bends its neck around to face the sun. Using its neck as an axis, it continues to face the sun all day long.

But in Lapland it's different. There the sun wheels around in the southern sky and stays aloft for months, so the sunflower of that latitude instead of simply bending over from east to west for a matter of twelve hours and then getting a good night's rest — instead of this humane Texas schedule, the Lapland sunflower's neck must twist itself around for months without any letup.

So it comes about that the traveler standing in a field of Lapland sunflowers at sunset is startled by the murmur of multitudinous little snapping, cracking, and swishing noises all about him. But be reassured, stranger from the South, there are no spooks nibbling at your ankles: it's only the sunflowers untwisting their necks for a long snooze in the coolish polar night.

I had this little legend from a botanist, Dr. William G. Whaley, on his return from a summer's stay in northern Sweden a year or so ago. If this is not genuine folklore, it is at least folksy and naturalistic enough to bring into focus points that are common to much of the folklore that appears in the field of natural history.

The fancy-factor in this idyl is more easily separated from its factual base than is the rule in most natural-history folklore. It is a fact that the common sunflower follows the sun, as certain other members of the great thistle family do, but folk generally reserve the name "sunflower" for only that species which most obviously exhibits this curious fondness for the sun. It is a habit of the folk mind to let its fancy dwell chiefly upon the more obvious features of natural phenomena, irrespective of whether or not the obvious is the essential. It is also a fact that in our temperate zone the sun holds a course across the sky, whereas in the polar regions it describes more or less of a circle based on the horizon.

Upon these botanical and astronomical data folk fancy goes to work somewhat as follows:

1. If the temperate-zone sunflower follows the sun willy-nilly, facing eastward in the morning, straight up at noon, and westward as the sun moves down from the meridian, then what

happens when the same sun-fascinated flower finds itself up towards the north pole where the sun simply circles around indecisively for a few months in the southern sky? What, indeed, could happen except that this sun-crazy plant must twist its neck throughout the months-long day to make the accommodation. That's what a man must do when he turns his face without altering the position of his body — he simply twists his neck. Twisting the neck in the same direction for any considerable period is a tedious and finally a painful process.

So, besides seizing upon the most obvious aspects of a natural occurrence, the folk mind here makes its interpretation upon an anthropocentric basis. It loves the pathetic fallacy quite as dearly as the formal rhetorician abominates it.

2. Now a human neck twisted steadily without letup all day leaves its owner in no condition at nightfall to enjoy his repose. Hence, when the sun sinks below the horizon and the hypnotic tension is released, the plant quickly untwists its neck just as a human being would.

3. At the end we find the touch of humor which makes the whole world of folklore kin. Accustomed all his life to the silent, deliberate behavior of the normal sunflower, the observer is placed by the legend in a whole field of Lapland sunflowers just at the moment when the last rays of the polar sun disappear. Presto! There ensue tiny snapping and swishing noises all about him, so he "jumps out of his skin," only to find that it's nothing but innocent sunflowers untwisting their necks, as anyone who knows anything about sunflowers would expect them to do. Poor dub, to be frightened at that! It's funny.

Maybe the "little noises" the Lapland sunflowers make are derived from the "growing" noises of corn, with which all rural folk in our Midwest are familiar. Transpositions or analogies of this sort often bob up in folk interpretations of natural phenomena. It will be noted that a sustained neck-twisting is also the mainspring of the well-worn folklore "Western" about the burrowing owl. The burrowing owl, by the way, doesn't burrow, but merely avails himself of the burrowing activities of his roommate. This is another instance of the careless, don't-give-a-damn acceptance of the obvious, and of the *non sequitur*.

The bird dives into a burrow, doesn't he? Ergo, he is a burrow-ing bird.

However, all your analyses of folk-thinking, your condescend-ing exposure of its innocent tricks, its naïve assumptions, its faulty observations, and its jumping at conclusions, fail to wean us away from it. Fact is, we're not ready to be weaned. The pap is pleasant and often nourishing to the very sciences which re-pudiate it. Particularly, as the machine more and more domi-nates our lives and an all-pervasive technology forces our think-ing into stern mathematical patterns, do we find pleasant re-lief in the wild freedom of the old brain-tracks, grooved long, long ago, a heritage from the primitive — from the Neanderthal or Java man, for that matter — who in turn took his thought-patterns from animal progenitors. "For we are indeed one with Nature; her genetic fibres run through all our being; our physi-cal organs connect us with millions of years of her history; our minds are full of immemorial paths of pre-human existence."[1]

The superhighways, motorcars, jet planes, and prospects of space travel really intensify the pleasure of winding along neighboring roads, or of following footpaths or even animal trails in the, alas, too few wilderness areas now left our sadly devastated domain. Just so the mind likes to follow along the old trails of primitive thinking, coursed on still dimmer ones of animal thinking. Especially in natural-history folklore do we like the diversity, the *non sequiturs,* the aimless meanderings, the dallyings, and those sudden juxtapositions of incongruous ideas which constitute the soul of much of its humor. It's like park-ing the car at last to get out of the dizzy traffic and away from the glare of an undeviating highway, in order to wander off into the woods with nowhere to go and no set time to return.

With this trail-theory in mind we shall examine other in-stances of how folklore tends to deal with natural phenomena. We find it incurably anthropocentric. I cannot vouch for the truth of Voltaire's statement that man created God in his own image, but there is little doubt in the mind of any naturalist that man does create animals in his own image. Science, how-ever, has invented a terrible word for this: *anthropopsychizing.*

[1]General J. C. Smuts, *Holism and Evolution* (New York, 1926), p. 336.

For instance, the anthropopsychist believes that birds sing generally because they are happy, as we ourselves whistle and sing because we are happy, or (in reverse) pour out our dismalest feelings into song as a necessary purgation.

The ancient Greeks, keen nature-observers and the most downright and practical people of whom there is any record — these unsentimental folk heard from the throat of a nightingale no warning to other nightingales to stay out of his territory, as the ornithologist of today interprets his song, but instead the most musical of mourning. In Greek legend the bird is a "bewildered mourner, bird divinely taught, for 'Itys,' 'Itys,' ever heard to pine."

Nowadays the really scientific ornithologist says "bosh" to all this. The song of the mocker or of the thrush, especially in the spring, is an expression of "territorialism"; that is to say, the sweetest and most seductive songs of these birds are only a warning to others of their own species to stay away, keep out, private property, posted, officer on guard. Twenty-five years ago it was "scientific" to attribute all spring bird songs to love, to the pretty little anthropocentric fiction of the male's serenading his faithful mate as she sits patiently hovering their eggs, a modest, home-loving little creature as all females in the world are or should be. And after this Victorian exposition, it was the fashion of the scientific person to get really profound and point out the importance of bird songs as a factor in sexual selection. Debunk, however, as much as you please, folk will continue to anthropopsychize bird songs and even fit words of human speech into the various rhythms of them; and I'm not so sure they are not getting nearer a vital truth than the scientists are.

Seriously, there is sometimes truth in folklore of higher quality and of greater importance than the mere facts-is-facts of science. In nature lore and especially in folklore about animals, our ancient kinship in mind and body with all animate nature is revealed; and the folk mind, wisely following the old trails here, refuses to exchange a sympathetic and therefore emotional for a purely intellectual apprehension of nature.

We are conditioned from childhood to doubt folk tales about animals. As we grow up we find there was never such a bird as the roc, no such animal as the unicorn, no mermaids, no centaurs. Science delights in debunking these folk creations and substituting, quite properly, "the fairy tales of science and the long result of time." We naturally become incredulous. Our first reaction is to discount any tale of mysterious occurrences in nature, and especially any behavior-story in which the lower animal exhibits human intelligence. Science is especially suspicious of such stories, since it has virtually assumed the role of defense attorney for *Homo sapiens* against any presumptuous animal coming into court to claim any part or parcel of that sacred psychological area known as human reason. Loyal to the human race, it is determined that we shall not be dragged down to the bestial level without a fight. Man may become bestial, but animals can't become rational.

It is, however, a mistake to become too skeptical. I have often pooh-poohed a folk story only to be compelled later to eat my own words. I rejected forthwith the account of a praying mantis capturing and biting into the throat of a hummingbird, but found that this does sometimes happen. And I didn't believe it when a friend told me he had seen a grackle fly two hundred yards with a crust of toast in his bill, dunk it in water and eat it just as some of us dunk our toast in coffee. But it's so. On the other hand, I accepted at once a story from an old woodsman explaining why the folk name for pileated woodpecker is "Lord God" or "Good God." Says he, "When a feller who ain't never seen one before sees a woodpecker as big as a crow, he just naturally says 'Lord God!' and that's the way the critter got its name." I published this as a probable origin of the East Texas name for this enormous woodpecker, and presently there came through the mails the following explanation from Dr. Irving McNeil, of El Paso:

One suggestion [he begins with disarming diffidence] that I think if I could have got to you before you published, you would have been glad to include about the folk name of the pileated woodpecker. The origin of the name "Good God" might be traced back a step further, to the section where I was brought up in northern Mississippi and West Tennessee. The Negroes there called the bird "Lord God." As a boy I thought it was awfully funny but it was not until I was grown and learned that another name for the bird was "log cock" (see Webster's *New International Dictionary*) that the explanation came to me. There it is: Repeat the two names out loud to yourself, and see how much alike they sound and see how easily the name "log cock" could be mistaken by the illiterate for the other. All that is needed to complete the gap is to consider that East Texas was settled by Tennesseeans.

I don't like to give up the old forester's explanation, but I am driven by "preponderance of evidence" to accept Dr. McNeil's, at least, provisionally.

The bullfrog's mouth and his hind legs are his most striking somatic characters; and, true to its genius for enlarging plausibly upon the obvious, folk fancy has developed a whole cycle of tall tales about this batrachian's capacity for swallowing and jumping. The surprising thing is that science comes along and proves that none of them is an exaggeration. Indeed, folk fancy seems for once a bit sluggish.

An old fisherman told me when I was a boy that he had seen a bullfrog swallow things "twict" his own size — apparently a self-contradictory exaggeration. We have all heard trotline stories of a fish swallowing a baited hook, of a larger fish swallowing him and then of a frog swallowing the larger fish, and so on until the fifty-two-pound yellow cat that was the final swallower was made to disgorge more pounds of fish and frog than the swallower himself weighed — *on the same scales*.

So when I heard that a bullfrog had swallowed one of Dr. M. R. Gutsch's ducks, I put it at once in the tall-tale class, of value only as illustrating folk disposition to exaggerate the function of an organ of abnormal appearance. I confronted Dr. Gutsch with the story, expecting an instant repudiation, but instead he told me that one day he saw a duckling disappear suddenly from the surface of his duck pond. When it failed to come up in a reasonable time, he seined the pond and found his missing duckling with its head in the belly of a bullfrog. True it was a duckling, not a duck, and the frog hadn't yet swallowed the whole of it, but the facts certainly furnish a good, sound basis for the story.

L. T. S. Norris-Elye writes to A. C. Bent: "We have had instances of frogs capturing and swallowing ruby-throats [hummingbirds], one at Gull Harbor and one at Gimli, Lake Winnipeg. The Gimli case was observed by my friend Hugh Moncrieff, who captured the frog (leopard) and had some boys cut it open and recover the bird, while he took some good motion pictures of the operation."[2] Think of this gross Caliban having the agility of leg and the expansiveness of mouth and gullet to engulf our little Ariel while he is hovering over the water on iridescent wings vibrating 200 strokes per second![3] Folk-fancy never invented an unlikelier story, and still competent scientific observers, eyewitnesses, assure us 'tis so!

Dr. Osmond P. Breland in his excellent book *Animal Facts and Fancies*[4] records a swallowing reported to him by Dr. W. Frank Blair, Associate Professor of Zoology, University of Texas, who had an eleven-inch alligator confined in the same cage with a five-inch toad. One morning he missed the alligator and noticed that the toad was rather distended and appeared unusually drowsy. He felt the toad's belly and there, sure enough, coiled neatly inside was his alligator.

And the dark, unfathomed caves of ocean bear some curious

[2]A. C. Bent, *Life Histories of North American Cuckoos, Goatsuckers, Hummingbirds, and Their Allies* (Washington, 1940; U. S. National Museum *Bulletin* 176), p. 349.

[3]According to Gordon C. Aymar, *Bird Flight* (New York, 1938), p. 133, the hummer makes "up to 200 strokes per second," apparently counting both downbeats and up-beats as strokes. A. C. Bent, on p. 345 of the work cited above, explains how the flight of the hummingbird has been studied by means of a high-speed camera. He states the results: "Dr. Charles H. Blake examined with great care the films taken of hummingbirds in flight and found that the birds beat their wings 55 times (completed strokes) a second when hovering, 61 a second when backing, and as rapidly as 75 a second when progressing straight-away. Probably this last figure would be found to increase as the bird gained speed, if the camera could keep the bird in focus." Since Blake is speaking of completed strokes, his figures would have to be doubled to make them comparable to Aymar's.

[4]Breland, *Animal Facts and Fancies* (New York, 1948), p. 182.

instances of the swallowing capacity of certain of its denizens. There is a dragonlike creature whose immense mouth and elastic body make it possible for him to swallow a fish actually larger than he is.[5]

So the old fisherman who repeated folklore about the swallowing capacity of frogs and fishes was really nearer the truth than he thought.

For more than a century science has found folk belief in the hibernation of birds harder to kill than a cat with its nine lives. Since the days of good old Gilbert White, and before, it kept bobbing up here and there in spite of scientific proof to the contrary. Science has told us repeatedly that birds migrate, and that the ignorant, not being familiar with the facts of migration, attribute the disappearance of birds in the fall to hibernation. Possums, bears, bats, and other animals hibernate for the winter, so why not birds? — such is typical folklore reasoning. The learned world for a long time has dismissed belief in the hibernation of birds as completely without foundation. Even as late as 1948 Dr. Breland says, ". . . a recently compiled list of books and articles dealing with the hibernation of swallows contained no less than 175 titles. Despite these early beliefs and the learned published articles, however, so far as is known there are no types of birds that hibernate."[6]

Yet facts were coming to light here and there which rather supported the folk belief. In the coast country of Texas there is record of a cold snap in late spring which reduced hummingbirds to a state of suspended animation. People picked them up in great numbers, and it was found that many of them recovered when brought into a warm room. There was for a long time a

[5]Edward W. Meyer, Jr., editor, *Natural History Magazine*, tells me that the label on an exhibit formerly existing in the Fish Hall of the American Museum of Natural History read as follows:

"*The Black Pirates.* These deep-sea pirates are not snakes but 'degraded eels,' that have lost almost everything but their voracious appetites. One of them has just swallowed a fish that is bigger than himself, which stretches him nearly to his elastic limit. His less fortunate mate, yawning fearfully, opens the dark gateway to a cavernous interior."

[6]*Op. cit.*, p. 111. Dr. Breland writes "learned published articles" with tongue in cheek.

question about the Carolina parakeet, colonies of which were found holed up in hollow trees during cold weather, but no reputable authority was willing to declare that it was a case of hibernation. Since this bird is now extinct, we shall never know whether or not his holing-up was hibernation or merely a case of temporary refuge. I read a year or more ago in the very reliable *London Illustrated News* an account by a scientist of a bird which nests in the far north of Europe and, after hatching its brood, is occasionally driven south by a late blizzard, leaving thinly clad nestlings unprotected for as much as a week at a time. Well, the nestlings are alive when the parent birds return! How is that possible? The scientist reports that he examined such a brood every day while the parent birds were gone and found that the little fellows were apparently asleep. Their blood temperature went down with the temperature of the air about them, which is a symptom of hibernation.

But the first actual proof of the hibernation of an adult bird generally accepted by the scientific world was recorded by Edmund C. Jaeger only this year (1953) in the February issue of the *National Geographic*. He found a poorwill sleeping away the winter in the hollow of a tree out in California, gave it all the hibernation tests, and solemnly pronounced it the real thing. So that's that: folklore right, science wrong, at least insofar as the poorwill is concerned. It is interesting to note that the poorwill belongs to the same order as the humming-bird, which we found exhibiting an inclination toward hibernation on the Texas coast.

Natural-history folklore is strong on function. Every organ of an animal is endowed, whether or no, with a function, and the more striking the organ the more functions are invented for it. Generally speaking, this is right: nature doesn't create an organ just for fun, and nature's disposition to economize makes her delight in multiple uses.

What, for instance, is the function of a rat's tail? It furnishes the sitting rat a prop for which a far shorter tail would serve, modeled, say, on that of the prairie dog, certainly the premier sitter of the rodent world. While climbing, the cautious creature sometimes takes a stabilizing twist with the pliable member around a small limb or other projection, but this very occasional convenience would seem to be more than offset by getting its owner caught in a snap-trap, although this is not always a fatal casualty. Many a time I have found about half or even two-thirds of the tail firmly clasped in the jaws of my trap, left there apparently as an insulting suggestion that the tail-owner had more intelligence than the trap-setter.

Some say that when a colony of rats in migration reaches a stretch of water lying across its route, a wise old bewhiskered member wades in while the next in line takes the tip of the leader's tail in his teeth. The second rat extends the same courtesy to the third rat, and so on in turn until the whole colony is strung chainwise across the water. Thus, it is said, many a weak one gets across a river who otherwise would be swept away in the current. I don't know whether this is science or folklore. Its picturesqueness suggests folklore, while the survival value would point to scientific speculation.

Dr. Gustav Eckstein, Professor of Medicine in the University of Cincinnati, quotes "a man from Guernsey" to the effect that he noticed the daily diminution of olive oil in a tall thin bottle on his pantry shelf.[7] Determined to solve the mystery, he watched through a hole in the door. About nightfall he saw a rat climb to the shelf above the bottle, seat herself at just the right point, lower her tail into the bottle, raise it, and lick it.

Since this is reported anonymously, I thought maybe Dr. Eckstein was just telling a story. But the incident in the next paragraph I could not dismiss so easily, for he saw it "with his own eyes." A great gray rat entered his kitchen. "One spring to the back of a chair. One spring to the middle of the table. And there, set there every afternoon to cool, stood a flat dish of milk. Carefully she swung her stern, carefully she fitted it to the rim, and, in a single sweep, the job was done." One may ask why she didn't take the cream direct instead of skimming it off with her tail. The only answer which occurs to me at the moment is that the fastidious creature didn't want to mess up her whiskers.

[7]From Eckstein's "Lives" (1932), in *The Book of Naturalists*, ed. William Beebe (New York, 1944), p. 358.

But these Eckstein instances, purely anecdotal (not folklore), are included here only as a possible suggestion of how folklore may get started from the observation of a unique event. My own experience with a praying pig, who, by the way, kept a prayer cushion, falls into this class, a seed of a possible folk tale which I shall now proceed to sterilize by publishing it. I quote it verbatim from an entry in my camp diary dated several years ago:

There's a pig running loose around my camp who gets all the table scraps from a neighboring farmstead, as much milk as he can drink, the constant attention of two boys who consider him a pet, and as much purslane and succulent roots as he can stuff in. I have never seen a rounder, cleaner, more self-possessed, or friendlier pig in all my life.

A talkative fisherman who drops by for a cup of coffee now and then tells me that this is a religious pig, that he prays almost daily and keeps a cushion to kneel down on. I tried to laugh this off as a "pig with a prayer cushion" but the man was serious. He told me about this praying act several times, and finally I decided to keep watch on the pig and see what activity of his justified my fisherman's conclusion. It took me about a week, for his praying habit proved to be irregular. I find these to be the facts:

This pig has attacks of bellyache from stuffing in too many table scraps and guzzling too much milk. His sides become bloated, and his grunts indicate discomfort. During such periods, he tries sinking down on his belly. That hurts, so he turns over on his side. That hurts, too, so he turns over on the other side. Still his belly hurts. Then he rests his great weight on the knees of his forelegs, but the place is littered all over with sharp oystershell, and the edges of it cut his knees, so he squeals a little, and rises, but his internal pain drives him to his knees again, which is apparently the only comfortable position he can assume. Again the cruel shell cuts him. Then he discovers an old castaway auto cushion in the corner of an open garage. He mounts this cushion, kneels down, and gives what I take to be a grunt of relief. He stays there kneeling on the soft cushion until the inner pain is over, and then with gratified grunts he goes his way again seeking what he may devour. This routine comes irregularly and I think only after gorging himself on some delightful dish, usually table scraps soaked in milk.

Animal folklore still adheres in its richest expression to two

New World animals: the vampire bat and the opossum. Both were unfamiliar to Europeans when early explorers returned laden with marvels collected during their wandering in lands beyond the seas. People were wonder-hungry and conditioned to believe anything. Rational processes were anesthetized and folk fancy was liberated to show what it could do. In the area of natural history it seized avidly upon these two animals concerning which there were no realistic inhibitions in the popular mind. As a result, the tales still current involving the form and behavior of the vampire bat and of the opossum would fill a good-sized volume: the one, an enormous flying mammal which sucks the blood of its victim while he sleeps; and the other, a curious fumbling, ambling, fuzzy, death-feigning quadruped equipped to nourish and bring forth at frequent intervals her litters of incubator babies.

Since there isn't room for both here, let's pass on by the vampire bat and take a look at the opossum. In 1717, Madam Merian published her drawing of a mother opossum carrying young on her back with their little tails coiled loosely around hers. A century or more later another creation appeared representing an "improved" folklore, showing the mother's tail arched grandly over her back and ending in a fine Spencerian flourish just over her head, while the babies, partially suspended by their tails, are strung along the mother's back from shoulder to rump. Another forty years of expanding folklore brought forth an "improvement" which transforms our sluggish, sleepy, dreamy marsupial into a really fearsome beast, tail more sharply arched over the back with the babies' tails twisted tightly around it and the whole litter holding on for dear life as the mother ranges madly like an enraged boar over the bumpy landscape.

Now this fictitious baby-carrying mechanism took such firm hold on the imagination of the people that it has not been loosened yet. The same type of illustration appeared in the schoolbooks and dictionaries of the last century, and may still be found in current editions of the Larousse foreign-language dictionaries.

A complete representation of evolving opossum folklore from 1516 on down may be found in a remarkable series of pictures reproduced in Chapters 18 and 19 of Dr. Carl G. Hartman's fine work, Possums.[8] Dr. Hartman assures me, by the way, that it is an anatomical impossibility for the opossum to arch its tail over the back in the manner shown in his four-century album of opossum pictures.

Hartman also tries to put to rest a tenacious bit of folk biology about how opossums breed and bring forth their young.[9] Many people still believe this egregious folklore version of the breeding and birth of this very common animal. Again, it is the folk imagination bent on assigning a function to match the peculiarity of form observed in the organs involved.

But the folk have never discovered one gruesome function of this marsupial's tail. It is used as a reserve food supply. When the going gets really rough — no paw-paws, no haws, no Mexican persimmons, no chicks, no eggs, no insects (the animal is omnivorous) — when just about to starve, the resourceful creature sometimes curls up and chews off his own tail right to the root. Science scores here over folklore in the account of Dr. Harold C. Reynolds, an eminent marsupial authority.[10]

The ancients believed in mashing up a quantity of ticks to secure a curative salve useful in the treatment of certain skin affections. Pliny the Elder recommends tick blood as a depilatory and as a curative ointment. It was also used as an aphrodisiac. I suppose very few sophisticated people consider this other than worn-out folklore coming down to us from unscientific ages. But Dr. Cornelius B. Philip, of the U. S. Public Health Service, doesn't think so.[11] Having spent his whole life studying ticks he now assures us that tick blood contains an antibiotic

[8]Carl C. Hartman, Possums (Austin: University of Texas Press, 1952).

[9]Ibid., p. 83.

[10]See Harold C. Reynolds, "The Opossum," Scientific American, CLXXXVIII (1953), 90.

[11]"Tick Talk," Scientific Monthly, LXXVI (1953), 77-78. See also Ludwick Anigstein, Dorothy M. Whitney, and Don W. Micks, "Antibacterial Factor in Tick Extracts," Texas Reports on Biology and Medicine, VIII (1950), 86-100.

that inhibits growth of many species of bacteria. So it is quite possible that, with a little more experimentation with the gore of the humble tick, folklore may be able to stick another feather in its cap and say, "I told you so."

Actual experimentation has proved that a vulture can take off from a tower or other eminence and fly for miles with a weight in his talons which he could not possibly lift up from a level surface. Tales of baby-snatching by eagles met their quietus in these experiments. Weight-lifting experiments and observations seemed also to discredit folk tales of how any decadent descendant of Reinecke Fuchs could make off with a ten-pound goose. But science, apparently, doesn't know its fox as well as folklore knows him, as will later appear.

The big owl, whose bulk is mostly hollow bones and feathers, has been accused of making away with much more than his weight of hen. Confronted by the skeptic who has actually seen a good-sized owl unable to lift a medium-sized fryer off the ground, much less a full grown hen, the believer might invent a very pretty little story which seems to obviate the difficulty.

True enough, you are told, no one of the big owls can get off the ground with the weight of a hen in his talons; but, being a very wise bird, the owl takes advantage of certain well-known laws of flight by snatching his hen on the wing.

You immediately object to this on the ground that hens fly very little during daylight hours, not at all at night when the owls are feeding.

"But you don't know your owl," comes the ready response. "The owl catches his hen as she flies down from the roost, and soars happily off without violating any laws of flight."

Now you think that you have your taletelling nature-faker backed up in a corner. "So," you say, with a triumphant air of a lawyer who has just trapped a troublesome witness, "you call the owl a wise bird, and still you would have her wait around the barnyard until daylight for a hen to fly down from her roost. A likely story! when the farmer is already up and feeding his horses. Wouldn't he make short work of an owl perched up in a tree waiting for one of his fat hens to fly down!"

But your witness slips out of the noose even as you begin to tighten it.

Oh, no, the owl doesn't wait until daylight — by no means. He simply flies quietly in about midnight and perches right beside his sleeping victim. You know owls fly very quietly. Presently he gives the hen a little nudge, which means "move over." The sleeper, accustomed as she is to being pushed around on the roost by members of her own clan, squawks a weak little protest and promptly moves over. The intruder now waits until the hen of his choice goes back to sleep. Then he gives her another nudge towards the end of the roost, and gets the same satisfying reaction, a little squawk and a little move over. Thus patiently and very gently he gets his "intended" right to the end of the roost. The brute now changes his tactics and gives his hen a violent shove off the roost and swoops down after her. At just the point where he has gained the necessary momentum, he fastens his talons securely in her back and away they go on his wide wings to the hungry brood hidden safely in the deep, deep woods, far, far away.

I had never thought of doubting this story until I became folklore-conscious. Then I found that I couldn't remember a single farmer who had ever "seen with his own eyes" this owl-hen drama occur. Owls hooted over in the bottom and next morning a hen was missing: "After this, therefore on account of this" — typical folk reasoning. I began cross-questioning everyone who told the story but failed to get even one eyewitness. There were those who had heard squawking and flapping in the old dead hackberry tree where the chickens roosted and had rushed out there *just after* that damned old owl had made off with the fattest hen on the place. And "surenuff" next morning feathers were scattered all over the place — surely light evidence to sustain so heavy an indictment.

In 1942 I struck a hot trail. Miss Edna McCormick, at that time professor of mathematics in the Southwest Texas State Teachers College at San Marcos, said her father had actually seen an owl do this very thing. My heart fluttered a little as I asked if her father were still living, for I needed a firsthand

observation from a living witness. Yes, he was alive, living in
Denton, Texas.

With reference to the owl and the chicken [his reply to my letter
began], your letter received and the facts are as follows:

At my father's home in Denton on a moonlight night, about 67
years ago, I was in the yard near an unfinished crib. The ridgepole
was exposed, and chickens were roosting on it. I saw an owl light
beside a hen, and begin pushing it. The owl tried several times to
push the hen off the roost, and every time the owl pushed the hen
would squawk. [These lovely details! what a witness!] The owl
seemed to know, the only chance to carry off the hen was to force
it off the roost, and catch it on the fly. [Here I drew a deep breath.
Now I have it nailed down, I muttered. But alas! there was a final
sentence.]

I frightened the owl away to save the hen.

> Very truly yours,
> W. L. McCormick.

James R. Simmons, Contributing Editor of *The Land*,[12]
quotes and flatly contradicts the eminent naturalist, Roy Chapman Andrews' debunkation of two folk stories: (1) that of how
handily a fox can make off with a fat goose; and (2) the old,
old story of the snake's swallowing its young.

Regarding the first, Simmons quotes Andrews as saying that
the fox never undertakes to make off with anything larger than
he can handle. His jaws and body size are not built for a quarry
as big as a goose, turkey, or heavy fowl.

Just the other morning [replies Editor Simmons], I saw a red fox
emerge from a timothy field, cross the farm road and disappear into
a patch of woodland, dragging a fowl that would weigh at least ten
pounds, and *I'll swear that it was slung from his shoulder!* I was
near enough to observe how this was accomplished . . .

Two reliable persons have recently told me that they saw a fox
carry off a goose, "on his back." One, a Canadian woman, has
described the entire procedure from kill to get-away, as she actually
saw it in the barnyard of her farm home.

How is it done? Not of course by main strength of body or jaw
but by sheer skill in the distribution of weight. The fox first kills the

12James R. Simmons, "From a Cabin in the Woods," *The Land*, Vol. VI
(1947), No. 1, pp. 42-43. Simmons paradoxically heads his discussion of the fox
and the snake "Myths That Are True."

goose. Then he grasps it by the neck, close to the head. With a clever twist he slides his body underneath. Then he rises and goes forward in a comparatively straight line. He never backs up, tugging at his load as a dog or even a man so often does. The quarry hangs across his shoulder somewhat as a man would carry a partially filled sack of grain. The body of the goose drags. But the weight of the pull is actually on the body of the fox.

Again, you see, Reynard the Fox comes up triumphant. Folk don't credit the fox with cleverness without warrant. He may have a fragile body, but what a mind!

As for the snake-swallowing story, Mr. Simmons quotes Roy Chapman Andrews as saying that many years of scientific observations fail "to produce evidence that a snake ever swallowed its young." Then Mr. Simmons gives an eyewitness account with himself on the witness stand.

"Recently," he reports, "I came upon a three-foot snake, stepped on its tail and held it captive for examination. The snake immediately opened its mouth and out wiggled four small specimens of the same species, each about two or three inches in length and in excellent health and vigor. . . . I can name other observers who have seen the same thing." J. Frank Dobie can, too. Mr. Dobie has flirted with acceptance of this story as true for years, and has speculated entertainingly about it in various articles, the most thoroughly documented of which appeared in the publication of the Texas Folklore Society for 1946, "Do Rattlesnakes Swallow Their Young?"[13] He contents himself here with quoting authorities. "I repeat," he concludes, "that I affirm nothing, that I merely transmit." Like Paul, Dobie appears at times "almost persuaded"; and the last time we discussed the matter, he was still wavering.

Mr. Simmons' account, in my opinion, would have been improved had he identified the species under his observation. He says definitely that the little fellows were the *same* species as the adult, but he does not say *what* species.

With these few samples of the kinds of folklore that pervade natural history and popular reasoning on the subject, I should

[13]*Mexican Border Ballads and Other Lore,* ed. Mody C. Boatright (Austin, 1946; Texas Folklore Society Publication XXI), pp. 43-64.

like to be able to draw certain profound conclusions relative
to the mind of man and the nature of belief. But alas! I must
content myself with that which is already apparent to any
reader, with pointing out that natural-history folklore consists
largely of folk fancy playing about irresponsibly with mere appearances; that folklore jumps at conclusions; that it seems
incapable of rational analysis; that it must give every organ
a function, whether or no; that its humor leans to the broad and
the grotesque; that it paints with a wide brush; that it has
an overwhelming yen for mysterious happenings in nature
(whence we deduce that man is a natural at wonder-monger-
ing); that folk interpretations of natural phenomena are incurably anthropocentric; and finally and marvelously, that folklore in the field of natural history often discovers facts or
principles at which science scoffs for some centuries only to be
forced at long last to accept them.

So, looking out from my own restricted field over the vast,
vast field of folklore, I am no longer amazed at its persistence,
its power, its philosophical implications, and its entertaining
qualities. Age cannot wither it nor custom stale its infinite
variety. I am appalled at the crude amount, at the mass and
smothering volume of that which we call folklore, including,
as it does, the traditional customs, vernacular ballads, sayings,
and beliefs, especially those of a superstitious or legendary
character, preserved unreflectively by a people. And, of course,
this mass is by no means homogeneous throughout the world.
Cross racial boundaries or language barricades, or change social
levels inside specific racial or language groups, and the character of much of the folklore is transformed. Indeed, it would
hardly be an exaggeration to say that folklore constitutes the
basis of 99 per cent of the mental and emotional life of 99 per
cent of the people.

On the time scale of evolution, mind itself is a late-comer,
while the modern mind's main instrument, reason, came on the
scene only day before yesterday. Considered in the large, that
is, taking into view mankind as a whole, reason as motivation
has established but limited sovereignty and that only in restricted areas of the vast jungle where human motives arise and

give impulsion to action. "Thinking," says Professor Toynbee, "is as unnatural and arduous an activity for human beings as walking on two legs is for monkeys."

Speculating on the universal appeal of folklore, I return again to my trail theory as a helpful analogy. All normal human beings like to wander through the woods following footpaths beaten out by the tread of savage feet, which, in turn, took them over from the hoofed or padded feet of animals. And so does the machine-age mind, tired of rational dictation, like to be turned loose to take its own way in the wilderness areas along brain-tracks scored in the primitive or even in the subhuman brain, and now appearing as inherited vestiges of a very ancient traffic.

Dim trails, they are, with twists and turns and many branchings-off, offering free choice at frequent intervals, including that always present one of back-tracking when the prospect no longer pleases. Here the vacationing mind may idle, entertain not-so beliefs, think as wishfully as it pleases without rebuke, indulge prejudices and prepossessions and, when the mood strikes, may even burlesque that great tyrant Reason with abandon. Here its hankering after "hunches" and other mental atavisms finds a congenial climate. This, I take it, makes for the wide appeal of folklore, and this may be its main contribution to sanity.

OIL

Paul Bunyan: Oil Man

My introduction to Paul Bunyan came during the summer of 1920 spent in the Hewitt field, near Ardmore, Oklahoma. I was learning the game as a "boll weevil" and so was the victim of many "sells," such as being sent for a left-handed monkey-wrench or the pipe-stretchers. The old-timers particularly enjoyed making casual references to miraculous time- and labor-saving practices that the powerful and ingenious Paul Bunyan used on his rig. There was nothing, however, like a cycle of stories; there were no extended tales.

A year later I returned to the oil field, this time near Breckenridge, Texas, where I worked for several months in a gasoline plant. At last I got a chance to go out as a tool-dresser or helper, on a standard (cable tool) drilling rig. Both my driller and the one on the opposite tour[1] were old heads, having started back in West Virginia twenty or thirty years earlier. Paul Bunyan was an old friend of theirs, and occasionally, in their lighter moods, they amused themselves and "kidded" me by calling to mind some of his exploits.

During a two years' absence from the field I learned to appreciate the Bunyan myth as folklore and went back not to work but to collect Bunyaniana. I drifted along the trail of the oil development through Ranger, Breckenridge, Eastland, Cisco, Big Lake, Best, and finally to McCamey, the latest fron-

---

[1]"Tour" is oil field argot for shift, and is invariably pronounced "tower." In the fields in which I worked the twenty-four hours of labor were divided evenly between two "tours."

tier. I had been having the typical luck of the folklorist —
picking up here and there a mannerism, an incident, or running
across a grizzled driller who knew Paul Bunyan but just couldn't
remember any stories right then. At McCamey, however, where
things were doing, I hoped to find Paul Bunyan in action.

My hopes were not justified by the results. Paul Bunyan did
not reign here and revel. I loafed about, raking up speaking
acquaintances with all who looked as if they might even have
heard of Paul and buying drinks for half the idlers in McCamey,
but I found no one who gave me more than a reminiscent
smile and perhaps a slight incident or two. I went out to the
camps, but I found no considerable body of narrative. Either I
failed to discover an old-time tale teller with the genuine crea-
tive fancy, or I lacked the key to unlock their word-hoards. My
efforts resulted in a heterogeneous mass of incidents that spoke
of Paul Bunyan more often as a rig-builder and driller, but
also as a pipeliner, a tank-builder, and even as a constructor of
telegraph lines.

These fragmentary incidents, I became convinced, were the
shreds of a widespread and varied legend of Paul Bunyan as
an oil-field hero; yet the legend, new as it was in a comparatively new industry, seemed to be succumbing to the machinery
of modern life so fatal to all folk creation. I have tried to give
this disjected material a semblance of coherence.

Paul Bunyan appears in the oil fields as a jack of all trades
who nevertheless is proficient in each far beyond the best of
his rivals. He is regarded by the different groups of workers
as having had a large part in developing the tools and methods
of their trade. His own huge strength and uncanny skill, however, enable him often to discard the slow and cumbersome
conventional practices. For instance, as a rig-builder, as the
oil-field carpenter is called, he demonstrated clearly that he
was supreme. He could sight so accurately that no plumb line
was necessary. The arduous and difficult job of "pulling,"
"running," and "sighting" a derrick, *i.e.*, building it, took Paul
only one day, thereby saving two days of the usual time, as
well as the labor of two men. The customary hatchet was too
light for him; his weighed eight pounds and drove any nail

to the head at a single blow. He could build a pair of the great wooden "bull wheels"[2] in half a day, hang the massive "walking beam"[3] by himself, and "skid a rig" (the whole derrick) several yards over by hand. If any timbers, or even the crown block,[4] fell off the structure in the process of building, Paul, who worked below, caught them in his hands to save the lumber as well as the heads of those who might be underneath.

Bunyan was such a powerful and tireless worker, and so considerate of his men, that he used to let them sleep half the tour while he did alone the work of the crew of five. His childish pride in his own ability led him to perform many stunts. One day without help he built a rig and "spudded in"[5] the hole with a Ford motor. He boasted that he could dig faster with a "sharp shooter"[6] than any crew could drill, but since he could never find anyone to call his bet, he did not try this feat. It was not uncommon for him, whenever he grew impatient in building a rig, to drive a sixteen-pound hammer into the ground so deep that the oil came to the surface without drilling. This practice was deplored by the operators because it called for the very inconvenient and wasteful task of dipping the oil out of the hole.

Sometimes Paul's fiery nature caused even greater losses. The visits of officious "high-powers"[7] often made him lose control of his hot temper. At these times the crew ran frantically for cover and left him to vent his rage in a wholesale smashing of derricks for a mile around. The most violent manifestation of this weakness brought him a fortune. One day while up in the derrick, he grew terribly angry at one of his crew who was below. Paul hurled his hatchet at the man with such force that, missing its aim, it penetrated the ground so far that oil gushed

[2]The "bull wheels" form the large reel on which the drilling cable is wound.

[3]The "walking beam" is a great wooden beam that is worked with a seesaw action by the engine, raising and lowering the tools in the hole for drilling.

[4]The crown block is the wooden block on top of the derrick; it holds the pulley wheels over which the steel cables run.

[5]"Spudded in" — i.e., started the hole. The first two or three hundred feet of hole is drilled in a special manner without the walking-beam.

[6]A "sharp shooter" is a long narrow spade.

[7]"High-powers" are officials of high rank in the company controlling the drilling.

up. Quickly forgetting his anger, Paul and his crew set about casing and cementing the hole. The well brought him a million dollars, every cent of which he spent for Mail Pouch tobacco.[8] He had conceived the scheme of soaking his tobacco in corn whiskey and making a "clean-up" by selling it to the oil-field "bullies." His own appetite got the better of him, however, and he chewed it all himself.

Paul did not waste his time with derricks of the usual size. His structures towered far above their conventional neighbors and had telephone connections for each member of the crew. After drilling started, the derrick man was able to come down only twice a month, for pay-day. On one occasion Paul determined to break his record for height. He built the structure up, up, up until it became so tall that he and his crew moved to Heaven and lived there while they finished their work. Paul determined to drill a well worthy of his derrick. He penetrated to China before he stopped drilling.

While building another tall rig, at Bakersfield, California, Paul had a remarkable experience. He was up on the derrick at work when a terrific wind storm carried him out to sea. His first conscious moment found him alone in the Pacific 500 miles from land with his hatchet in his hand, astride a board. A whale appeared and attacked him. Paul fell into the water, killed the big fish with a single blow of his hatchet, and, mounting the dead whale, paddled with his plank back to California.

As a driller Paul Bunyan is quite as striking a figure. He was equally at home on a rotary or on a standard rig; in fact, he devised most of the implements and practices of the trade. His naïve humor is seen in the names used by every driller, toolie, and roughneck: the "headache post"; "Maud," the heavy breakout tongs; "bull wheel" and "calf wheel"; the "lazy-bench," and many other names.[9] On his own rig, when he was using a rotary, he did not unjoint the drill-stem in small sections, to be stacked in the derrick, but simply ran the 2,000 feet of

[8]Mail Pouch chewing tobacco is perhaps the favorite brand in the oil field; Beechnut is a close second.

[9]For explanation of the terms see "Oil Patch Talk" by James W. Winfrey in this volume.

steel pipe up into the air and held it in his hands until the bit was changed. For his own convenience, to allow him to leave the rig, he invented a way of winding the drill pipe around a big drum. He thus saved many days of the time usually required to drill a well. His boilers were so big that anyone who carelessly went near the injectors[10] was sucked up inside. If a boiler blew up, Paul jumped astride it and rode it back safely to earth; he would not be baffled by such annoyances as that.

His experiences on a standard tool rig were often bizarre and colorful. One time while drilling in a mountainous country, he ran on to a "granite-rock" and pounded for a week without making any apparent progress. He put on an extra set of jars[11] without any effect; a third and a fourth set of jars did not help materially, and he finally put on fifteen sets in a desperate effort to save the hole. The terrific pounding jarred the whole lease up fifty feet above the surrounding land before he broke through the rock. On another mountainside location Paul drilled what seemed to be a very deep hole. Finally he ran into "soft diggin' "[12] and decided to set casing before going any farther. He started putting in the casing; it kept going down until it seemed that it wouldn't stop. At last one of the crew who had gone over to another location on an errand came running back to tell him that the pipe was coming out the other side of the mountain. Paul discovered that the "tough diggin' " had deflected the tools; he had drilled through the mountain; the casing had run out and made a pipeline for two miles down the valley. Another experience was more tragic. Paul was drilling in Mexico this time. There was a heavy flow of rubber that drenched the whole rig and cooled before it could be washed off. The poor toolie, who was up in the derrick, could not keep his hold on the slippery boards and fell. He hit the rubber-covered floor and bounced for three days and nights.

[10]The injector sucks water, usually from a depression in the ground, forcing it into the boiler.

[11]The jars are two heavy steel links attached above the drill stem, allowing several inches of play and therefore increasing the shock of the blow.

[12]"Soft diggin' " and "tough diggin' " are common expressions for soft and hard rock.

They finally had to shoot him to keep him from starving to death.[13]

Perhaps the strangest of all Paul's experiences came as the result of an accident. One day he carelessly allowed himself to be caught in the steel drilling cable while the bit was being lowered into the hole. Before he could be stopped he found himself at the bottom of the well in a large cavity in a very warm atmosphere. "It was hot as Hell down there," Paul described the atmosphere later. He soon found that he actually was in Hell. Walking on deeper into the mountain cave, he met the Devil, who greeted him warmly, as if the famous driller were perfectly known to him. The Devil took him all around the place, and at last showed him the harem. The beauties were so ravishing that Paul tried to carry one along, and the Devil in a rage chased him back up the well. Before Paul left, however, he settled a certain question that had been bothering him. Some time before, a "roustabout" who had a grudge against him had sneaked up behind him, cut off his leg, and thrown it down the well. Paul had never grown accustomed to his wooden leg; so while down in Hell he asked about his lost flesh-and-blood limb. The Devil told him it was already roasting on the coals and that he could not have it.

Paul Bunyan would never admit defeat until forced to do so, and then he always made the best of his losses. A particularly good example of his pertinacity and grit is seen in an exploit of his out on the California coast. He was shooting a well,[14] but the charge of five hundred quarts of nitroglycerine exploded while going down the hole. A terrific flow of oil caught the crew altogether unprepared to take care of it. Before they could think, Paul jumped to the well and sat upon the pipe, stopping the flow. The incredible pressure of gas and oil thus restrained forced the casing out of the ground, carrying Paul up in the air so high that he stayed three days before a derrick could be built to rescue him. The well was capped and the oil

13Cf. the story of Pecos Bill's "bouncing bride," "Pecos Bill," in *Century Magazine*, October, 1923.

14"Shooting a well" is exploding a charge of nitroglycerine, "soup," at the bottom of the hole to break up the sand and stimulate the flow of oil.

saved. Paul lost only two holes in his long drilling career. The first loss occurred in the Texas Panhandle. He drilled into an alum bed and the hole shrank up tight, catching the tools so firmly that they could not be released. The second misfortune was just a "piece of hard luck" that Paul could not help. He had been drilling for several months on the top of a very high hill. One night just before the "graveyard shift"[15] came on, a fearful windstorm struck the location, driving with such velocity that it blew all the dirt away from the hole. There was nothing for Paul to do but saw the well up and sell it for post-holes. Another of the rare failures of Bunyan was his attempt to transplant "dry holes"[16] to Europe. They were of no use over here, and besides saving a lot of drilling over there, they might make wells. They were all warped, however, in the rough trip over the waves and had to be thrown away.

Paul Bunyan is known in practically all phases of the oil game, as well as in other trades where he can find hairy-chested bullies for comrades and workers. He is never seen in a "white-collar" job, but is always out where there is "somethin' doin'," with no time for effeminacies of dress and manners. The pipe-liners, the roughest crew to be found in the oil fields, tell of Paul's big camp for which he laid a pipeline to furnish butter-milk for his men. According to them, he was a giant with only one arm, and that in the middle of his chest. His tongs were so heavy that four men were required to carry them. The tank-builders say that Paul's first tank was so high that a hammer which he dropped from the top one day wore out two handles before it hit the ground. Among the telegraph construction men Bunyan also stands out as the leader of them all. They speak of him boastingly as the builder of the Mason and Dixon line.

These various manifestations of the Paul Bunyan theme evidence its vitality and suggest that it is thoroughly and typically native. Paul Bunyan of the oil fields, like Paul Bunyan of the logging camps, is another addition to American folklore. In the homogeneity of their interests and in their relative isola-

15The "graveyard shift" works from twelve at night till twelve noon.
16A "dry hole," a "duster," is one which did not produce oil.

tion from books and other distractions of civilization, hairy-chested American laborers of the twentieth century have made him their superhero.

▼▼▼▼▼▼▼▼▼

Pipeline Diction

ORLAN L. SAWEY

As in many other industrial fields, the pipeliner is gradually being pushed into the background by ever-developing machinery which takes the place of manual labor. Welded pipelines are being used more than screw-joint lines, and machines are digging even the short ditches once dug by hand. There is still, however, in the oil fields much work that can be done only by hand, and there are still several pipeline companies near Corpus Christi that regularly employ pipeline maintenance men.

The two-fisted, rough-and-ready pipeliner, who was once the toughest man in the oil fields, now seems to be found mostly in legend. He has been replaced by the farm boy who plans to settle down ultimately on a small farm and take it easy, or by the disappointed college man. However, there are a few who still hold to the old tradition of Saturday night drunks, empty pockets and a headache on Monday morning.

All types of men are found in oil field work, possibly because it generally pays more than most semiskilled labor. I remember one seven-man crew which consisted of a Jewish refugee, the son of an Arkansas cotton planter, two ex-college men, an ex-soldier, and two farmers. I know a pipeline foreman, an old-timer who spins mighty yarns of Burkburnett and the other early oil fields, and crochets beautiful bedspreads and table-cloths. He plans to crochet a bedspread for each of his grand-children.

Pipeliners have their own special language which consists mostly of technical terms and coined words. Many of these terms are used in the oil field as a whole, but some of them are peculiar to pipelining.

The pipeline maintenance crew, whether it consists of two men or twenty, is invariably called the "gang." For the ambitious pipeliner the gang is only a steppingstone to a better job, but many men content themselves with "roustabout" work and plan to remain in the gang until they get "bumped," or fired.

The straw boss of the gang is called the "pusher." He usually knows quite a bit about pipe fitting and is able to direct such work. He often works with the rest of the men, especially if the gang is short-handed. The foreman, who does the hiring and the firing, is called by the simple title of the "Man," spoken with a capital letter. The superintendent, much more revered, is called the "old Man," and anyone higher than he is called a "Big Shot."

There are pipeliners of varying importance, the least of them being the "boll weevil," or the new man. The roughest and the dirtiest work is thrown his way, but he endures it until another boll weevil enters the gang. Some men, however, because of their inability or their reluctance to learn the trade, always remain boll weevils. Any mistake made by a pipeliner is a "boll weevil stunt," and the penalty for "pulling" such a stunt is the drinks for the gang. A shorter name for a mistake, derived from the penalty, is "coffee."

Another type of pipeliner is the "snapper," the man who always looks for the easiest job, or the "snap." A snapper once told me that snappers could always be found walking the streets, but a man who "hit the ball" always had a job. He was looking for a job the next week. Equally detested is the man who seeks after "pull," in order to win promotion. A man who works steadily and efficiently is a "real pipe hand."

Any job, no matter how small, is called a "contract." The contract most detested by the pipeliner is ditch digging, and he would much rather lay pipeline all day than to dig. The first thing the ditch digger does is to "spud in," this term being used universally in the oil fields, especially in the drilling. To begin digging any hole or ditch is to spud in. The tools used by the ditch digger are the long-handled shovel and the "sharp shooter," a slender-bladed digging spade with a short handle. The first layer of the ditch is dug with the sharp shooter, and the dirt that is left is "crumbed" or "doodled" out with the shovel, and the ditch is left clear of dirt. In especially hard ground a pick is used.

Another contract less distasteful to the pipeliner is the repairing of pipeline leaks. When the line walker "spots" fresh oil near a pipeline, the gang is sent to find the leak. The man who finds it says that he has "got production." A "clamp" is usually placed on the leak, but sometimes it is patched by an electric welder.

The laying of the "screw-joint" line is an interesting procedure. The joints of pipe have threads on each end, and both ends are screwed into a "collar," the name used to designate the simplest form of union. The collar is usually already screwed firmly on one joint of the pipe, the end of which is raised from the ground and placed on the "lazy board," a square piece of lumber with a broken spade handle attached for convenience in carrying. The "stabber" fits a small pipe wrench in one end of the joint of pipe which is to be "rolled in," and the other end of the joint is placed in the collar. The joint is lined up so that it will "roll" easily, and then the "jack," a crude two-legged wooden tool, is placed under the joint next to the stabber, who screws the pipe in as far as it will roll.

The tools usually used in "making the pipe up" are pipe wrenches called "chisel tongs" because a square metal key, or chisel, placed in the jaws of the tongs, grips the pipe. A common type of chisel tongs is the "scissor tongs," so called because the hands open like scissors. One pair of these tongs, the "back ups," is placed behind the collar and the lazy board, with the handles on the ground to keep the pipe from recoiling. Two other pairs of tongs are placed "on top" the joint of pipe to make it up and each is operated by from one to three men, depending on the size of the line.

The pusher usually "pounds" or "packs" the collar with a hammer and the "hook men" "hit" the hooks in time with the beats of the hammer. When the pipe rolls easily, the hook men "break out," or hit at alternating beats of the hammer, but when the pipe rolls harder, they "break in," or strike in unison. When the pipe is made up, the collar packer "rings 'em off," and the whole gang moves on to the next joint.

A pipeline gang usually consist of the back-up man, the collar pounder, who is also the lazy-board man, the hook hitters, the jack man, the stabber, and two or three men who manhandle the joints of pipe and "spell off," or relieve, the other men. Every man in a gang is usually capable of handling any job. If there is more than one man on each pair of hooks, the one on the end of the handles is called the "hook pointer."

There are usually connections to be made in the laying of a line, possibly in the "tying in" of a "battery," a group of small field tanks, near the well. Other tools used in connection work are "chain tongs" and various pipe wrenches. The gripping of the chain tongs is done by a chain which fits around the pipe. They hold much better than chisel tongs, and are easily adapted to the size of the pipe, but chisel tongs are easier to handle. The pipe wrenches are spoken of according to their length in inches, i.e., a "24," "36," or "48."

If a connection is unusually hard to make up or loosen, a short piece of pipe called a "cheater" is placed on the end of the wrench, so there will be more leverage. In loosening a connection the man using the wrench will sometimes take it off the fitting and remark that it should be "handy," meaning that it should be loose enough to be taken off by hand. His companion will then try it and, if it is too tight, will remark, "You pulled it green, Bud. It may be handy for Paul Bunyan, but not for me." This is a favorite expression among pipeliners, and any job too difficult for a man to do is considered a good one for Paul Bunyan, strong man of the oil fields, and pipeliner de luxe.

Strangely enough, the "doghouse" is the place where the pipeliner likes best to be. There are two meanings to this expression. The first kind of doghouse is a canvas shelter over a pipe framework on top of the work truck, constructed to shelter the men from the cold and the rain. The other doghouse is the tool room, or, perhaps, the pump station office. It is there that tales are told about oil-field heroes, the greatest of whom is Paul Bunyan, and about former contracts, which are always larger than those held now. The past is always more glamorous than the uninteresting present, and in the past pipeliners were mightier than they are today and could do unheard-of amounts of work. It is in the doghouse that the pipeliner becomes a superman, loath to return to his everyday task of keeping the oil flowing.

▼▼▼▼▼▼▼▼▼▼

Oil Patch Talk

JAMES W. WINFREY

Oil-field hands use a large vocabulary of names and expressions which apply to the work and life that go with drilling for and producing petroleum. As is true with working men away from women in all industries, many of their most colorful phrases are salted with unprintable words, a large portion of them referring to the questionable parentage of almost anything. However, there remain a great many interesting expressions, some that are meaningless outside an oil field, others that are from the soil and would be understood by any Texan. All of this talk recorded here has been picked up in the Texas Gulf Coast.

"Get the job done" is an expression common among oil-field hands from the roustabout to the general superintendent. It is traditional in the "oil patch," a colloquial variation of "oil field" or just "the field," not to back off from any job no matter what the difficulties or how dangerous. "Do something, if you do it wrong."

If a roustabout or roughneck complains about wages or hard work to a fellow worker, he will probably be told, "You hired out to work, didn't you? There is a fellow up town living on a cracker a day that wants your job." The reply may be, "I was looking for a job when I got this one," or, "I've got my sack full anyhow," or, "I've got it made." The last two expressions mean he is independent, doesn't need a job. He may say, "I'm ready to drag up (quit), I've got money in the bank and cattle out west." If this man is really a trouble maker, he may get "run off" (fired). He might just get "eat out" or take a "reaming" from his boss, the driller.

If there is a smart aleck in a crew who is always "popping off," there is usually some other roustabout or roughneck who will "put the packoff on him," or shut him up. This expression is from a device used to control the flow of a well.

At the end of a hard day one of the hands will probably say, "I gave 'em an honest jump today," or "Another day, another dollar. In a million days I'll be a millionaire." He may be told, "Well, boy, you be back here in the morning without a pain in your body, 'cause you're gonna keep your head down and your rear up if you make it on this job."

If you have to work overtime, you are "stuck." When you are in a big hurry, you "hull out" or "gin" (gin a bale).

Anything heavy around a drilling rig, especially the drill pipe, is called "pig iron." When "the man" is advising the driller he is doing a job wrong, if he is an old-timer, he will say, "That ain't well diggin'."

An evasive answer to an inquiry as to a hand's whereabouts is, "He went to Fort Worth with a load of goats."

Regardless of the occupation, whether drilling, production, or in the office, to "make a hand" means to be a competent, efficient worker.

One of the most universally used terms is "boll weevil," which means an inexperienced man. "Boll weevil tongs" are chain tongs that even a boll weevil cannot put on the pipe wrong. One manufacturer calls his tubing head a "boll weevil tubing head" because it does not require an experienced man to land it. A shop-made device that injects lubricating oil into the steam line on a drilling rig is a "boll weevil lubricator." A boner in any kind of work is a "boll weevil stunt."

If a man is dumb or forgetful, he is "like a goose, wakes up in a new world every day."

One of the less offensive names for a man who plays up to

his boss for special favors is a "graper," who is held in very low esteem.

You are in a "boom" if a lot of work is going on, whether drilling or production. If you cannot handle your job, it "eats you up." If you get in trouble, you are in a "bind." When you try to do a job and it goes wrong, you may be told you "twisted off," which comes from the name for a drill pipe failure. This expression is common in poker games. When a player draws to a straight or flush and misses, he will say, "I twisted off."

If any kind of equipment fails, the operator will say it "swarmed" (as a bee colony separates) or more commonly, it "cratered." This last word comes from the description of the worst kind of "blowout" or wild well, where a huge crater is formed.

When a man says he is ready to "flange up" he is about through. This common saying comes from the necessity of using a flange union to complete nearly all pipe connection jobs.

During an active drilling campaign (a boom), when the edge of the field is discovered by a rig encountering the pro-ducing sand below the salt water horizon, they have "hit the Gulf of Mexico" or "the suitcase sand." The roughnecks know that before long there will be a "suitcase parade" of layoffs or transfers. This will usually start as "roughneck talk" (rumors).

A well which fails to produce oil or gas is a "duster" or "dry hole." A gas well is a "blue whistler." A well or field that has to be pumped is "on the beam," the "walking beam," that is.

A roughneck who loses his girl to another has been "drilled around." If someone passes him up for a better job, he has been "sidetracked" or "by-passed."

An oil company that has a hard time financially and has to use patched-up equipment is a "po' boy (poor boy) outfit." The community of houses built up around a major oil company head-quarters is called the "camp." The company-owned houses built to accommodate the key men are usually in a group. The privately owned houses where the "hands" live are officially the "employees' camp," but the people who live there sometimes call it the "po' boy camp," although many of the "po' boys" have a nicer "spread" than the company houses.

Any kind of faked or altered reports are "boiler housed," referring to the alleged practice of pumpers "gauging their tanks in the boiler house."

Occupation names are as colorful as the rest of the oil-field diction. All officials from the main office are "pressure," or "big shots." The manager of a field is officially the district super-intendent, but the hands will refer to him as the "kingfish," "head roustabout," "head knocker," or "the man." Anyone with authority has "stroke." The "stroke department" includes the district superintendent, tool pushers, and farm bosses. The engi-neers are called, among other things, the "brains department" or just "brains."

A tool pusher is in charge of one or more drilling rigs. The name originated in the days when his main job was to keep the rig supplied with drill bits or tools and the day driller was king of the rig. Now the bits are handled by a truck driver known as the "junk hustler," and the tool pusher has authority over all drilling crews.

A farm boss is in charge of producing and treating oil after the wells are completed. All gangs and pumpers work under him. The name probably started in the early days when a producing unit, now referred to as a lease, was called a farm, which it usually was.

A rotary driller is foreman of a drilling crew. He is more often called a "rig runner," "well digger," or "digger." Speaking of a day driller, a roughneck will say he is "running days." The 4:00 P.M. to midnight shift is called "evening tour" (pronounced tower), and midnight to 8:00 A.M. is "morning tour" or the "graveyard shift." The driller operates the drawworks and rotary to drill the hole or run pipe in or out.

Next to the driller is the derrick man, who works in the derrick when pipe is being run in or out of the hole. He is also pump repair man. They say he "works derricks."

The two rotary helpers are the legendary "roughnecks." When making a "trip" (out and in the hole with the drill pipe) one is "pipe racker," who guides the stand of drill pipe coming out of the hole to its proper place on a platform and "stabs" it in the joint hanging in the rotary going in the hole. He also latches the breakout tongs and helps handle the slips. The other roughneck works the "boll weevil corner," which is always the first job for an inexperienced man. He latches on the backup tongs coming out of the hole and the makeup tongs going in the hole if a star post is used. A roughneck is emphatically a skilled laborer.

The fifth man in a drilling crew is the fireman or "pot fireman." He fires the boilers with gas or oil, repairs the boiler feed pumps, and helps out the roughnecks during trips. Two of his most important jobs are to make coffee and to wash the crew's overalls in a "blow barrel," usually a fifty-five gallon oil drum connected up to water and steam. It is rough on the overalls, but gets them clean.

The foreman of a gang is a roustabout gangpusher. His crew consists of three more roustabouts. Their duties are to connect oil wells to the gas-oil separators and lease-stock tanks, maintain all producing equipment, and keep the producing properties cleaned up. A gangpusher is said to be "pushing a gang" while a roustabout is "in the gang."

A lease pumper is called a pumper even though every well in the field is flowing. It is his duty to regulate the flow of the wells, gauge the tanks into which the wells produce, treat oil water emulsion, and report on "gauge tickets" all oil.

A rig builder erects and dismantles derricks and has nothing to do with the drilling rig. The name originated in the days of wooden derricks when the rig builders built the derrick and then hewed out a walking beam, made a bull wheel and sampson post for "standard" pumping rig.

A "dry watchman" watches a rig that has been shut down or "stacked."

The "crum boss" is custodian of the bunkhouse. I do not know the origin of the name, but "crum" is an archaic form of crumb.

A "swamper" is a truck or tractor driver's helper, but the name is often used for any kind of helper. The "dauber" is a welder and a "pump doctor" is a pump repair man.

Equipment and tools used in the field also have their peculiar names, some functional, some fanciful. The steam, gas, or diesel engine driven hoist which raises and lowers pipe in the hole by means of a wire rope run through a "crown block" on top of the derrick and a "traveling block" moving in the derrick is called the "drawworks." While running or pulling pipe the "hook" below the "traveling block" supports the "elevators," a device that latches around the pipe by means of steel loops called "elevator bails." While drilling or "making hole," the drill pipe is supported by a "swivel" and "kelly joint" or "grief stem" suspended from the hook and screwed into the drill pipe. The "kelly joint" is a square, hexagonal, or grooved hollow forging, which slides through and fits snugly in the "rotary drive bushing." The "rotary" is a turntable controlled by the driller and usually turned by a chain from the "drawworks." The "rotary hose" connects the "swivel" to the top of the "standpipe," a pipe run up a corner of the derrick. The bottom of the standpipe connects to reciprocating "slush pumps" or "mud hogs" and drilling fluid or "mud" is pumped through the drill pipe and bit all the time it is rotating on bottom.

If a well is being drilled and the drilling fluid (mud) pumped down the drill pipe enters the formation instead of flowing back up the hole, you "lose returns." When the end of an old catline or bull rope is raveled out it becomes "soft line." A chaise longue-looking affair is made by a fireman out of 2 x 12 boards for his personal use in front of the boiler and is called his "lazy bench." When pipe is being measured (tallied) the man who holds the end of the tape to one end of the pipe has the "ignorant end." The cross beam at the top of the draw-works is the "headboard." The vertical columns which support drawworks bearings are "jack posts." The opposite end of the drilling line from the drawworks drum is tied down to a "dead man."

The "rathole" is a joint of casing stuck through the derrick floor a few feet from the rotary and drilled down into the ground. When the kelly is not being used to drill it is lowered in the rathole and does not have to be laid down. When the size of the bore hole is reduced while "coring" the small hole is also called "rathole."

Heavy pieces of pipe which run adjacent to the bit on bottom of the drill pipe are "drill collars." Any kind of adapter used between two sizes of pipe is a "sub." When anything is lost in the hole, it is a "fish" and all devices used to recover material dropped in the hole are "fishing tools." If it is to go inside the fish, it is a "spear," but if it fits over the fish, it is an "overshot." A "bulldog spear" is one that cannot be released. One type of sucker rod overshot used on pumping wells is called a "mousetrap." There are innumerable kinds of patented fishing tools.

Several years ago when heavy tool joints were first being used to connect joints of drilling pipe, operators did not put them on every joint. A tool joint "box" went on top of a stand of pipe and a "pin" on bottom. If the stands were "doubles" a drill pipe coupling connected the two joints; if they were "thribbles" two couplings connected the three joints of pipe. While drilling it is necessary to make single joint connections each time you "make the kelly down." To accomplish this one joint was equipped with a box and pin for stringing doubles and two such joints for thribbles. These were the "grey-hounds." They were used as follows: make the kelly down, pull it out and run in a greyhound; make the kelly down, pull it out, lay down the two greyhounds and run in a thribble; repeat the process. Since every joint of drill pipe is now equipped with a box and pin, greyhounds are obsolete.

Now when drill pipe is removed from the hole, it is stood on end with two to four pieces screwed together. They are referred to as "doubles," "thribbles," or "fourbles," a "stand," or "a set back." The platform the derrick man works on is called the "double board" or "fourble board" but rarely the "thribble board." Each piece of drill pipe is called a "joint" or "stalk." Short pieces of line pipe are "nipples." Short joints of casing or tubing are "pup joints." Short sucker rods are "pony rods." The connections between joints are "tool joints." Two methods used in racking the drill pipe back are the "hayrake method" and "finger and monkey board method." The platform around the top of the derrick is the "water table" and the cross beam above it is the "gin pole."

A driller knows how much weight is on the bit in the bottom of the hole by watching the weight indicator attached to the drilling line. If it has a weight recorder on it, the roughnecks call it a "stool pigeon," because the tool pusher by looking at the chart can tell not only whether the rig has been shut down in his absence, but the exact time.

The boilers are the "pots" and the automatic firing control on the boilers is the "nigger boy." Steam is sometimes called "smoke."

A wide, smooth-faced, flanged pulley on the end of the drawworks lineshaft is the "cathead" and the rope (usually 1½ in.) which runs on it by friction is the "cat line."

A very heavy set of chain tongs used only on hard-to-break drill collars is called "Old Maude" or the "bull tongs." A rotary made so that the center can remain still while the outside turns is called "double deck." When it is used to make up pipe going in the hole the chain tongs are engaged by an erect tool called the "star post" which fits into the moving outside ring of the rotary while the weight of the drill pipe in the hole is carried by "slips" resting in the rotary. Some rigs make up their drill pipe with a "spinning line" which turns it by friction and is pulled by the "cathead."

Most drawworks are equipped with a hydraulic device on the drum shaft to take part of the load off the brakes going in the hole. This is called the "water brake" or "yo yo" from its resemblance to the well-known toy.

When a hole is started, it is "spudded in" from the "grass roots." The first pipe cemented in the hole is "surface casing," usually 9⅝ in., 10¾ in., or 13⅜ in. in diameter. The casing head, sometimes called "braden head" from one of the early manufacturers, is screwed on the surface casing. The "blowout preventer" flanges to the top of the casing head and is designed to stop the well from flowing from around the drill pipe when it is in the hole. The last string of casing run is the "oil string" and the small pipe suspended in it is "tubing."

If someone asks a driller how deep he is, the stock answer is "deep as a tree."

Should a "pay sand" be encountered and oil string casing set, a strainer of smaller diameter than the casing will usually be set adjacent to the oil sand and held down by "liner" and a "packer." The strainer is called "screen" regardless of its construction. The liner is pipe of the same diameter as the screen; the packer is a patented device usually employing canvas to seal between the screen setting and casing. After the screen is set, the blowout preventer is removed, and the tubing swung from the "tubing head." The well is finally closed in with a manifold of valves and connections universally known as the "christmas tree." It may consist of only one valve or a dozen valves and other elaborate control equipment.

Tools used by a roustabout gang are practically the same as described by Orlan L. Sawey in his article "Pipeline Diction" in the present volume. A gang will connect the pipe "flowline" to the "christmas tree" at a well so the oil can flow to the tank "battery," a group of tanks where all oil produced on a lease is measured and "run" to a pipeline company which transmits it to the refinery. Rate of production of a flowing well is controlled by a restriction in the flowline called a "choke." Natural gas is separated from the oil by a gas-oil separator usually called a "trap." If the well produces salt water with the oil, it is usually "treated out" by flowing through a "gun barrel," a tall tank with a vertical "flume" in the center. In recent years many operators use a "flow treater" instead of a gun barrel. It is an elaborate patented device containing several compartments and a heater. One pumper calls his "the Rice Hotel," because it has so many rooms in it.

When pressure is released from a well or pressure vessel, it is "bled off." A long-handled shovel is a "canal wrench." A device used to grip guy lines so they may be tightened is a "come along." A hand-operated brace for drilling holes in steel by hand is "the old man." A steel load binder for tightening a chain around the load on a truck is a "boomer."

A pumper's office is his "dog house" and the territory he covers is his "beat." A device he uses to take oil samples from a tank is a "thief." A small opening in the top of a tank is the "thief hatch."

A heat exchanger used on gas lift wells to prevent the gas choke from freezing is a "watermelon." A well that flows intermittently "heads."

A hand-operated pump used to lift water out of a "cellar" (the hole around a well head while it is being drilled) is a "one armed Johnnie."

A malodorant added to natural gas so that leakage may readily be detected by smell is "skunk oil." An individual gas odorizor used on isolated houses is a "stink bomb."

Some of the older fields in the Gulf Coast still pump wells with "standard rigs," that is, cable tool drilling rigs. The wire line drum, drum pulley, and brake wheel make up the "bull wheel." When "sucker rods" (also called sucker poles) are pulled, the bull wheel is connected to the "band wheel" in the "belt house" by the "bull rope," a heavy manila rope or small wire line. The band wheel is belt driven by some kind of prime mover. While the standard rig is "bobbin'" (pumping) the pump down in the well is suspended from the end of the "walking beam" by the sucker rods and "beam hanger." The walking beam rocks on the "sampson post" riding the "saddle bearing." A post set under the walking beam to catch the weight of the sucker rods in case the pitman breaks on a standard rig is the "headache post." On modern rigs a steel segment of a circle on the rod end of the walking beam is the "horsehead." The beam hanger is a "bridle." The oscillating motion is transmitted from the prime mover through a crank to the beam by a vertical member called a "pitman."

Among the transportation equipment, a tractor is a "cat" and a large flat bed semi-trailer truck is a "dance hall." A short-bed four-wheel truck is a "bob tail." The boom on a crane truck is the "stinger." A removable semi-trailer truck bed is a "float."

When a roustabout thinks a connection is screwed up tight, he says, "That'll do me." I believe that flanges me up.

Aunt Cordie's Ax and Other Motifs in Oil

MODY C. BOATRIGHT

In all the oil regions of the United States there circulate certain archetypical stories which are told as truth and often printed in good faith, but which in many instances prove to have little or no basis in fact. Such stories are not without interest in themselves; and if they are folklore (as I believe they are) a study of their content and distribution should throw some light upon the development of folklore in a literate and increasingly industrial society. Pending a more thorough study, which must await further collecting, I offer this account as a preliminary report on some of these tales. In it I shall deal with only three typical and widely distributed motifs.

One of these is the story of the new ax. It is meant to be comic, the humor depending upon the discrepancy between the wants and the means of the formerly poor but now rich landowner. I first heard the story in the McClesky version from Ranger, Texas.

In 1917 Uncle John and Aunt Cordie McClesky, as their neighbors called them, were living on a farm a mile south of Ranger. They had an unpretentious but substantial farm house with a garden and orchard, for, like most of their neighbors, they produced much of their food at home. For cash income John McClesky grew cotton and peanuts, and worked as a bricklayer on the rare occasions when there were any brick to be laid in the little village. He was not used to handling large sums of money, but his condition was hardly one of poverty. The owner of property valued at some $20,000, he ranked among the more prosperous farmers of his community.

It was upon his farm that the Ranger discovery well came in on October 22, 1917, with a flush production which gave him an income of about $250 a day. Some weeks after his good fortune he built a cottage in Ranger, where the McClesky Hotel, representing the first sizable investment of his oil money, was under construction.

It was at this time that a newspaper woman from Fort Worth

called upon Mrs. McClesky for an interview. The reporter quoted her as saying that when the well came in, her husband asked what he might buy for her. Mrs. McClesky replied, "Well, the blade of the old ax has a nick in it and I would like to have a new one to chop kindling with."[17]

I have heard this story in several variants (in one the handle of the ax is so old and rough that it leaves splinters in her hands) from at least a dozen informants who believe it to be true. I accepted it as truth myself until a few years ago when on the trail of Gib Morgan I found the same story in Pennsylvania. I have since heard it from Desdemona, where a farmer is reputed to have said that he was going to get not only the best ax that money could buy, but also a grindstone and a gasoline engine to turn it. Then he was going into a thicket and see how it felt to attack a post oak with a really sharp ax.[18] Bob Duncan has a version of the ax story from Beaumont.[19] Haldeen Braddy heard it in Vann. George Sessions Perry must have heard it, for in one of his short stories he has a character say to another who had oil land in East Texas, "He's got so much money he can't hardly spend it. He bought three new axes an' a barrel of lamp oil an' a barrel of flour, that didn't even make a dent in his money."[20]

Doubts therefore arise as to whether or not Mrs. McClesky did in fact ask her husband for a new ax. She and her husband are dead and their children have left the state. Among their neighbors the story is widely believed, but I have found no informant who will vouch for its authenticity. Mrs. Hagerman, the widow of the first mayor of Ranger, for example, said that since Mrs. McClesky did not consider herself too good to go to the woodpile and cut up an armful of wood, the story was not impossible. She said, however, that many stories were told about the McCleskys which she knew to be false. She said that at one time in the Ranger-Breckenridge area " a McClesky"

[17]Boyce House, *Were You at Ranger?* (Dallas, 1935), p. 15.
[18]*Ibid.*, p. 78.
[19]Bob Duncan, *The Dicky Bird Was Singing* (New York, 1952), p. 268.
[20]George Sessions Perry, *Hackberry Cavalier* (New York, 1944), p. 42.

was used as a common noun to designate any comic story of
the newly rich.

John Rust, who lived on the farm adjoining the McCleskys
and was twelve years old when the well came in, said in a
tape-recorded interview:

Yes, I heard the story and I've always doubted that it's true.
It could be true certainly, and I'm not sitting here to say that
it's not a true story. . . . I will tell you that I didn't hear her
make the remark, but then of course she could have made it . . .
without my presence. But knowing her . . . and her husband as
I have known them for years, all my life, and the kind of people
they are . . . I just don't believe that she made the remark at
all. She might have made it, however, in a joking sort of way,
just for fun. But to seriously make the remark, I doubt if she
would make it.

I know that they didn't do silly things with their money; they
were good, thrifty people. They always had plenty to eat and they
looked presentable in their clothes. Old John McClesky was the
kind of man that didn't have his ax blade gapped up anyhow. He
had an old-fashioned grindstone — I remember where it used to sit
— and I've been over there before the oil boom at their home, and
maybe old John would be gone somewhere or out in the field working or something, and Aunt Cordie would need some wood to cook
the evening meal. I've gone out there and picked up that ax, and I
remember that it always had a sharp blade.

And I just have every reason to kind of doubt that she made the
remark.

Joe Weaver, retired oil operator who came to Texas from
West Virginia by way of Oklahoma, and who was beginning
operations in the Ranger area before the McClesky well came
in, said that he did not believe the story. Then he said he
would tell me what he called "an old West Virginia story."
Oil was discovered on a widow's farm, "and her boys went
to Harpersburg to celebrate. They had had a tough time and
the widow had been a very hard worker. And the boys were
enjoying themselves when one turned to the other saying, 'We
must take mother a gift,' and the other one said, 'Well, what
in the world will we take her?' And the first suggested, 'I know,
we will take her a new ax.'"

Tradition does not indicate that the first purchase of every suddenly enriched landowner was an ax. It might be a stalk of bananas, a cookstove, linoleum for the kitchen floor, a XXXX beaver Stetson. But the ax seems to be the most constant symbol of the new status. Its appeal may rest partly on irony. Oil brings a new fuel and makes the family chopping ax obsolete.

Another motif is that of the lucky breakdown. As drilling equipment is being moved to a wildcat location made by a geologist, transportation fails and the well is drilled at the scene of the breakdown. It is a producer, but when the original location is later drilled, the well is a duster.

This story, observes Samuel W. Tait, Jr., "has been related about every oil field I know, whether it be sandy desert, boggy swamp, muddy prairie, or rocky mountain, and it has probably happened in every one of them."[21] The one instance that Tait vouches for happened in the sandy desert of California in 1895.

There are several occurrences of the story in Texas. Of these I have been able to verify only one, and it is little known. J. R. Webb of Albany, Texas, entered into a partnership with a relative to drill a well in Shackelford County, where oil, when found at all, was encountered at shallow depths. The partner, a geologist, now a man of high position in an oil company, made the location on the top of a hill. When machinery arrived it was found that the trucks could not be driven up the grade, and in those pre-bulldozer days the construction of a road involved more money than they cared to risk. They set up the rig at the base of the hill and got oil. Part of the returns from this well were used to build a road to the original location, where drilling brought a dry hole.

Few people have heard of the Webb-Crutchfield experience, but nearly everybody in Texas and Oklahoma knows the legend of the Fowler Farm Oil Company.

S. L. Fowler, owner of a large and rich cotton farm in the Red River Valley just north of the little town of Burkburnett, Texas, in 1918 decided to give up farming and become a ranchman. He figured that the proceeds from the sale of his farm would buy sufficient grassland to sustain a herd large enough

21Samuel W. Tait, Jr., *The Wildcatters* (Princeton, 1946), p. 113.

to make him a good living. The only difficulty was that Texas has a community property law, and Mrs. Fowler would not consent to the sale. She was quoted by one journalist as saying: "I believe there's oil under our land, and I won't agree to dispose of the farm until a test is drilled. If oil isn't found, I'll sign the papers; but the people of this section have undergone so many hardships with such patience that I just know there is something good in store for them."[22]

Finding his spouse adamant, Fowler decided that the only way to sell the farm was to meet her condition, so he called on his neighbors for help. He figured that it would take $12,000 to put down a well deep enough to satisfy his wife. He put up a thousand dollars and his friends subscribed varying amounts until the sum was raised. One of the subscribers was Walter Cline, a drilling contractor who happened to have an idle rig in North Texas at the moment. In exchange for a thousand-dollar interest in the venture, he agreed to furnish the rig and the services of his drilling superintendent.

A geologist was employed, according to legend, who staked out a location in the cotton field. The wagon hauling the first load of equipment bogged down in the sand. "Oh well, unload her here," Fowler said, since for his purpose one place was as good as another.

The well came in and opened the Burkburnett Field. After a few months the Fowler Farm Oil Company sold out for $1,800,000, paying the shareholders $15,000 for each one hundred invested.

The figures are history and a part of the legend is true. Neighborliness did enter into the formation of the company. Sand had something to do with the location of the well, and a well drilled later north of the discovery produced only salt water. The rest is imagination.

As Walter Cline remembers, the project began to take shape one day in front of Luke Staley's drug store, "where we usually congregated and did our whittling and settling really heavy problems."

[22]Boyce House, *Oil Boom* (Caldwell, 1941), p. 39.

S. L. [Fowler] broke the news to the bunch [Mr. Cline continues] that he wanted to dispose of his cotton land and get him a piece of ranch land but that his wife thought they ought to drill a well on the land and that he didn't have money enough and he was going to have to get some help, and he wanted to know if any of us would be interested. Well, there was nothing particularly favorable to encourage anyone to want to spend any money or time or effort on the Fowler land. On the other hand, there was nothing that definitely condemned it. So we sat around and decided that just as friends and neighbors, we'd just do our boy scout good turn by putting in a little, not enough to hurt any of us, but maybe enough to poorboy a well down. . . .

And we got enough money committed to look like we could afford to drill a well. The question of location then came up and we decided there wasn't any use in pulling a whole lot of sand, going way out in this cotton patch, and we'd drill it reasonably close to town. So we went right north of the hog pen that was east of S. L.'s house with a lane through there and a gate, drove out in the field where we had driven a stake and drilled there.

I'd like to interject here the statement that there's been very few discovery wells brought in that the myth hasn't started that they decided to drill a well on a given ranch or a given farm or on a given part of ground and they started out and it rained like the devil or they broke the wagon wheel or the truck broke down, and they were already on the property where they wanted to drill and they were a half-mile or a mile from the location, and they said, "Oh well, hell, let's just unload it. One place is as good as another. We're on the right land. We'll drill it here."

Well, now I heard that. I've heard it about the Fowler well and I've heard it about practically every discovery well that's been drilled in Texas in my time, and I have yet to find a single instance of where that's true. I just don't think there's a bit of truth in it. I know it's not true so far as the Fowler well is concerned. We drilled the Fowler well right where we intended to drill it, and right where we drove our stake. And that definitely settles the Fowler well.[23]

Another and more elaborate version of the lucky breakdown story is the one concerning Santa Rita, the discovery well in the Big Lake Field, the first of the oil fields to be opened on the endowment lands of the University of Texas.

The earliest published version of this story that I have found

[23]Tape-recorded interview, Wichita Falls, August 13, 1952.

is that of Owen P. White in the New York *Times* for May 3, 1925.

> When the lease was signed Krupp [Hyman Krupp, organizer and president of the company] went to work. He hired expensive oil experts ... to go out and locate the proper anticlines for him and then after this had been done, busied himself in getting together enough money to drill the well. ... The months flew by until the date on which the lease would automatically expire was dangerously near. Krupp redoubled his efforts and finally, with only a few days to go, he took the road with three trucks loaded with drilling equipment.
>
> When Krupp was still several miles away from the precious stake, which had cost him several thousand dollars to have driven in the ground, one of his trucks broke down completely, and—there he was! At that time, as the story goes, he had only two days left. What should he do? There was no possibility of being able to reach the desired destination with his outfit. The breakdown had occurred on land covered by his lease and so, with no high-salaried geologist at hand to advise him, but merely because the ox was in the ditch and he had to act at once to prevent forfeiture, Krupp set up his rig at the scene of the disaster and went to work.

Another version of the tale was included in the general report of the Sun Oil Company covering operations in West Texas and New Mexico up to November 1, 1929. A paragraph reads:

> An unusual incident occurred when the Big Lake Field in Reagan County was discovered in 1923. Location for their first test was made some two miles westward, but owing to a breakdown while transporting the materials to the location, they unloaded just where the incident happened, and this well, while it led to a small producer, led to the discovery of the Big Lake Field. Had the first test been drilled where the location was originally made, possibly new chapters would have been written regarding the field. Subsequent tests have proven their first location would have been a failure.[24]

A writer in the *Daily Texan,* student newspaper of the University of Texas, for February 9, 1940, told the story as follows:

> The site, in the southwestern part of Reagan County, at which the first oil well was completed in May, 1923, was chosen purely by acci-

[24]This and the two newspaper stories following are quoted by Martin Schwettman, "The Discovery and Early Development of the Big Lake Oil Field," M. A. Thesis, University of Texas, 1941.

dent. The drilling party, headed by Frank Pickrell, was bogged down. Since the lease was to expire in a few hours, members decided to drill where they were stranded.

They drilled not on their own lease, but on a part of the 2,000,000 acres provided by the Constitution for the University endowment fund and now known as the Big Lake Field.

But for a real professional handling of the story, we turn to the Austin *Statesman* for January 23, 1940.

The ragged country with its old worn jutting hills, crouched beneath the terrible drenching from the rains. Little rivers ran where dry gulches with their platted grasses formerly cut through the terrain.

In slicker and chewing the end of an old cigar, a man named Frank Pickrell peered from the switch house into a torrent of rain, walked impatiently back and forth.

"All right, boys," he said, "I've got a lot of money tied up in this. We've got to take a chance. We've got to get this machinery going."

And the boys got up and in the heavy rain began loading the rig and drilling machinery on the cumbersome wagons. In a little while they got started.

Mud clawed at the wheels and sucked at the mules' feet. The animals grunted and strained at the traces and the wagons creaked through the slime over the treacherous roads.

"Just seven miles to go," encouraged Mr. Pickrell. The rain poured. The men cursed and cracked whips, and wiped the mud from their eyes.

The geologist had said that oil would be found on a certain spot. Mr. Pickrell was determined to reach that spot. Then the rain came down in torrents. It almost hid one team from another. West Texas had never seen it rain like that before.

Up front there was much cursing. Hazy figures floundered here and there. Mr. Pickrell stalked up front. The lead wagon was mired. There wasn't any use, the straining mules could not budge it.

"We'll have to wait," said Mr. Pickrell. The boys huddled together to wait. The skies were puffed and swollen with clouds, and the rain chattered along the gullies and around the wagons.

They waited all day. Mr. Pickrell knew his West Texas. "Boys," he said, "this thing'll keep up. Another day and we'll be here two weeks getting to that place. Unload her here. We'll dig our well right here."

Now the testimony gathered by Schwettman from Pickrell and other participants in the event is to the effect that (1) it was not raining when the equipment was being moved; on the contrary, the ranchers were complaining about a long dry spell, (2) horses rather than mules or trucks were used to draw the equipment, (3) there was no breakdown, (4) the well was located where the geologist had driven the stake.

Pickrell had previously certified that the well had been located at the stake driven by the geologist and that it was upon the recommendation of the geologist that the well had been drilled. Moreover, the breakdown story became an issue in a lawsuit in 1926. The court found the story false and so stated in its judgment.[25] This, however, did not dispose of the legend. Three of the four written versions I have quoted came after the decision, and folks in Texas still talk about the lucky breakdown that first brought oil to their university.

The third motif is that of the million-dollar drink. This is no Coal Oil Johnny episode in which a million dollars is spent; instead, a million dollars is gained, though not for the celebrant.

In one form of the story that celebrant is a geologist. He is called upon to make a hurried decision, when, unfortunately, he is too drunk to study his data. He makes a random mark on the map, and when he sobers up he realizes that it is not on the structure as he had plotted it. He remains silent, however, and hopes for the best. The best happens, and subsequent drilling on the location he would have made had he been sober results in a dry hole.[26]

In the more common form of the story, the big brass in a distant city decide to abandon a well. But the driller or someone in the chain of authority between him and the president of the company fails because of drunkenness to see the order carried out. Drilling continues a few hours longer and a million-dollar sand is tapped.

This tale is told of the McClesky well, but it has met with no wide credence in the Ranger area.

The classical Texas example, like that of the lucky breakdown, comes from the Big Lake Field and involves Frank Pickrell. In 1928 a deep test known as University 1-B was being

25Schwettman, op. cit., p. 20.
26Duncan, op. cit., pp. 37 ff.

put down with cable tools. At a depth of 8,245 feet the bailer hung, the sand line parted, a long and expensive fishing job ensued, and the company decided to abandon the well. The order was not carried out, and the discovery of a new producing horizon resulted.

The reason the order was not carried out, according to a widely circulated report that reached print in the San Angelo *Standard-Times* for May 28, 1933, was the million-dollar drink.

Late in November, 1928 Frank Pickrell, Texon vice president, ordered a halt at 8,343 feet. The deep wildcat had cost over $100,000. Cromwell reported that the formation looked promising and argued successfully that drilling continue. On Saturday, Dec. 1, the bit reached 8,518 in black lime. Pickrell again telephoned and this time insisted that work stop. Cromwell stopped to revive his spirits with what someone later aptly termed "a million dollar drink," and decided he could notify the crew the next morning. Meanwhile the drill kept pounding.

Early the next morning the driller phoned Cromwell that the well was spraying oil. "Hit 'er another foot," Cromwell instructed and No. 1-B began to flow for a new world's record depth of 8,525 feet.[27]

Schwettman also investigated this legend. What basis it has in fact is indicated by a letter he received from Waldo Williams, chief driller.[28] Williams said that the "big boys had a meeting in New York and decided that $140,000 was enough to spend on a non-paying well." They ordered Pickrell to stop drilling at 8,500 feet. Pickrell then called Cromwell by telephone and gave the order. Cromwell then talked over the prospects of the well with Williams, and was so confident of success that he said instead of giving the order he would disappear for a few days. On the second day of December the well flowed forty barrels of oil.

Williams began trying to locate Cromwell. After two days he was found at an editors' convention in Sweetwater. In a few hours after he received the message, he was on the location directing the completion of the well.

These are some of the local exemplifications of some of the motifs that seem to be coextensive with the oil industry in the

[27]Quoted by Schwettman, *op. cit.*, pp. 101-3.
[28]*Ibid.*

United States. The tales have been only meagerly collected, and little can be said with assurance concerning the localities of their origin. Although I have not been able to verify any instance of the ax or the million-dollar drink stories, it is not improbable that they, like the legend of the lucky breakdown, have happened somewhere, perhaps more than once.

The stories I have dealt with and many others have been disseminated through both the spoken and the written word. The mobility of the personnel of the oil industry and the high rate of circulation of newspapers and magazines among the American people account for their wide diffusion. In no case have I been able to determine with certainty whether a local version was circulated first in oral or in written form. The newspaper account of Mrs. McClesky's ax followed so close upon the discovery of oil that my informants cannot say whether or not the tale had been previously in oral circulation. My belief is that the reporter had heard the story before and was the first to apply it to Mrs. McClesky.

The story of the lucky breakdown in connection with the Big Lake discovery was in oral circulation by midsummer following the completion of the well in May, 1923. The earliest version I have found in print is that of May 3, 1925. The earliest printed version of the million-dollar drink story that I know of was published May 28, 1933, nearly four and a half years after the event. The reporter intimated that the tale was then in oral circulation.

Whichever preceded, the history of these tales illustrates the manner in which the spoken and the printed word complement each other in the development of one type of folklore in a literate society.

Like most folk motifs, they involve the unusual, the unexpected. Yet why some stories are interesting and are widely repeated and others are not cannot be fully explained. But in any group there will be those who know a good story when they hear one and are not too strictly bound by facts to alter them if it makes the story better. And there will always be feature writers who are not averse to changing and embellishing facts to make salable copy.

Appendix

Selections in this book located by volume numbers in the
Publications of the Texas Folklore Society

PEREZ, SOLEDAD
  Dichos from Austin. XXIV.
  Ratoncito Pérez. XXIV.
  Susto. XXIV.
  The Weeping Woman. XXIV.
SAWEY, ORLAN L. Pipeline Diction. XVIII.
SONE, VIOLET WEST. Rope-Jumping Rhymes. XVIII.
SONNICHSEN, CHARLES L. Mexican Ghosts from El Paso. XIII.
STORM, DAN. The Little Animals. XIV.
STRECKER, JOHN K.
  The Folklore of Texas Birds. VII.
  · Texas Reptiles in Popular Belief. V.
TAYLOR, PAUL S.
  Corrido de Texas. XII.
  Deportados. XII.
THOMAS, GATES. Six Negro Songs from the Colorado Valley. V.
TURNER, TRESSA. The Human Comedy in Folk Superstitions. XIII.
WEBB, WALTER PRESCOTT. The Legend of Sam Bass. III.
WINFREY, JAMES W. Oil Patch Talk. XIX.
WOODHULL, FROST. Ranch Remedios. VIII.

Publications of the Texas Folklore Society

I.   *Round the Levee.* 1916.
II.   *Coffee in the Gourd.* 1923.
III.   *Legends of Texas.* 1924. Out of print.
IV.   *Publication No. IV.* 1925. Out of print.
V.   *Publication No. V.* 1926. Out of print.
VI.   *Texas and Southwestern Lore.* 1927.
VII.   *Follow de Drinkin' Gou'd.* 1928.
VIII.   *Man, Bird, and Beast.* 1930.
IX.   *Southwestern Lore.* 1931. Out of print.
X.   *Tone the Bell Easy.* 1932.
XI.   *Spur-of-the-Cock.* 1933.
XII.   *Puro Mexicano.* 1935.
XIII.   *Straight Texas.* 1937. Out of print.
XIV.   *Coyote Wisdom.* 1938. Out of print.
XV.   *In the Shadow of History.* 1939. Out of print.
XVI.   *Mustangs and Cow Horses.* 1940. Out of print.
XVII.   *Texian Stomping Grounds.* 1941.
XVIII. *Backwoods to Border.* 1943. Out of print.
XIX.   *From Hell to Breakfast.* 1944.
XX.   *Gib Morgan, Minstrel of the Oil Fields.* 1945. Out of print.
XXI.   *Mexican Border Ballads and Other Lore.* 1946.
XXII.   *The Sky Is My Tipi.* 1949.
XXIII. *Texas Folk Songs.* 1950.
XXIV.   *The Healer of Los Olmos.* 1951.
XXV.   *Folk Travelers: Ballads, Tales, and Talk.* 1953.
          All volumes still in print may be obtained from:
          Southern Methodist University Press, Dallas 5, Texas.

Index